TECHNOLOGY AND EDUCATION: ISSUES IN ADMINISTRATION, POLICY, AND APPLICATIONS IN K12 SCHOOLS

ADVANCES IN EDUCATIONAL ADMINISTRATION

Series Editor: Richard C. Hunter

Volume 1–5:   Series Editor Paul W. Thurston
Volume 6–7:   Series Editor Richard C. Hunter

ADVANCES IN EDUCATIONAL ADMINISTRATION   VOLUME 8

TECHNOLOGY AND EDUCATION: ISSUES IN ADMINISTRATION, POLICY, AND APPLICATIONS IN K12 SCHOOLS

EDITED BY

SHARON Y. TETTEGAH

Department of Curriculum and Instruction, University of Illinois at Urbana-Champaign, USA

RICHARD C. HUNTER

Department of Educational Organization and Leadership, University of Illinois at Urbana-Champaign, USA

ELSEVIER
JAI

Amsterdam – Boston – Heidelberg – London – New York – Oxford
Paris – San Diego – San Francisco – Singapore – Sydney – Tokyo

ELSEVIER B.V.	ELSEVIER Inc.	**ELSEVIER Ltd**	ELSEVIER Ltd
Radarweg 29	525 B Street, Suite 1900	**The Boulevard, Langford**	84 Theobalds Road
P.O. Box 211	San Diego	**Lane, Kidlington**	London
1000 AE Amsterdam,	CA 92101-4495	**Oxford OX5 1GB**	WC1X 8RR
The Netherlands	USA	**UK**	UK

First edition 2006

British Library Cataloguing in Publication Data
A catalogue record is available from the British Library.

ISBN-10:   0-7623-1280-7
ISBN-13:   978-07623-1280-1
ISSN: 1479-3660 (Series)

∞ The paper used in this publication meets the requirements of ANSI/NISO Z39.48-1992 (Permanence of Paper).
Printed in The Netherlands.

CONTENTS

**PART II: TECHNOLOGY, POLICY, AND
PHILOSOPHY: WHAT ALL SCHOOL DISTRICTS
SHOULD KNOW**

FOREWORD: RETHINKING EDUCATIONAL TECHNOLOGIES AS ARCHITECTURE AND AESTHETICS

That teaching and learning with technology has no meaning apart from teachers and learners is the important message of this fine collection of essays. The editors, Sharon Tettegah and Richard Hunter, are to be commended for their timely volume entitled, *Technology and Education: Issues in Administration, Policy, and Applications in K-12 Schools.* While the message that machines are meaningless without human minds seems self-evident, there is something about computerized technologies – in schools especially – that undermines and over-rides this important insight. At a time when the wonders of "wireless" and "wiki" distract more than ever from the main educational game, this wide-ranging anthology presents a persuasive and powerful testimony reaffirming the fundamental principle that educational technologies are only as effective as the curriculums, the pedagogies, and the assessment practices that frame their usage.

Technology and Education brings together 19 engaging chapters asserting this timeless educational axiom. Important social dimensions of learning technologies canvassed by the chapters include administration, policy, philosophy, school reform, professional identities and continuing learning, equity and access, standards and accountability, and school-community partnerships. Empirical research projects and grounded case studies provide insights into differentiated ways in which technology shapes and is shaped by educational milieu. Because the histories and futures of school communities – and hence the social and educational needs of students – are different in Thomasboro (Illinois) from those of Tacoma (Washington), so too are the opportunities, challenges, uses, and outcomes of learning technologies. Just as the social imperatives of Bellerose (New York) differ from those of Buffalo (Texas), so too technology needs to be planned, administered, and applied differentially in these locations. This is the important message of *Technology and Education.*

The scattered geographical location of the contributors in itself shows how new technologies have changed educational research. That the editors invited an Australian to write this Foreword testifies to the increasing internationalization of knowledge production through the power and scope of communications technologies. While Sharon and I are colleagues, we have never met face-to-face.

This paradoxical notion of the social and local embeddedness yet powerful reach of technology reminds me of the songlines used by Australia's indigenous people. Songlines were sung maps that provided markers of identity, location, and time for aboriginal people as they traversed this great landmass (see Fox, 2003). For thousands of years before European colonization, these sophisticated systems of sung language were used as modes of social organization, communication, and navigation. Customary knowledge of the tracks was established during the Dreamtime – a time before living memory when ancestral beings in non-human and human form created the land. Knowing the songs meant knowing who you were, where you were going, and where to find food and water. Musical tracks crisscrossing what was otherwise a featureless landscape enabled the people to maintain an ecologically sustainable relationship with the land and with each other. Similar to the magic of wireless transmission and the Internet today, strings of words, musical notes, and footprints coded and spoke the land into physical being and spiritual meaning for its inhabitants.

Following British colonization and the destruction of aboriginal language and culture, this highly functional communication system disintegrated. My point here is that because of the intimate connection of songline technology to the linguistic and cultural customs of the people, and because adults taught children the songs down through the generations, it is somehow easier to think of them as patterns of social and pedagogical practice than current communications technologies. Yet, the songlines may have more features in common with the digital devices of *Technology and Education* than is readily apparent. The latter may be more tangibly material – consisting of metal objects sitting on desks or fitted snugly into the palm of the hand – yet they too constitute and co-construct culturally differentiated social languages, codes, logics, and value systems.

Technology and Education's message of the social embeddedness of technology resonates with the work of contemporary architect, Reinhold Martin (2003). His study, *The Organizational Complex: Architecture, Media, and Corporate Space*, locates historically and theorizes socially the office buildings of corporations built in the United States after the Second World War. Martin integrates objects, images, knowledges, and discourses to analyze these seemingly neutral buildings and to show how corporate and computer networks dominated social relations and city landscapes in the postwar period. Linking economics and politics to the logics of digital technology, Martin connects the military–industrial complex with the distinctive architecture and aesthetic of big business like General Motors and IBM.

Martin's ideas can be applied to the socio-technical networks of schools. Typically understood as designed structure, the term architecture refers also to the operating systems of computers and their networked interactional exchanges. Digital software and the learning it supports are composed of linguistic, symbolic, and numeric codes. These codes, in turn, comprise discourse (see Fitzgerald, 2000). As discourse, the techno-social and pedagogical architectures of schools variously embody a certain kind of aesthetic in their application and use. The term aesthetic refers here to an underlying set of principles manifested by a style of action and interaction. In large part, school leaders, principals, administrators, and teachers define and construct the kinds of social philosophies and technical policies (i.e., architectures) and the kinds of aesthetic (i.e., actions, interactions, and practices) they believe are required for the communities they serve. These are the focus of *Technology and Education*.

While the physical places of schools continue for the main part as industrial-model built environments, clearly they are undergoing huge transformations in other ways. Mobile and online technologies are changing how schools are organized socially and spatially in what are now global educational communities. Studies like *Technology and Education* provide important, critically reflective snapshots of this transition. They show how, in some ways, schools are postindustrial educational equivalents of Martin's modernist, techno-economic corporate office. Notions of "SMART classrooms," "digital libraries," "teacher as brand," "bullying through blogs" and "digital photo journals" speak new architectures and aesthetics of learning and teaching with and around new textualities and technologies. The authors of *Technology and Education* invite the reader to reassess and reexamine tired assumptions about technology through the reaffirmation that technological change is necessary though not sufficient unless accompanied by whole-school curricular and pedagogical reform. I unreservedly recommend this text as a significant new resource for administrators and educators who seek to contribute to this epochal wave of social and educational change.

REFERENCES

Fitzgerald, B. (2000). Software as discourse: The power of intellectual property in digital architecture. *Cardozo Journal of Arts and Entertainment Law Journal, 18*, 337–386.

Fox, M. (2003). *Songlines: Emerging Queensland indigenous artists*. Brisbane: Keeaira Press.

Reinhold, M. (2003). *The organizational complex: Architecture, media, and corporate space*. Cambridge, MA: The MIT Press.

Cushla Kapitzke

INTRODUCTION

In the age of billion-dollar baby dolls, dot.com enterprises, software giants, MP3 players, cell phones, personal digital assistants, cyber viruses, digital libraries, knowledge management, and computer-aided testing, school district personnel struggle with No Child Left Behind and technology integration. The 21st century has brought multiple challenges for k12 schools and higher education, with numerous educational tools and technology at the forefront of every industry, public and private school (International Society for Technology in Education, 2003).

Every aspect of information communication technologies affects our schools. Current headlines indicate more than ever, educators should be prepared for leadership, policy, and curricula changes involving information communication technologies (ICT), and instructional technologies in schools. As we concern ourselves with No Child Left Behind, homeland security, online aggression, and the effects of natural disasters on our communities and schools, it is expected that K-12 schools will be leaders in the dissemination and education of information through communication technologies. For example, recently hurricane Katrina displaced many families causing school districts to place victims of the hurricane in schools all over the United States. Schools throughout the United States used the Internet and the World Wide Web to provide outreach and donations for displaced families and to locate relatives and friends. Additionally, wireless technologies, global positioning systems, handheld units are now used in schools to investigate and record various ecosystems. While simulations and virtual reality applications are currently used to help improve teaching and learning practices to meet the needs of students with a variety of problems, including attention deficit hyperactive disorder and bullying situations, most educators are using technologies as productivity tools (Pflaum, 2004; Tettegah, 2005). These are only a few examples of how schools are using ICT, yet, as technology advances so will the need for better understanding of its impact on education.

A recent article in the New York Times maintained, more than ever, students, at home, are using more electronic games to learn basic reading and math skills, while educational software purchases are at an all time low (Richtel, 2005). Internet technologies and electronic games have become the dominant way to learn for many students. While many students engage electronic games others engage in virtual fieldtrips to learn about historical and current events. Are we using multiple types of technologies? Yes, we are using technologies for learning in multiple ways other than the Internet, as schools continue to argue about which technologies are most appropriate for teaching and learning.

As we struggle to deal with these issues of emerging risks of online aggression and violence; we also struggle with the integration of curriculum and technology, as well as, appropriate uses of information communication technologies for classroom knowledge management. From digital libraries to administrative policies to the use and misuse of technologies, this book documents how such issues and behaviors using multiple technologies affect our schools. Our book is organized into three parts. Part I discusses schools, administration, and presents various uses of technology. Part II presents information about what school districts should know about technology, as it relates to policy and philosophy. Part III is about applications of practice and strategies to better use technology in schools.

PART I: TECHNOLOGY, SCHOOLS, AND ADMINISTRATION: RAISING AWARENESS

David M. Marcovitz suggests that public education has not changed very much in the last 100 years, in spite of information and communication technology (ICT). Is ICT simply another educational fad or will it have a lasting impact on K-12 education? Lisa C. Yamagata-Lynch and Sharon Smaldino maintain there have been several examples of effective uses of technology in K-12. However, the inability of public schools and higher education to properly train teachers has severely limited the success of using computer technology in most public schools. Sharon Tettegah, Diana Betout, and Kona Renee Taylor describes cyber-bullying, as a phenomenon that is creating difficulty for educators and has led to the humiliation of many students across the nation. David Williamson Shaffer and Kurt D. Squire argue that researchers of educational technology should study Pasteur's Quadrant for "use-inspired basic research" to create better models to evaluate educational practices and the use of technology. John Keller and Matthew J. Stuve discuss teacher quality, a topic that has taken on greater importance since NCLB. They also talk about the use of "teacher as brand" as a construct to further affect teacher quality. In connection, branding has been a very successful venture in the commercial context.

PART II: TECHNOLOGY, POLICY, AND PHILOSOPHY: WHAT ALL SCHOOL DISTRICTS SHOULD KNOW

Considering recent discussions involving intellectual property, school district accountability, copyright and digital divide, this section provides readers with some much needed information and discussion on policy, and other legal aspects associated with technology and schools. David M. Marcovitz reviews recent court rulings on the copyrighting of intellectual properties in technology. He suggests that authors might consider placing their works in the public domain to facilitate greater usage by educators. Nicholas C. Burbules, Thomas A. Callister, Jr. and Claudine Taaffe maintain the digital divide metaphor is lacking because it fails to capture problems associated with other dimensions derived by student's unequal access to computer hardware. Dawn G. Williams, Nicole S. Clifton, and Tawana L. Carr maintain the elimination of the digital divide will produce stronger assurances that all students will be better prepared for the 21st century. Kona Renee Taylor, Eun Won Whang, and Sharon Tettegah raise awareness about Acceptable Use Policies (AUP), related AUP content and who decides on the content. Saran Donahoo and Michael Whitney discuss the influence technology and accountability have had on K-12 education. They examine costs, success, and the impact technology has had on the work of administrators. Mustafa Yunus Eryaman reviews the central themes of integrating technology into education and recommends the use of a hermeneutic approach toward implementing educational policy and technology.

PART III: TECHNOLOGY, APPLICATIONS AND PRACTICE: ACTIONS AND STRATEGIES

This section presents different ways technology is used in school. Authors argue why technology integration is critical for effective teaching and learning practices. Technology integration is at critical points for schools. This section describe ways current technologies are transforming teaching and learning while others discuss integration of technology in schools. Marcia A. Mardis and Ellen S. Hoffman discuss digital libraries as a means of transforming the contemporary teaching and learning landscape in public education. Barbara Hug and George Reese describe a professional development effort to assist teachers in changing their practice in integrating technology into a local educational community. Bryan Carter presents the theory behind collaborative learning and discusses technology projects from the St. Louis Science Center and the children's museum of Manhattan. Barbara Monroe argues telementoring as a means of enhancing communication among teachers, students, and professors. She shares data from a recent study from Johns Hopkins University that reveal 40–60% of all high school students are disengaged in their learning. Karen Swan, Dale Cook, Annette Kratcoski, Yi Mel Lin, Jason Schenker, and Mark van't Hooft remind us that although digital technologies have changed work in business and industry, they have had little impact on classroom teaching and learning. They discuss Weiser's idea of "ubiquitous computing" and argue that simply putting more computers in schools will not create a ubiquitous computer environment. Cynthia Carter Ching, X. Christine Wang, and Yore Kedem raises the dilemma that early childhood educators are experiencing in deciding what to do regarding the use computer technology in their classrooms. These teachers are experiencing difficulty deciding whether to use computers in their instruction. Renee Clift and Judith A. Federmeier remind us that the majority of students do not have access to computers for instruction. They discuss their experiences in implementing a computer-intensive curriculum in a high school. Richard C. Hunter talks about the pressure schools are under to integrate computer technology into their curricula. He also presents several leadership strategies for public school superintendents to increase the integration of computers into classroom instruction.

REFERENCES

International Society for Technology in Education, (2003). Retrieved September 10, 2005, from http://www.iste.org/.

Pflaum, W. D. (2004). *The technology fix: The promise and reality of computers in our schools.* Alexandria, VA: ASCD Publications.

Richtel, M. (2005). Once a booming market, educational software for the pc takes a nose dive.*The New York Times*, Retrieved September 10, 2005, from http://www.nytimes.com/2005/08/22/technology/22soft.html?pagewanted=all.

Tettegah, S. (2005). Technology, narratives, vignettes and the intercultural and cross cultural teaching portal. *Urban Education, 40*(4), 268–293.

Sharon Y. Tettegah
Richard C. Hunter
Editors

PART I:
TECHNOLOGY, SCHOOLS, AND ADMINISTRATION: RAISING AWARENESS

CHANGING SCHOOLS WITH TECHNOLOGY: WHAT EVERY SCHOOL SHOULD KNOW ABOUT INNOVATION

David M. Marcovitz

ABSTRACT

Change is constant in schools. Educational fads come and go while many believe that schools of today have changed little over the last hundred years. Enter information and communication technology (ICT). Is it just another fad that will pass? Is it window dressing for schools that are fundamentally the same? A quick "yes" to these questions fails to understand the nature of ICT, the nature of schools, and the nature of innovation in schools. This chapter explores models of innovation to help schools understand the change process and how to use models of change to support innovation with ICT.

INTRODUCTION

Quick, easy, and verifiable results are what everyone hopes for in innovation. Unfortunately, innovation rarely works that way. Hall and Hord

Technology and Education: Issues in Administration, Policy, and Applications in K12 Schools
Advances in Educational Administration, Volume 8, 3–15
ISSN: 1479-3660/doi:10.1016/S1479-3660(05)08001-7

(1987) teaches us that change is a process during which people go through several stages of concern and levels of use. Rogers (2003) teaches us that some people are quick to adopt innovations while others are slower and still others resist innovations. Bruce (1993) teaches us that if we are looking at some idealized innovation, we've missed the point of the innovation in a complex social system as that idealized innovation is reinterpreted and recreated by the actors in the situation. That is, change is not quick; it is not easy, and results are hard to verify. To put it another way, there is no magic bullet.

Understanding the change process is important because too many people think there must be a magic bullet, and when an innovation isn't quick and easy, and the results aren't identical to what was expected, they write it off as another fad gone wrong ... and by the way, why are classrooms of today so much like those of the past (Cuban, 1986, 1993).

As we think about innovation in schools, we need to think about innovations, individuals, and school cultures. By understanding these three aspects of the change process, we are better able to effect lasting and meaningful change. If we focus on one area and ignore the others, our change is unlikely to have an impact.

INNOVATIONS AND AN
INNOVATION-CENTERED VIEW

We commonly think that innovations come into situations and change things. In this innovation-centered view, innovations are the chief actors. We simply need to bring in the right innovation, and it will solve our problems. Bruce (1993) states:

> Sometimes the new technology is viewed as sufficient unto itself to effect the desired changes. In that case, we succumb to technocentrism (Papert, 1987), the tendency to conceive technology independent of its contexts of use. With this mindset, we assume that if only teachers and students had access to the power of the new technology, all aspects of the wonderful vision would be realized (p. 9).

This leads us to a view of an ideal innovation. That is, the innovation will come into the situation and do certain things. As implementers of the innovation, our job is to get the innovation to look as close as possible to the ideal. Any variation from the ideal is bad. In this view, the details of the situation are secondary, or at best obstacles to be overcome, and in the end, all successful implementations of this innovation will approximate the ideal.

As Cuban (1996) discusses, this is the view of "techno-reformers" who believe that all we need to make the innovation successful is to bring in more machines and help the teachers use them better.

As Bruce (1993) states:

> In reality, the innovation is but one small addition to a complex social system. Instead of seeing it as the primary instrument of change, it is better to see it as a tool that is incorporated into ongoing processes of change. We are thus led to a different model for implementation of innovations. In this model, the active agents are not innovations, but the participants in the setting in which the innovation is placed. Participants interpret the innovation and then re-create it as they adapt it to fit with institutional and physical constraints, and with their own goals and practices (p. 17).

This leads us to focus on the complex social situation in which the innovation is placed, including the participants or individuals and the culture of the school.

INDIVIDUALS

As we move away from a focus on the innovation, we move to a focus on the individuals who implement the innovation in context. Many researchers have recognized that individuals, even individuals in a similar situation, are not the same. Rogers (2003) divides individuals into categories: innovators, early adopters, early majority, late majority, and laggards. The categories are based on how quick individuals are to adopt innovations.

Several authors have recognized that change is a process (Hall & Hord, 1987; Dwyer, Ringstaff, & Sandholtz, 1990; Szabo, 2002; Sherry, Billig, Tavalin, & Gibson, 2000), and individuals do not simply jump into full implementation of an innovation. In the Concerns-Based Adoption Model (Hall & Hord, 1987), individuals are viewed along two dimensions: stages of concern and levels of use. Each dimension is defined by seven stages or levels. Stages of concern include: awareness, informational, personal, management, consequence, collaboration, and refocusing. However, these can be grouped to leave three primary foci for concern. That is, an individual may be focused on him/herself, on the task, or on the impact of the innovation. Levels of use include: non-use, orientation, preparation, mechanical use, routine, refinement, integration, and renewal. This complex model is an excellent tool for researchers and for detailed analyses of the status of innovations, but a simpler model might be more useful for schools trying to understand their innovation processes.

The model developed from the Apple Classrooms of Tomorrow (ACOT) study (Dwyer et al., 1990) contains five stages: entry, adoption, adaptation, appropriation, and invention. For any given innovation, teachers travel through the stages in a more or less linear fashion with two exceptions. First, teachers might move back and forth throughout the process, progressing to one stage and backtracking to an earlier stage. Keeping in mind that the innovation and the teacher are situated in a context, it is only natural for other demands to take precedence and require a teacher to focus less on this particular innovation. Second, some teachers will never progress through all the stages of the model, reaching a plateau, for example, at the adaptation stage.

In the entry stage, teachers find "themselves facing first-year-teacher problems" (Dwyer et al., 1990, p. 5). That is, they struggle with the disruptions the innovation brings to their classroom routine. In the adoption stage, the disruptions have subsided, and the innovation has fit more or less into the previous classroom routine. For example, lectures use PowerPoint and drills are transferred to the computer. In this phase, the change is symbolic (Fullan, 1991) as the routine is altered but only to accommodate the technology. By adaptation, Dwyer et al. found that the increased efficiency of the technology, still being used largely to support the same style of teaching as before the innovation, allows for "increased opportunities for teachers to engage students in higher-order learning objectives and problem solving in math" (p. 6). While the technology has some direct impact on the focus of instruction, the indirect impact can be more positive. In the appropriation stage, the technology is no longer a focus of instruction as the teachers begin to use it effortlessly and are able to adopt new models and methods of teaching (such as team teaching and interdisciplinary project-based instruction). The invention stage represents a shift in teacher beliefs about education, expanding on the benefits of the appropriation stage to encompass a new belief in the way instruction should be. For Dwyer et al., this represents a shift from an instructionist view of learning to a constructivist view.

The key to understanding an individual's progression with innovation is to understand that there are stages and that creative and inventive application of the innovation does not take place immediately. With that in mind, an even simpler model suggested by Szabo (2002) has three stages: play, use, and create.

> First, people "play" with it, to find out its capabilities and limitations. In the second
> stage, they use the technology to assist them in their daily chores and responsibilities. In
> the third stage, they begin to use the innovation to help address new opportunities or

problems which have not been addressed before the innovation, problems previously
though[t] unassailable (p. 10).

These models give a good introduction to the idea that innovation takes
time. One might judge an innovation's success early on, but only if one
recognizes that in the early stages, teachers are likely to be playing with the
innovation, adopting the innovation, and at best, relegating it to mechanical
use, possibly doing the same kinds of things they could do before without
the innovation. Without recognition of the process, judging an innovation in
the early stages is likely to lead to an unfavorable assessment. It is only in
the later stages of create, appropriation and invention, and integration and
renewal that innovations will tend to have a significant positive impact. As
Hall and Hord (2001) puts it:

> Over the years a pattern has developed: introduce a new program, give it a year to take
> hold, immediately assess its effectiveness, and reject it when no increased program out-
> comes are found. School staff soon catch on to this annual cycle and conclude, "Don't
> put any energy into this one; it, too, will go away," And, sure enough, it does (p. 31).

While the "give it a year" time frame varies based on the nature of the
innovation, giving individuals adequate time to use the innovation and
progress through the innovation process is necessary for seeing results.

CULTURE

Now that we recognize that the innovation itself is important and that
individuals are the primary actors, who redefine the innovation as they go
through a process of change, we must understand how those individuals fit
into a context and culture of the school. Cuban (1996) decries the innovation-centered model:

> Just suppose, though, that the techno-reformers have it backward. Maybe the limited
> classroom use of new technologies is rooted in how reformers have framed the problem.
> Maybe their exaggerated claims for what the technology can do, their disregard for the
> social organization of schools, their ignorance of classroom realities, and their power to
> frame both the problem and the solution are all parts of why there are so few serious
> users of these new technologies.

Cuban argues that as we blame teachers, and even innovations, for failing,
we miss the point of the need to redefine the culture of the school so that
innovations can succeed.

Hall and Hord (2001) offers definitions for climate, culture, and context:

> 1. *Climate* is the individuals' perceptions of a work setting in terms of a priori established concepts that can be measured empirically.
>
> 2. *Culture* is the individually and socially constructed values, norms, and beliefs about an organization and how it should behave that can be measured only by observation of the setting using qualitative methods.
>
> 3. *Context* ... is comprised of (a) culture (as defined above) and (b) ecological factors (as defined in James and Jones' discussion of situational variables above) (p. 194).

Dexter (1999) defines culture by way of Emile Durkheim's concept of collective representations "to describe the influence of a group's understanding of itself on the social forms and structures it creates." That is, the collectively agreed upon policies and procedures make up part of the "moral" code of a group, and the moral code is further defined by the social norms of acceptable behavior within the group. While Durkheim is referring to larger societies, Dexter brings this to the scale of smaller groups and organizations, such as schools, by discussing the idea of frames, which are individual situations in the larger social context:

> Because frames encompass a shared understanding of a situation, they also carry rules of behavior for the participants. When individuals follow rules of behavior (or what Durkheim would call moral representations), they are not only agreeing with a particular framing of a situation, but they are also reinforcing their commitment to a specific image of self and to a culture. Management of personal behavior is, in effect, communication with the group that reaffirms both how individuals will be perceived and their role within the group. When group members respond accordingly to the image an individual presents, it is an acknowledgment, acceptance, and reinforcement of that culture.

Dexter (1999) takes us beyond a view of innovation and resistance to innovation in a way that shifts the emphasis from perceived shortcomings of the teacher or even a noble struggle of a teacher uneasy about replacing old methods that work with those that are unproven. "'Proper' student and teacher behavior doesn't just obey the collective representations of that culture, it embodies and reinforces them." Significant change in practice requires either a culture that is accepting of that change or a change in the culture.

A high school teacher wanted to teach an innovative, advanced science class. Plans were made for the class, but as the beginning of the semester approached, not enough students enrolled in the class, and the class was cancelled. The innovative teacher was "rewarded" for his effort by being assigned to teach one period of in-school suspension (clearly recognized as the worst teaching assignment in the school). The constraints of the situation dictated that teacher resources needed to be used wisely. The principal had an available teacher and a slot of in-school suspension to cover. The teacher accepted his assignment without resistance. All of these actions go beyond a simple matter of the needs of the school and speak to the culture of the school. The school culture was open to innovation to a limited degree, but the policies and procedures and social norms, which make up the culture of the school, were reinforced in this instance and limited the possibility of future innovation.

In another example of culture and innovation, Marcovitz (2000) reports the caution of a computer coordinator who was having difficulty distributing computers in the school. As is typical in many schools, he had to balance the cultural norm of equity with the needs and aspirations of specific teachers. The odd design of the building (a few classrooms that were separated from others by a few steps, preventing access to computers on carts) allowed a small imbalance in the distribution of computers. The cultural value of equity was the overriding factor, and overcoming the inequity of the steps, not a desire for innovation, was the concern that allowed a shift in the equal distribution of computers.

Dexter (1999) provides a broader example of the conflict of culture and innovation.

> Because information age classrooms are inquiry-based, with an emphasis on authentic, real-world-based activities, curriculum is often more interdisciplinary in nature and assessment more performance oriented than is the case in most schools. Instead of an emphasis on content, the purpose of assignments may be equally, or even mostly, related to process skills. To institute these ideas would mean considerable change in teachers' thinking and planning processes. It would require developing new measures of progress, new routines for managing their and their students' work, and new unit and lesson plans requiring locating and adapting new resources for student use.

And Dexter (1999) contends that the change in roles that is required for this kind of innovation, requires that "the collective – teachers, administrators, students, and parents – must all come to a shared understanding of any new approach to teaching and learning." That is, implementation of technology in this way requires a cultural shift.

SHIFTING THE CULTURE

Recognizing the magnitude of the problem is the first step. In the previous sections, we came to understand that the individuals must go through a process of change, but that must happen with the support of a culture that is receptive to that change. Dexter (1999) refers to the "cargo cult" in which a culture goes through the motions of innovation without understanding how the change is meant to bring about improvement. Fullan (1991) discusses "*symbolic* rather than *real* changes" (p. 28) in which, much like in the cargo cult, change involves surface adjustments to practice without any meaningful change. Moller (as cited in Szabo, 2002) refers to "second-order change" as the kind of change that requires a "paradigm shift in the culture of the organization" (p. 7).

Dexter (1999) relates many schools' use of information and communication technology (ICT) to the cargo cult. In a cargo cult, indigenous cultures saw settlers building airports. The airports were the source of many goods, that is, cargo. The indigenous people would clear fields for runways and build buildings that resembled airports in hopes that they, too, would get cargo. Likewise in schools, we often bring in hardware and software and have all the trappings of a technology-rich environment in hopes that education will improve. Of course, these symbolic changes have little or no impact unless they are accompanied by real changes that transform the way we teach. In referring to lessons that use the Internet, Harris (1998) asks two questions (which could easily apply to all use of ICT):

1. Will this use of the Internet enable students to do something they *couldn't* do before?
2. Will this use of the Internet enable students to do something they *could* do before, but better? (p. 9)

In other words, what is the *real* impact of our use of ICT? Has the teacher who has always lectured and now lectures with PowerPoint made a *real* change or a *symbolic* change? Those who do not teach with technology often think of adding technology as a *paradigm shift*, but in reality, the PowerPoint lecturer has not passed beyond the adoption stage of Dwyer et al.'s (1990) model of change.

When our goal is a significant improvement in education and our change is symbolic, the change has failed ... or has it? That would be true if change were easy and uniform and a short-term process. But our PowerPoint lecturer has reached one point on one path along the way to meaningful change. If the path stops there – and too often it does – perhaps the change has failed. If the path continues on through adaptation, appropriation, and possibly invention, then the change has a chance to make a positive difference. The PowerPoint lecturer may be satisfied to stop there or unwilling and/or unable to move beyond spicing up a lecture with technology, but if we view the spiced up lecture as a step in the process and give the teacher the support and encouragement to continue the process, real change is possible.

CONDITIONS OF SUCCESSFUL CHANGE

Ely (1990) points to conditions of successful change. This section focuses on Ely's model and his eight conditions for success.

> Change is difficult because it is riddled with dilemmas, ambivalences, and paradoxes. It combines steps that seemingly do not go together: to have a clear vision and be open-minded; to take initiative and empower others; to provide support and pressure; to start small and think big; to expect results and be patient and persistent; to have a plan and be flexible; to use top-down and bottom-up strategies; to experience uncertainty and satisfaction. Educational change is above all a very personal experience in a social, but often impersonal, setting (Fullan, 1991, p. 350).

Ely (1990) attempts to tame the dilemmas, ambivalences, and paradoxes by describing eight conditions that facilitate the implementation of change: "dissatisfaction with the status quo, knowledge and skills, resources, time, rewards, participation, commitment, and leadership" (p. 298). Surry, Porter, Jackson, and Hall (2004) found that these conditions vary in importance based on the specific situation. Wizer and McPherson (2005) found five forms of administrative support needed to foster technology use in schools: "faculty development, financial expenditures, organizational structures, personal commitment, and leadership support" (p. 15). While these authors believe that change cannot be a top-down process, it is critical for the administration to provide an environment that is welcoming to change and supportive of change.

The eight conditions can be used to assess the environment and need for change in advance of adopting an innovation and for assessing and improving the environment for change once the innovation has been adopted (Ely, 1990). We need to know if the current situation is unsatisfactory to the participants; that is, if everyone is happy with how things are, change is less likely to be successful. Surry et al. (2004) suggests stirring the pot a bit by encouraging dissatisfaction by showing teachers what is possible. This can take the form of technology fairs or other forums designed to showcase excellent uses of ICT, from inside or outside the school, with the intent of creating dissatisfaction with the status quo.

We need to know if teachers have the knowledge and skills to implement the innovation and find ways to provide knowledge that is lacking. This, of course, is the first step in any staff development process: the needs assessment. Not only is it unfair to expect teachers to use an innovation without adequate training, appropriate training must target the real needs of the teachers. Relevant support and training is a critical factor in the success of innovation (Marcovitz, 1999).

"Resources are broadly defined as those tools and other relevant materials that are accessible to assist learners to acquire learning objectives" (Ely, 1990). Innovations are less likely to succeed if adequate resources are not provided. Numerous schools expect teachers to check email during the school day. Schools in which teachers have access to email in their own classrooms are more likely to be successful at this than schools in which teachers have to find a computer elsewhere in the building to check email.

Time is a separate condition for success because it is vitally important to the process of change (Ely, 1990). Teachers who are expected to change what they do and how they do it must be given time to play, use, and create (Szabo, 2002). This involves a long period of time to follow the process of innovation as well as time at each step of the process to explore and adapt the technology to the needs of the classroom.

Ely (1990) discusses the importance of rewards and incentives. Just like with our students, intrinsic motivation is better than external rewards, but done properly, rewards become an appropriate balance of "support and pressure" (Fullan, 1991) that can serve to counterbalance, if not overcome, disincentives that are an inherent part of the system. Generally, teachers want to do the best for their students, and if they view the innovation as helping that mission, they want to be part of that. But the system is full of disincentives to change. A critical part of Ely's condition of rewards and incentives is the removal of disincentives. Surry et al. (2004) warns, "Instead of valuing failure, rewarding innovative efforts that fail, and learning from failure, we often ignore failure and, at worst, punish people who try innovative things that fail" (p. 1421). Surry et al. recommends that schools will only be innovation friendly when they embrace failure and accept that good things will happen only if we allow risks to be taken and accept that some of those risks will fail.

When developing a technology plan, a school will often appoint one individual to go off and write the plan. When I ask the teachers in my classes about their school's technology plan, if they have one at all, it was often written by one individual and gathers dust in a filing cabinet. The key to making a technology plan work is buy-in. As Ely (1990) puts it, "Participation is expected and encouraged ... . The important message here is that each person feels that he or she has had an opportunity to comment on innovations that will directly affect his or her work." Without this opportunity, the important people who have to implement the innovation will not buy into it and will not put forth the needed effort to implement it successfully.

The last two conditions for successful implementation of innovations have to do with the direct actions of the administration and leadership (Ely, 1990). Administrators need to show a commitment to the innovation, and they need make sure that leadership is evident. This aligns with Wizer and McPherson's (2005) keys to success:

> Personal commitment refers to key administrators who use, value the use of, and expect the use of technology throughout the school for improved instruction and more effective operations. In some situations this is achieved when administrators are avid supporters or cheerleaders (p. 16).

By supporting and encouraging technology leaders in the school, and by leading by example, administrators demonstrate the commitment and leadership that is an essential condition of success for innovations. Administrators who pay lip service to technology, don't use it themselves, and show no evidence that it matters (e.g., through low expectations of its use and limited incentives for its use) are likely to find that it is used by only a handful of teachers in any way that goes beyond symbolic change.

While Ely (1990) recognizes that all eight of the conditions are rarely fully in place, success will only be achieved if most of them are in place. Using suggestions of Ely, Surry et al. (2004), and Wizer and McPherson (2005), we cannot ensure that change will be successful, but we can work to set up an environment that promotes real, meaningful, and positive change.

CONCLUSION

Innovation in schools is possible, but it is difficult. We must focus on the innovation, the people, and the culture of the school. To make real, rather than symbolic, change (Fullan, 1991), we must heed the warnings of Hall and Hord (1987), Dwyer et al. (1990), and Szabo (2002) that change is a process. Innovations don't enter situations and change everything immediately. Real change takes time. Further, we must heed Bruce's (1993) warning that the innovations aren't the key actors. Instead, we must focus on the participants in the situation who will reinterpret and recreate the innovation. In order for the innovation to be successful, we must be mindful of Ely's (1990) conditions for success that help us focus on the teacher and teach us that change is possible if the participants are dissatisfied with the current situation, are provided with appropriate training to get the needed knowledge and skills, are provided with the appropriate resources, have the time available, are true participants in the decision-making process so they buy into the innovation, and see commitment and leadership from the administration in the school. Building a "cargo cult" (Dexter, 1999) is easy. Having a true impact on the education of our students is difficult, but it can happen if the conditions are in place.

REFERENCES

Bruce, B. (1993). Innovation and social change. In: B. C. Bruce, J. K. Peyton & T. Batson (Eds), *Network-based classrooms: Promises and realities* (pp. 9–32). New York: Cambridge University Press.

Cuban, L. (1986). *Teachers and machines: The classroom use of technology since 1920.* New York: Teachers College Press.

Cuban, L. (1993). *How teachers taught: Constancy and change in American classrooms* (2nd ed.). New York: Teachers College Press.

Cuban, L. (1996). Techno-reformers and classroom teachers. *Education Week*, October 9 [Electronic version]. Retrieved May 17, 2005, from http://www.edweek.org/ew/articles/1996/10/09/06cuban.h16.html

Dexter, S. (1999). Collective representations and educational technology as school reform: Or, how not to produce a cargo cult [Electronic version]. *Educational Technology & Society*, *2*(4). Retrieved May 17, 2005, from http://www.ifets.ieee.org/periodical/vol_4_99/sara_dexter.html

Dwyer, D. C., Ringstaff, C., & Sandholtz, J. H. (1990). *Teacher beliefs and practices* (ACOT Report #8), Cupertino, CA: Apple Computer, Inc. Retrieved May 17, 2005, from http://www.apple.com/education/k12/leadership/acot/pdf/rpt08.pdf

Ely, D. P. (1990). Conditions that facilitate the implementation of educational technology innovations. *Journal of Research on Computing in Education, 23*(2), 298–307.

Fullan, M. with Stiegelbauer, S. (1991). *The new meaning of educational change.* New York: Teachers College Press.

Hall, G. E., & Hord, S. M. (1987). *Change in schools: Facilitating the process.* Albany, NY: State University of New York Press.

Hall, G. E., & Hord, S. M. (2001). *Implementing change: Patterns, principles, and potholes.* Boston: Allyn and Bacon.

Harris, J. (1998). *Virtual architecture: Designing and directing curriculum-based telecomputing.* Eugene, OR: International Society for Technology in Education.

Marcovitz, D. M. (1999). Support for information technology in schools: The roles of student teachers. *Journal of Information Technology for Teacher Education, 8*(3), 361–374.

Marcovitz, D. M. (2000). The roles of computer coordinators in supporting technology in schools. *Journal of Technology and Teacher Education, 8*(3), 259–273.

Rogers, E. M. (2003). *Diffusion of innovations* (5th ed.). New York: Free Press.

Sherry, L., Billig, S., Tavalin, F., & Gibson, D. (2000). New insights on technology adoption in schools. *T.H.E. Journal, 27*(7). Retrieved May 17, 2005, from http://www.thejournal.com/magazine/vault/A2640.cfm

Surry, D. W., Porter, B. E., Jackson, K., & Hall, D. (2004). Conditions for creating an innovation friendly environment in K-12 schools. *Technology and Teacher Education Annual, 15*, 1418–1425.

Szabo, M. (2002). Educational reform as innovation diffusion: Development of a theory and test of a model using continuing professional development and instructional technology. Paper presented at the Informing Science conference, June, Cork, Ireland. Retrieved May 18, 2005, from http://www.quasar.ualberta.ca/IT/research/Szabo/Szabo-Educa.pdf

Wizer, D. R., & McPherson, S. J. (2005). The administrator's role: Strategies for fostering staff development. *Learning & Leading with Technology, 32*(5), 14–17.

CYBER-BULLYING AND SCHOOLS IN AN ELECTRONIC ERA

Sharon Y. Tettegah, Diana Betout and
Kona Renee Taylor

ABSTRACT

Recent reports in the news media indicates a vast majority of children are connected to the Internet and the World Wide Web. As more children connect online, they bring their behaviors that were once principally face-to-face, to the Internet. This chapter is concerned with online aggression, specifically school age bullying. Children's capacity to bully their peers is growing because of increased use of electronic and wireless information communication technologies. Anonymity provides a venue to engage in risky cyber-bullying for today's children. Schools district need to be aware of the dangers and psychological effects of cyber-bullying.

INTRODUCTION

Recent media and literature have publicized the problems that schools in the United States face related to aggressions linked to peer victimization and bullying (Boulton, 1997; Bosworth, Espelage, & Simon, 1999; Keith & Martin, 2005; Ybarra & Mitchell, 2004). What is bullying? What is Cyber-bullying? This chapter will define bullying and Cyber-bullying,

Technology and Education: Issues in Administration, Policy, and Applications in K12 Schools
Advances in Educational Administration, Volume 8, 17–28
ISSN: 1479-3660/doi:10.1016/S1479-3660(05)08002-9

present anecdotal incidences, and address the dangers for the victim and the victimizer, as well as what educators and parents can do to protect children in online environments.

BULLYING

What is bullying? Bullying can include physical aggression, name-calling, teasing, verbal threats, and social exclusion (Boulton, 1997). The aggressive behaviors associated with bullying can result in psychological, emotional, or physical harm of its victims. Research indicates that aggression through bullying is prevalent; current estimates suggest that as high as one-third of American students are involved or engaged in some type of bullying or victimization (Nansel, Overpeck, Pilla, Ruan, Simons-Morton, & Scheidt, 2001a). As many as 25% of student, in US schools, admit to bullying or being bullied with some regularity, within school environments (Nansel et al., 2001a). In addition when students are asked about bullying without identifiying bullying as such, 20% of the students report some type of bullying behaviors (Nansel et al., 2001a).

Bullying in schools is not a new phenomenon, however the intersections between information communication technology and bullying is new in schools. Cell phones, instant messaging, text messaging, emails, and online chat forums have made their way into the world of bullies. Not surprisingly, children's capability to bully their peers is growing in complexity due to a combination of technological advances and the growing accessibility of the Internet and the World Wide Web (WWW). Access to technology in schools, and resulting Cyber-bullying has created much difficulty for schools. The next section highlights the problems associated with cyber-bullying.

CYBER-BULLYING

What is Cyber-bullying? Cyber-bullying, as defined by Shek (2004) is

> ...sending or posting harmful, cruel texts or images on the Internet through e-mails, instant messages (IM), chat rooms or "blogs" or through other digital communications devices such as cell phones. Contents of the messages can vary, from poking fun of someone's physical attributes to disclosing a victim's sensitive personal information, often sexual behaviors (p. 1).

Ultimately, cyber-bullying involves the same content as traditional bullying, but it depends, through the use of the Internet and the WWW, upon the form of communication used and the audience who is privy to the bullying behavior.

Through the use of the Internet, the WWW, and cell phone wireless technologies, cyber-bullying can manifest itself in the following ways:

- Sending cruel, vicious, and sometimes threatening messages.
- Creating web sights that have stories, cartoons, pictures, and jokes ridiculing others.
- Posting pictures of classmates online and asking students to rate them, with questions such as "Who is the biggest (add a derogatory term)?"
- Breaking into an e-mail account and sending vicious or embarrassing material to others.
- Engaging someone in instant messaging (IM), tricking that person into revealing sensitive personal information, and forwarding that information to others (Cyberbully.org, Cyberbullying., n.d.).

Recent research stated more than 42% of students report online bullying, while as high as 35% reported being threatened online, and 57% of students said someone said hurtful things to them online (Keith & Martin, 2005). When bullies victimize their peers over the Internet and the WWW, there is a certain amount of anonymity that enables the bully to detach him or herself from the damage caused to their victims. In face-to-face aggression, the individual causing the harm must have visual contact and see how their actions are affecting the victim. This is not the case with cyber-bullying. Cyber-bullies can victimize others in the safety of their own room and they may never have to cope with the consequences of their actions (Blair, 2003). Yet, victims may suffer emotionally and their actions can have a lasting impact.

The acts committed by cyber-bullies are extremely harmful to the victim. One example of how detrimental cyber-bullying can be involved students who created a web sight to harass a fellow student, Scott Mitchell.[1] The students at Scott's school posted the website and several months went by without Scott knowing anything about the website or the negative things on it. Scott finally learned of the site when he received an email from a classmate asking him to take a look, and he was shocked to see the content. His picture was posted along with several web pages designed to make fun of him and his family, including accusing Scott of being a rapist and a pedophile. Yet, the harassment did not end with the web site after the initial posting of the photos. After it's posting, Scott began to receive e-mails that were equally damaging, telling him things such as no one liked him. Scott's mother felt that this type of harassment had more affect on Scott than face-to-face harassment.

Scott's mother stated, "It's a cowardly form of bullying, it's like being stabbed in the back by somebody (and) you have no way of ever finding out who they are, or defending yourself against the words they say. So it's more damaging than a face-to-face confrontation with somebody who is clearly willing to tell you what he or she thinks of you"(Leishman, 2002). In a sense, the victim is defenseless, unable to fight back against the nameless and faceless bully (or in some cases bullies). Yet, the worst part is the rate at which a bully can pick on their victim and the wide reaching audience who have a front row seat for the incident.

Franek (2004) wrote about the speed in which victimization can occur through the Internet. A specific example involves using a cell phone with a built in digital camera and Internet access. Using their camera phone, the bully can photograph the victim in the locker room or restroom as they are undressing, and instantly upload the picture onto a website for thousands to view. Once the photograph is posted, the damage is irreversible even if it is removed from the website. The Internet and the WWW has made pulling harmful pranks as fast as pushing a button. Unfortunately, with advancements in technology, children no longer have time to think about the consequences of their actions, because of the ease of which that have access. What is worse is that for the victim it is virtually impossible to getaway from their bullies.

Before the Internet children were able to escape their bullies by going home to the safety of their family, but with the emergence of cyber-bullying children have no place to escape. A recent news article cited the words from a victim:

> Rather than just some people, say 30 in a cafeteria, hearing them all yell insults at you, it's up there for 6 billion people to see. Anyone with a computer can see it, and you can't get away from it. It doesn't go away when you come home from school. It made me feel even more trapped.
>
> (Leishman, 2002)

A school safety violence specialist recently discussed the current trend that has come about with the new "always-connected" generation. The children of today have grown up in an environment where the Internet is widely accessible (Wendland, 2003). Children who do not have access to the internet are in the minority compared to those children who not only have access to the internet from their own computer but also from cell phones.

Consequently, this access to technology and ease of use makes it extremely difficult for children to get away from bullies, which can be very harmful emotionally for the victim.

THE DANGERS

A child who is bullied is more likely to suffer from depression and develop low self-esteem that can last into adulthood (Nansel et al., 2001a; Ybarra, 2004). Other side effects may include, post-traumatic stress disorder, substance abuse, social, and personal relationship problems. Additionally, victims are also affected academically. They are more likely to have low attendance and when they are able to attend school they are often too upset to concentrate, which in effect lowers their grades and causes more emotional trauma (Ybarra & Mitchell, 2004).

An example of the wide reaching effects of bullying can be seen in the case of Mahmoud Fazal, a 15-year-old boy who has learned this first hand how easy it is to be victimized online. Several of his classmates posted a tape that he had filmed of himself mimicking a Star Wars fight scene. Mahmoud soon became a worldwide celebrity and renamed the "Star Wars kid" by the media. The two-minute clip was down loaded by millions and manipulated by animators who place the student in a variety of environments. Mahmoud was humiliated by this incident and had to undergo counseling. He and his parents have also sued the classmates who posted the tape (Snider & Borel, 2004).

Documentation supporting the harmful nature associated with bullying shows when children experience bullying during k-8 school years it can have lasting effects (Nansel, Simons-Morten, Scheidt, & Overpeck, 2001b). Dr. Spivak recently explained, "that it's important not to dismiss bullying as a normal part of childhood – we know now that there are serious short and long-term consequences for both the bullies and the bullied. Bullying behavior should be viewed as a red flag that something is wrong with the child or children who are bullying other children" (Haahr, 2004).

Recent research documents the psychological implications of children who are bullies or commit bullying offences. They are more likely to engage in criminal behavior as they grow into adults (Nansel et al., 2001b). In addition, Nansel et al. (2001a, b) found that bullies are more likely to engage in drinking alcohol and smoking cigarettes. She also found that male bullies are four times more likely and female bullies are eight times more likely than their peers to commit suicide.

Seth, a 13-years-old boy learned first hand about the damaging effects of cyber-bullying when he and a group of friends created a hit list. The boys who created the list were known to be good students and wanted to change that image. While they did not intend to hurt anyone, they created a list and titled it "People We're Gonna Whack". This list was posted onto the Internet and when the boys began to brag about the site at school, students began to complain. Several of the students who were on the list went directly to the police. Seth's computer was confiscated and the police questioned him. When his mother spoke of the incident, she described her son as being hysterical and clinging onto her as he was sobbing (Wolfe, 2003). This story illustrates that it is not just the victim that is affected by cyber-bullying, and that the perpetrator him or herself can be equally affected. Unfortunately, cyber-bullying can be as damaging to a child as face-to-face bullying, but is often more complicated for adults to detect or prevent (Blair, 2003). Recognition or detection of cyber-bullying could be due in part because adults and children relate to technology in different ways (Snider & Borel, 2004).

Adults use technology as a tool while children use it as a lifeline that connects them to their friends and allows them to create a virtual social world. When a child is harassed online they are impacted on levels that are not always apparent to adults. When engaged in the virtual world it becomes very real to young people. Some young people even form their own virtual identity that may or may not be different from their physical identity. Educators need to be aware of the numerous ways students are using technology so that they can watch for possible signs, and problems associated with cyber-bullying and victimization. They should teach students how to protect themselves while on-line, especially when children are using such devises as e-mail, chatrooms, message boards, instant messaging (IM), and weblogs to connect with other human beings.

Huffaker (2004) investigated how children are using weblogs to communicate and express themselves. Weblogs are virtual diaries that are posted on the Internet. His study showed, young people are more likely to reveal personal information on weblogs when compared to chatrooms or forums. While looking at the different technological devises students are using, educators need to realize that a child's virtual identity can be an important part of their self-worth. Therefore, cyber-bullying can put a child's well-being at risk, which can greatly affect their ability to learn and function at school.

While educators need to be aware that cyber-bullying is covert and difficult to identify, likewise, administrators need to be careful not to fall into the current trend of taking a defensive stance in dealing with individual cases of cyber-bullying. According to Shariff (2004), this stance is due to emerging litigation. When parents of victims approach school officials for help, school administrators often take one of three stances. The first is to assume the victim has caused the abuse and is partly to blame. The second is that the victim is exaggerating the abuse. Finally, the third assumes that the school's written anti-bullying policy is all that the school can do to protect the victim, and the school is not responsible for actions that happen outside of school grounds. These defensive stances are due to the lack of understanding of the complexities that are involved in bullying and victimization. To overcome this defensive stance schools' officials must take steps to educate themselves and parents, as well as establish reasonable methods to prevent and deal with cyber-bulling.

Schools that have attempted to take a stand against cyber-bullying have often had difficulties determining their responsibilities and their legal rights regarding discipline. Decisions such as these are best if decided before there is a problem because federally funded schools have certain legal responsibilities that they must respond to or face litigation. According to Conn (2002), there are three important laws for school district personnel to be aware of:

- Children's Internet Protection Act of 2000, mandates adoption of technology protection of measures on all computers purchased with or supported by federal funds to prevent both children under 17 and adults from accessing certain objectionable visual materials on the Internet (p. 13);
- Title VI of the Civil Right Act of 1964, providing that no persons shall be excluded from, denied the benefits of, or subjected to discrimination under any program or activity receiving federal assistance because of race, color, or national origin; and
- Title IX of the Education Amendment of 1972, providing that no person shall be excluded from, denied the benefits of, or subjected to discrimination under any program or activity receiving federal assistance because of sex or gender (p. 72).

It is vital that educators not only be aware of these laws, but also know how they are to be implemented in the school setting.

The Children's Internet Protection Act of 2000 states that schools must protect children when they are on the Internet. To comply with this act schools often set up electronic filtering and blocks, which restricts access to certain web sights. In addition to this, some schools give students a password that enables educators to track how students are using the Internet (Beckerman & Nocero, 2003). While most teachers and administrators are aware that communication through the Internet is traceable, but not all students do. Regardless, this traceability makes it possible for schools to track down the student or students responsible for bullying behavior.

Therefore, schools should be conscious of Title VI[2] and Title IX[3]. If a public school student feels that he or she has been discriminated against to a degree that hampers their education, they have the right to sue that student and that student's family. The student may also sue the school for hostile environment harassment. In order to win this litigation the student must prove that the school was aware of the situation, had the power to stop the harassment, and chose not to. Despite difficulty in proving hostile environment discrimination, the courts have ruled for the students in the past (Conn, 2002). The most important way that schools can protect themselves is to create an acceptable use policy that articulates in writing what students are allowed to do and not do (Lawson & Comber, 2000).

An East coast school has taken an active stance in combating improper use of technology. The school set up a system in which the office can monitor students using the computer in real time. If students are caught misusing the computers, they lose the privilege of working on them. Similarly, a midwest-based software company has designed a system that enables administrators to view messages that fall into certain categories such as violence or adult content (Shek, 2004). Yet even with safety procedures in place children are still at risk. Many students have access to an unsupervised home computer. While schools can track and intercede in situations that take place on school grounds, they do not have control over what students do at home. A matter that complicates this problem is that some situations occur both on school grounds and at home. These cases can get difficult for educators especially when the incident is hampering student safety or learning. When schools begin to investigate these situations, they can run into roadblocks when trying to resolve the problem.

Roadblocks can include finding the culprit, removing the harmful material, and disciplining the guilty party. A specific roadblock occurs when two students share their screen name with each other. If an argument stirs between the two friends, the possibility of misuse is strong. The shared screen name could be used by one of the friends to impersonate the other friend over the Internet. The shared screen name can cause trouble for both the victim and the school who is trying to resolve the problem (Beckerman & Nocero, 2003).

The first thing schools can do to combat this problem is to educate students on the facts and consequences associated with cyber-bullying. School district personnel should explain to students, the penalties associated with misappropriate use of the information communication technologies.

Students need to know that what they say over the Internet can be harmful to others and they are not operating anonymously. Many students do not realize it is possible for their actions to be tracked and in some cases punishable by law. Schools should be very clear about computer expectations. Rules should be written in student handbooks, parents should be given copies, and they should be posted onto the school's website. Not only should expectations be written, but also the punishments if those expectations are not followed (Franek, 2004).

Some schools are using creative means to combat cyber-bullying. Wasek Community School uses the same technology that bullies often use, but to help victims. Harassed students have the opportunity to report incidents through a text message. This system is great for students who normally are too embarrassed or scared to turn to an adult for help. It allows them to send a text message and be heard (Wakefield, 2005).

Educators can also help parents take an active role in preventing cyber-bullying by providing informational brochures or other educational devises to help parents become more Internet savvy. Parents can play a major role when it comes to protecting their children from cyber-bullying by staying informed and asking their children questions. The most basic suggestion to give parents is to keep in mind that the same behavior expected in day-to-day living should also be expected in Cyberspace (Franek, 2004).

Beckerman and Nocero (2003) suggested parents use the following guidelines to keep their children safe on the Internet and the WWW:

- Set rules for computer use;
- Never give out personal information (e.g. name, age , address, phone number, school);
- Never meet anyone face-to-face;
- Don't respond to threatening, suggestive, or obscene messages-report them to the internet Service Provider (ISP);
- Do not accept messages from people who are not on your buddy list;
- Do not believe everything you read online-individuals who post online may not be who they say they are;
- Don't share your screen name and password;
- Change your user name and password frequently;
- Do not use a screen name that is gender specific.
- Parents also need to familiarize themselves with technology lingo that their children are using. One example is "POS" that stands for "Parent Over Shoulder". Children use this term and similar terms to communicate secretly with each other.

All of these examples are important for parents to understand, as well as watch out for when their children are on the Internet at home. It is also important that the children understand why following rules on the Internet are significant.

Other useful information school district personnel can give to parents involves what to do if they find their child is being victimized on the Internet. Administrators should inform the parents that there are several steps to keep in mind. First, do not panic and take away the child's computer privileges because this may prevent the child from disclosing future dilemmas. Parents should inform their child not to respond to a cyber-bully and help their child block the unwanted messages. If a student believes the messages are coming from peers that attend their child's school, parents should contact school officials. If the messages are threatening contact the police and file a report. If the harassment continues, contact Internet providers and explain the situation. It is possible to block messages coming from a particular machine regardless of what e-mail address is used (Snider, 2004). All of these steps will ensure school personnel, parents, and the child feels better prepared to deal with possible victimization and to feel more in control of the situation if it occurs.

CONCLUSION

With new advances in information communication technology, bullies have become more aggressive due in part to the anonymity associated with the Internet and the WWW. These technologies also provide a range of new tools for bullies to victimize their peers through instant messaging, web-pages, blogs, and text messaging just to name a few. Children's ever increasing accessibility to the Internet makes these tools fast and highly damaging. Cyber-bullying not only affects the victim, but it also has an adverse affect on the bully. Administrators and teachers need to be aware of how students are using technology to victimize their peers and what to look for in schools. In accordance with this, schools need to have a written acceptable use policy and they need to educate both parents and children on what is acceptable, what will not be tolerated, and what to do if cyber-bullying does occur.

NOTES

1. Scott Mitchell is a pseudonym. All persons and places are represented as pseudonyms.

2. Title VI prohibits discrimination based on race, color, and national origin receiving federal financial assistance (see http://www.usdoj.gov/crt/cor/coord/title-vi.htm for more information).

3. Title IX: No person in the United States shall, on the basis of sex, be excluded from participation in, be denied the benefits of, or be subjected to discrimination under any education program or activity receiving Federal financial assistance (See http://www.dol.gov/oasam/regs/statutes/titleix.htm for more information).

REFERENCES

Beckerman, L., & Nocero, J. (2003). High-tech student hate mail. *Education Digest, 68*(6), 37–40.

Blair, J. (2003). New breed of bullies torment their peers on the Internet. *Education Week, 22*(21), 6–9.

Bosworth, K., Espelage, D., & Simon, T. (1999). Factors associated with bullying behavior among early adolescents. *Journal of Early Adolescence, 19*, 341–362.

Boulton, M. J. (1997). Teachers' views on bullying definitions, attitudes and ability to cope. *British Journal of Educational Psychology, 67*, 223–233.

Conn, K. (2002). *The Internet and the law.* VA USA: Association for Supervision and Curriculum Development.

Cyberbully.org, Cyberbullying. (n.d.). Mobilizing educators. Parents, students, and others to combat online social cruelty. Retrieved March 26, 2005 from http://cyberbully.org

Franek, M. (2004). Rise of the cyberbully demands new rules. *Christian Science Monitor, 96*(115).

Haahr, M. (2004). *Lichtenstein Creative Media.* Bullying Retrieved September 10, 2005, from The Infinite Mind Web site: http://www.lcmedia.com/mind309.htm

Huffaker, D. (2004). *Gender similarities and differences in online identity and language use among teenage bloggers.* Master's Thesis, Georgetown University, Retrieved September 11, 2005 from http://cct.georgetown.edu/thesis/DavidHuffaker.pdf

Keith, S., & Martin, M. E. (2005). Cyber-bullying: Creating a culture of respect in a cyber world. *Reclaiming children and youth, 13*(4), 224–228.

Lawson, T., & Comber, C. (2000). Censorship, the Internet, and schools: A new moral panic? *The Curriculum Journal, 11*, 273–285.

Leishman, J. (2002, October 10). Cyber-bullying. *CBC news.* Retrieved March 26, 2005, from http://www..cbc.ca/news/background/bullying/cyber_bullying.html

Nansel, T., Overpeck, M., Pilla, R., Ruan, W., Simons-Morton, B., & Scheidt, P. (2001a). Bullying behaviors among US youth: Prevalence and association with psychosocial adjustment. *Journal of the American Medical Association, 285*, 2094–2100.

Nansel, T., Simons-Morton, B., Scheidt, P., & Overpeck., M. D. (2001b). Systemic vs. individualistic approaches to bullying. *Journal of the American Medical Association, 286*(7), 787–788.

Shariff, S. (2004). Keeping schools out of court: Legally defensible models of leadership. *The Educational Forum, 68*(3), 222–233.

Shek, K. (2004). Faceless 'cyberbullies' pose new challenges to schools. *Education Daily, 37*(201).

Snider, M. (2004). How to cyberbully-proof your kids. *Maclean's, 117*(21/22), 77.

Snider, M., & Borel, K. (2004). Stalked by a cyberbully. *Maclean's, 117*(21/22), 76–78.

Wakefield, J. (2005, February 16). Hi-tech answers to pupil problems. *BBC News.* Retrieved April 16, 2005, from http://news.bbc.co.uk/go/pr/fr/-/1/hi/technology/4268203.stm

Wendland, M. (November 17, 2003). Cyber-bullies make it tough for kids to leave playground. *Detroit Free Press.* Retrieved April 9, 2005, from http://www.freep.com/cgi-bin/forms/printerfriendly.pl

Wolfe, M. (June 2003). Cyber brats: bullies who taunt their peers with the click of a mouse. *Parenthood.com.* Retrieved April 9, 2005, from http://parenthood.com/articles.html?article_id=4335

Ybarra, M. L. (2004). Linkages between depressive symptomatology and Internet harassment among young regular Internet users. *Cyberpsychology and Behavior, 7*(2), 247–257.

Ybarra, M. L., & Mitchell, K. J. (2004). Online aggressor/targets, aggressors, and targets: A comparison of associated youth characteristics. *Journal of Child Psychology and Psychiatry, 45*(7), 1308–1316.

CRITICAL SUPPORT FRAMEWORK FOR K-12 SCHOOL AND UNIVERSITY TECHNOLOGY PARTNERSHIPS ☆

Lisa C. Yamagata-Lynch and Sharon Smaldino

ABSTRACT

It has been well documented that the successful use of technology in K-12 education improves student achievement. However, both K-12 schools and higher education institutions have not been able to systematically provide preservice and inservice teachers with adequate training and support. This chapter will examine the K-12 school–university partnership literature, and identify critical support elements that are necessary for successful change related to technology both in higher education and the K-12 classrooms. Additionally, we will introduce two characteristics from the NCATE Partnership Standards and how schools and universities can use them to guide relationships and how they approach the school technology reform process.

☆This project was funded by the Northern Illinois University 2005 Research and Artistry Grant.

Technology and Education: Issues in Administration, Policy, and Applications in K12 Schools
Advances in Educational Administration, Volume 8, 29–42
Copyright © 2006 by Elsevier Ltd.
ISSN: 1479-3660/doi:10.1016/S1479-3660(05)08003-0

In this chapter, we will address the systemic obstacles for mutually beneficial technology partnerships and what the critical elements are to overcome them. We will begin the discussion by examining the K-12 school–university partnership literature. Then we will identify elements that are critical to support successful technology integration into the K-12 and preservice curriculum. Finally, we will introduce the learning community and collaboration characteristics from the National Council for Accreditation of Teacher Education (NCATE) Professional Development School Standards and how schools and universities can use them to guide relationships to approach the school technology reform process.

When designed and implemented appropriately, technology integration in the K-12 classroom enhances student achievement (CEO Forum on Educational Technology, 2001; Schacter, 1999). Researchers and practitioners agree that technology can be used as an educational tool that offer learners rich and stimulating experiences otherwise difficult to achieve. For example, technology has been used to support: (a) computer-supported collaborative learning (Koschmann, 1996), (b) learner-centered mediational tools for student thinking (Bonk & Cunningham, 1998), (c) visualizing and modeling complex science interactions (Barab, Hay, Barnett, & Keating, 2000a; Barab et al., 2000b), (d) student inquiry based learning (McKenzie, 1998; Singer, Marx, Krajcik, & Chambers, 2000; Wallace, Kupperman, Krajcik, & Soloway, 2000), (e) supporting virtual learning communities (Barab, Kling, & Gray, 2004), and (f) encouraging student learning through video games (Gee, 2003; Squire & Jenkins, 2003).

To facilitate the above technology integration activities, K-12 schools and universities have both put effort to provide sound technology integration training to preservice and inservice teachers. Businesses, funding agencies, and educational policy makers have been supportive of the above efforts and have provided funding to improve technology infrastructure and teacher technology training programs (CEO Forum on Educational Technology, 2000; National Council for Accreditation of Teacher Education: Task force on Technology and Teacher Education, 1997). For example, the US government has put funding priority in: (a) equipping schools and public library with technology hardware and software (Webre, 1998), (b) clarifying the skills necessary for teachers to integrate technology into the classroom (National Educational Technology Standards, 2000), and (c) building partnerships between universities and schools for providing sound technology training to both preservice and inservice teachers (U.S. Department of Education, 1999).

Despite these efforts both schools and universities are still blamed for not adequately providing quality technology training that address issues pressing in the K-12 classrooms (Zhao, 2003). Therefore, providing technology equipment, skills, and opportunities for professional development do not facilitate change in classroom use of technology. Unfortunately, activities such as the above do not address the necessary support that schools and universities need to sustain mutually beneficial relations for effective technology integration. In other words, they do not address the organizational obstacles in both schools and universities that prevent teachers and students from taking advantage of the available technologies (Cuban, 2001; Cuban, Kirkpatrick, & Peck, 2001; Russell, Bebell, O'Dwyer, & O'Connor, 2003).

For example, once in the school environment, teachers are rarely given the opportunity to meaningfully integrate technology into the school curriculum. This presents a dissonance between what is taught at the university level in preservice and inservice education programs and what is practiced in K-12 classrooms (Strudler & Grove, 2002). Inevitably, this perpetuates the belief from teachers that university faculty are unappreciative of what really takes place in their classrooms, and university faculty belief that teachers do not appreciate or practice what is best for student learning. Additionally, these beliefs are an indication of the cultural conflicts between schools and universities stemming from the different sets of work expectations, responsibilities, and ultimately how teachers and university faculty define good teaching practices (Cochran-Smith, 2000).

UNIVERSITY–SCHOOL PARTNERSHIP OBSTACLES

Researchers and practitioners have identified school and university partnerships as a possible solution to better prepare qualified teachers (Clark, 1999; Goodlad, 1994). In many past partnerships, universities typically believed that there was something wrong with the schools and their staff, and prescribed solutions to fix the problem in a top-down manner (LePage, Bordreau, Maier, Robinson, & Cox, 2001). Recently, many professionals within the teacher education and partnership community agree that these traditional relations have consistently not been able to meet their goal for enhancing teacher education and teacher professional development programs (Day, 1998; Lieberman & McLaughlin, 1992; Simpson, Robert, & Hughes, 1999).

Fortunately, traditional types of partnerships are becoming less popular. Instead, many partnership programs now strive to maintain a collaborative relationship that involves (a) university faculty's active presence in schools identifying knowledge situated within teachers' work context and

(b) university faculty identifying and attempting to meet everyday teacher needs (Day, 1998). However, the unequal relations of past school–university partnerships developed a sense of mistrust and they are finding it difficult to re-establish collaborative relations (Clark, 1999).

Due to the mistrust and fundamental cultural differences between universities and K-12 schools there are many uncertainties about how to facilitate collaborative partnerships (Perry, Komesaroff, & Kavanagh, 2002). These uncertainties have made it difficult for schools and universities to find mutually beneficial relationships (Teitel, 2003a). Additionally, these uncertainties have instigated many instances of miscommunication between schools and universities, which ultimately have hindered participants from attaining the goals that they set out in the first place.

Currently, universities are blamed for not reciprocating what they gain from partnerships to schools. For example, in many cases partnership-based research that faculty conduct do not necessarily have results relevant to teachers' daily classroom activities and student achievement (Teitel, 2003b). When they are relevant the educational innovations do not have a systematic implementation strategy that will allow them to become everyday classroom practices (Blumenfeld, Fishman, Krajcik, & Marx, 2000). In other words, what university faculty bring to schools through partnerships are in many cases unusable for classroom teachers. Consequently, partnership research is not making immediate results to inform practice.

NCATE PROFESSIONAL DEVELOPMENT SCHOOL STANDARDS

The National Council for Accreditation of Teacher Education (NCATE) published the Standards for Professional Development Schools to clarify many of the uncertainties involved in partnerships. Specifically, the standards were prepared to: (a) better align school reform efforts targeted for improvement in student achievement with teacher quality enhancement professional development activities, (b) narrow the gap between research and practice on school reform, and (c) bring better articulation between what preservice teachers learn in universities and what they see practiced in schools (National Council for Accreditation of Teacher Education, 2001). NCATE anticipates that the use of the professional development schools standards will bring rigor to the nature of university–school partnerships and provide a framework for conducting evaluations and research of partnership outcomes.

The NCATE standards are structured into five key characteristics and four developmental guidelines. The characteristics include: (a) learning community; (b) accountability and quality assurance; (c) collaboration; (d) equity; and (e) diversity, and structures, resources, and roles. Each of the above characteristics has performance expectation descriptors based on developmental levels that include beginning, developing, at standards, and leading. In this chapter, we will specifically focus on supportive elements for learning community and collaboration.

The standard on learning community states the following:

> The PDS is a learning-centered community that supports the integrated learning and development of P–12 students, candidates, and PDS partners through inquiry-based practice. PDS partners share a common vision of teaching and learning grounded in research and practitioner knowledge.... The PDS partnership includes principal and supporting institutions and individuals. The principal PDS partners are members of the P–12 schools and professional preparation programs who agree to collaborate.
>
> (NCATE, 2001, p. 9)

In other words, the policies and practices within a partnership need to support members to learn about each other, K-16 students, and about both universities and schools as an institution. Partnership members need to be able to exchange ideas regarding the above matter. Additionally, the activities in the partnership need to make immediate improvement in the policies and practices of both schools and universities. These immediate results need to be disseminated within the members as well. Finally, the above standard identifies critical support members of partnerships that need to be included in partnerships and need to be in communication with one another.

The collaboration standard states the following:

> PDS partners and partner institutions systematically move from independent to interdependent practice by committing themselves and committing to each other to engage in joint work focused on implementing the PDS mission. They collaboratively design roles and structures to support the PDS work and individual and institutional parity. PDS partners use their shared work to improve outcomes for P–12 students, candidates, faculty, and other professionals. The PDS partnership systematically recognizes and celebrates their joint work and the contributions of each partner.
>
> (NCATE, 2001, p. 13)

In other words, partnerships need a structure for all members to explore a new work culture that allows them to work together toward the mission. The partners need to develop interdependence to achieve the mission. All members need to democratically decide what organizational structure and roles are critical for accomplishing the above. In order to improve K-16 student outcomes, partners need to share resources, ideas, and celebration events for their success.

In the following sections we will introduce our supportive framework for technology integration partnerships. Our framework is based on insights from past research on school–university partnerships, and the NCATE partnership standards on learning community and collaboration. The framework does not suggest a specific model for approaching partnerships, but instead suggest elements that need to be attended if K-12 schools and universities are going to successfully build mutually beneficial partnership culture for technology reform.

PARTNERSHIP SUPPORTIVE FRAMEWORK FOR TECHNOLOGY INTEGRATION

The core to quality learning experiences is the people who are involved in the teaching–learning process (Oppenheimer, 2004). Within teacher education, preservice teacher candidates encounter two different groups of people, university faculty and K-12 teachers. While they are both educators at their center, they are worlds apart in their culture. A key to understanding the successful relationship between these apparently dissimilar partners is to garner an understanding of their common goal, that of improving the quality of the teacher candidate as a first-year teacher.

In the context of technology integration, the disparity between universities and K-12 schools is further exacerbated. The K-12 schools often are either well endowed with technology resources or have little or no innovative resources, while the university is often not able to keep up with current trends due to lack of funding or to having to serve a diversity of courses and programs. Thus, university faculty complain they are unable to prepare students for all eventualities, and K-12 teachers complain that preservice teacher candidates are woefully under prepared to make technology decisions. This disparity of concerns creates a disconnect that entangles the preservice teacher candidate in a maze of confusion.

We have identified four critical contributory support elements in our partnership support framework that include (a) leadership, (b) participant interaction, (c) program coordination, and (d) program integration as shown in Fig. 1. Partnerships need clearly identified leadership teams representing both the school and university. Without this leadership, partnership members become confused to who is in control of partnership activities. Additionally, without a strong leadership, university faculty and K-12

Leadership   Participant Interaction

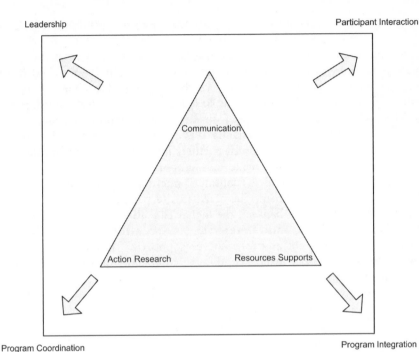

Program Coordination   Program Integration

Fig. 1.   Graphical Representation of Critical Support Framework.

teachers are left on their own to mend the cultural conflicts between their work settings. In these situations it quickly becomes unclear as to what the mission of the partnership was initially.

When participants are unclear of the reason to why they are maintaining partner relations, they become reluctant to interact with each other. Participants find it difficult to see any added value that the partnership brings to their individual work. This lack of interaction between teachers and faculty then allows the partnership to become fragmented and uncoordinated. When the partnership program itself is uncoordinated, schools and universities are not able to integrate faculty research, teacher research, teacher preparation practices, and K-12 teaching practices to inform one another for simultaneous renewal.

We believe that without the critical contributory elements, schools and universities will not find reciprocity in their relationships. Furthermore, on a daily basis the lack of the above support elements result in: (a) redundancies in the preservice and inservice education program, (b) complicated program procedures for teachers to navigate, (c) preservice program with a lack of connection to the field, (d) professional development programs that do not meet immediate teacher needs, (e) insufficient preservice teacher field supervision, and (f) programs that do not reflect university faculty and K-12 teacher interaction in its activities. We believe that it is time for higher education institutions to implement strategies to overcome partnership obstacles and maximize the benefits from the critical support elements.

When examining support elements, it is a reasonable goal to provide the necessary support structure for all partners involved in the partnership relationship. The factors that relate to a supportive framework that enables quality partnerships include: (a) continued internal communication between higher education departments involved in the partnership and continued partner communication between the higher education institution and partner schools, (b) collaborative preservice, inservice teacher, and university faculty action research, and (c) resource support to the daily activities of preservice and inservice teachers and university faculty in their research and teaching activities.

Communication

One key factor in our supportive framework is communication. Whether it is internal communication within university and within K-12 school settings or organizational communication between universities and schools, the issue of ensuring that all members are involved in the communication process is essential to successful partnerships. In order to bring about the types of teacher education programs desired, all participants must be involved in the communication process. All participants need to understand the desired outcomes, how teacher education is managed at all levels, the tools necessary to arrive at the outcomes, and the priorities and concerns of all those involved (Ellsworth, 2000).

Communication must be viewed as a two-way process. Historically, teacher education has been viewed as under the domain of the university setting. Teacher candidates attended classes, learning theory and application in a series of seemingly disconnected courses. For example, most preservice teacher candidates take technology courses too early in their program of study. This can be blamed as a result of university faculty perception that technology is a prerequisite for preservice professional courses. Furthermore, these professional courses are sequenced very tightly to fit as many as possible before student teaching; therefore, there is no room to fit curriculum technology integration courses into the professional preservice education semesters. For many students, learning technology skills early in their program leave them with limited knowledge and skills that they can apply at the time of student teaching. This situation is painfully exacerbated because shifts in technology occur rapidly and preservice teachers become further behind in being able to integrate technology into their teaching.

Internal Communication
The lack of communication among and between faculty further worsens the teacher education curriculum disconnect. In the past, faculty in content areas and methods courses felt the need to focus on their subject, leaving technology aside under the tag of the "technology course." For many years the prevailing view that a technology course in the teacher education program of study was fine (Mehlinger & Powers, 2002). However, over time this view has sifted to one where there needs to be an integration of technology throughout the entire teacher preparation program. However, faculty in content areas or methods courses are often ill-prepared to teach with technology themselves. With the advent of newer NCATE standards as they relate to technology integration, the apparent shift in the area of technology has been demonstrated in improved communications among faculty.

In the K-12 setting the internal communication is important to ensure quality clinical and student teaching experiences. Often within the K-12 setting, decisions are made at an administrative level that is not clearly communicated to the classroom teachers. Thus, many times the teachers feel as if they are not part of the decisions regarding their participation in a school–university partnership experience. Communication within the K-12 setting requires that everyone who is involved in a partnership is included in the discussion surrounding implementation of expectations related to that partnership.

Organizational Communication

Teacher education programs are incorporating protracted field-based programs so that preservice teacher candidates have more opportunities to participate in school settings as part of their preparation. This type of field-based participation requires that faculty communicate with schools to ensure a variety of participation experiences for preservice teacher candidates. Therefore, organizational communication is a key factor in supporting quality school–university partnerships.

Further, communication between the K-12 school and the university are necessary because schools are an essential part of the total learning experience of the preservice teacher candidate. Without their active participation and communication in the learning process, the teacher candidates will not have the quality experience necessary to see theory in practice (Ellsworth, 2000). This synergy of school–university practice is at the core of teacher education. Without the communication between the schools and the university, the essence of the experiences for students is lost because the connections between the two settings are unclear and the quality of the outcomes cannot be assured.

Action Research

Guided by the NCATE inquiry-practice standard, another factor in ensuring a quality partnership relationship is to examine ways in which faculty and teachers, along with preservice teacher candidates, can engage in classroom-based action research. The outcomes of these action research activities need to inform K-12 and university technology education teaching and learning practices. The collaborative nature of action research provides a foundation to achieving outcomes for all participants (Henderson & Hawthorne, 2000). In this process, teachers need to address instructional questions, faculty need to engage in applied research within their fields of study, and preservice teacher candidates need to learn the inquiry process as part of their professional development.

In many partnerships, the collaboration between partners is apparent, but the research efforts can be lost in the bustle of field-based experiences. Further, faculty is often pressured to perform quality research and publish in top journals, while classroom-based research is often seen as low-grade research. Field-based research projects can be complicated with the sensitivity of today's Internal Review Boards, along with the need to maintain parental acceptance of research on minors.

Communication plays a critical role at this level as well. Faculty and teachers must meet and decide on what needs to be studied and how to address the complicated procedures involved in partnership research. They must concur on the researchable questions or areas of inquiry, collaborate on the methodology, and identify the resources to engage in their study (Henderson & Hawthorne, 2000). Both the universities and the schools need to meet the requirements for research approvals. Therefore, faculty and teachers need a reliable communication method to work together and simplify the above complications involved in partnership research.

Resource Support

The final factor in a school–university partnership is supportive resources to ensure the sustainability of the partnership. Both the university and the school must agree that the value of supporting the relationship is necessary to success. One can view supportive resources akin to where "the rubber meets the road." The institutions must be willing to contribute to the activities of the partnership, in terms of time, money, and supplies. Again, communication is a key to ensuring that this factor is not lost in the fray.

Technology is a resource where there needs to be a connection between the partners because preservice teacher candidates can become confused and concerned that their preparation is inadequate for their particular school context. Schools often have specific types of hardware or software in their classrooms, while universities are often partnering with many schools, and thus are unable to provide an exact match with specific schools. Under these circumstances, many preservice teachers find that there is a discrepancy between the technology hardware and software they use at the university and what is available at K-12 schools.

Creativity is often called upon to find resolutions to the above disconnect (Ellsworth, 2000). When faculty put time into the school setting in the form of observing students or in collaborative teaching, they can locate the types of resources that might be useful in their university coursework. Further, faculty can engage their school-based teaching partners to assist them in teaching preservice teacher candidates to use technology. The partnership relationship between the school and university might enhance the manner in which technology is integrated into teacher education.

SUMMARY

The thrust of this chapter has been to introduce a partnership support framework that emerged from the partnership literature and addressed the key characteristics of learning community and collaboration from the NCATE partnership standards. We believe that without a strong leadership, participant interaction, program coordination, and program integration schools and universities will not be able to find desirable outcomes from their partnership agreements. Additionally, the key elements that affect the above structures on a daily basis that need to be addressed by all partners include internal and organizational communication, teacher and faculty action research, and resources support. With these factors at work a quality partnership relationship can evolve into one that fosters the development of quality teacher candidates.

REFERENCES

Barab, S. A., Hay, K. E., Barnett, M. G., & Keating, T. (2000a). Virtual solar system project: Building understanding through model building. *Journal of Research in Science Teaching, 37*(7), 719–756.

Barab, S. A., Hay, K. E., Squire, K., Barnett, M., Schmidt, R., Karrigan, K., Yamagata-Lynch, L., & Johnson, C. (2000b). Virtual solar system project: Developing scientific understanding through model building. *Journal of Science Education and Technology, 9*(1), 7–25.

Barab, S. A., Kling, R., & Gray, J. H. (2004). *Designing for virtual communities in the service of learning.* New York: Cambridge University Press.

Blumenfeld, P. C., Fishman, B. J., Krajcik, J., & Marx, R. W. (2000). Creating usable innovations in systemic reform: Scaling up technology-embedded project-based science in urban schools. *Educational Psychologist, 35*(3), 149–164.

Bonk, C. J., & Cunningham, D. J. (1998). Searching for learner-centered, constructivist, and sociocultural components of collaborative educational learning tools. In: C. J. Bonk & K. S. King (Eds), *Electronic collaborators: Learner-centered technologies for literacy, apprenticeship, and discourse* (pp. 25–50). Mahwah, NJ: Erlbaum.

CEO Forum on Educational Technology. (2000). Teacher preparation STaR chart a self-assessment tool for colleges of education. *CEO forum on educational technology.* Retrieved December 15, 2004, from the World Wide Web: http://www.ceoforum.org/downloads/tpreport.pdf

CEO Forum on Educational Technology. (2001). Building blocks for student achievement in the 21st century. *CEO forum on educational technology.* Retrieved December 15, 2004, from the World Wide Web: http://www.ceoforum.org/downloads/report4.pdf

Clark, R. W. (1999). School–university partnerships and professional development schools. *Peabody Journal of Education, 74*(3/4), 164–177.

Cochran-Smith, M. (2000). The future of teacher education: Framing the questions that matter. *Teacher Education Quarterly, 11*(1), 13–24.

Cuban, L. (2001). *Oversold and underused: Computers in classrooms.* Cambridge, MA: Harvard University Press.

Cuban, L., Kirkpatrick, H., & Peck, C. (2001). High access and low use of technologies in high school classrooms: Explaining an apparent paradox. *American Educational Research Journal, 38*(4), 813–834.

Day, C. (1998). Re-thinking school–university partnerships: A Swedish case study. *Teaching and Teacher Education, 14*(8), 807–819.

Ellsworth, J. B. (2000). *Surviving change: A survey of educational change models.* Syracuse, NY: ERIC Clearinghouse on Information and Technology.

Gee, J. P. (2003). *What video games have to teach us about learning and literacy.* New York: Palgrave-MacMillan.

Goodlad, J. I. (1994). *Educational renewal: Better teachers, better schools.* San Francisco: Jossey-Bass.

Henderson, J. G., & Hawthorne, R. D. (2000). *Transformative curriculum leadership* (2nd ed). Upper Saddle River, NJ: Merrill/Prentice-Hall.

Koschmann, T. (Ed.) (1996). *CSCL: Theory and practice of an emerging paradigm.* Mahwah, NJ: Earlbaum.

LePage, P., Bordreau, S., Maier, S., Robinson, J., & Cox, H. (2001). Exploring the complexities of the relationship between K-12 and college faculty in a nontraditional professional development program. *Teaching and Teacher Education, 17*(2), 195–211.

Lieberman, M. W., & McLaughlin, W. (1992). Networks for educational change: Powerful and problematic. *Phi Delta Kappan, 73*(9), 673–677.

McKenzie, J. (1998). Grazing the net: Raising a generation of free-range students. *Phi Delta Kappan, 80*(1), 26–31.

Mehlinger, H. D., & Powers, S. M. (2002). *Technology & teacher education: A guide for educators and policy makers.* Boston: Houghton Mifflin Company.

National Council for Accreditation of Teacher Education. (2001). *Standards for professional development schools.* Retrieved June 10, 2005, from the World Wide Web: http://www.ncate.org/documents/pdsStandards.pdf

National Council for Accreditation of Teacher Education: Task force on Technology and Teacher Education. (1997). *Technology and the new professional teacher: Preparing for the 21st century classroom.* National Council for Accreditation of Teacher Education. Retrieved December 15, 2004, from the World Wide Web: http://www.ncate.org/accred/projects/tech/tech-21.htm

National Educational Technology Standards. (2000). *National educational technology standards.* Retrieved December 15, 2004, from the World Wide Web: http://cnets.iste.org

Oppenheimer, T. (2004). *The flickering mind: Saving education from the false promise of technology.* New York: Random House.

Perry, C., Komesaroff, L., & Kavanagh, M. (2002). Providing space for teacher renewal: The role of the facilitator in school–university partnerships. *Asia-Pacific Journal of Teacher Education, 30*(3), 243–257.

Russell, M., Bebell, D., O'Dwyer, L., & O'Connor, K. (2003). Examining teacher technology use: Implications for preservice and inservice teacher preparation. *Journal of Teacher Education, 54*(4), 297–310.

Schacter, J. (1999). The impact of education technology on student achievement: What the most current research has to say. *Milken family foundation.* Retrieved, December 15, 2004, from the World Wide Web: http://www.mff.org/publications/publications.taf?page=161

Simpson, F. P., Robert, M., & Hughes, S. (1999). Using information and communications technology as a pedagogical tool: Who educates the educators? *Journal of Education for Teaching, 25*(3), 247–263.

Singer, J., Marx, R. W., Krajcik, J., & Chambers, J. C. (2000). Constructing extended inquiry projects: Curriculum materials for science education reform. *Educational Psychologist, 35*(3), 165–178.

Squire, K., & Jenkins, H. (2003). Harnessing the power of games in education. *INSIGHT, 3,* 5–33.

Strudler, N., & Grove, K. J. (2002). Integrating technology into teacher candidates' field experiences: A two-pronged approach. *Journal of Computing in Teacher Education, 19*(2), 33–38.

Teitel, L. (2003a). *The professional development schools handbook: Starting, sustaining, and assessing partnerships that improve student learning.* Thousand Oaks, CA: Corwin Press Inc.

Teitel, L. (2003b). Using research to connect school–university partnerships to student outcomes. In: D. L. Wiseman & S. L. Knight (Eds), *Linking: School–university collaboration and K-12 outcomes* (pp. 13–27). Washington, DC: American Association of Colleges of Teacher Education.

U.S. Department of Education. (1999). *Preparing tomorrow's teachers to use technology (PT3)*. Retrieved December 15, 2004, from the World Wide Web: http://www.ed.gov/programs/teachtech

Wallace, R. V., Kupperman, J., Krajcik, J., & Soloway, E. (2000). Science on the Web: Students online in a sixth-grade classroom. *The Journal of the Learning Sciences, 9*(1), 75–104.

Webre, P. (1998). *Federal subsidies of advanced telecommunications for schools, libraries, and health care providers. CBO Paper*. Washington, DC: Congressional Budget Office.

Zhao, Y. (2003). What teachers need to know about technology?: Framing the question. In: Y. Zhao (Ed.), *What should teachers know about technology?: Perspectives and practices* (pp. 1–14). Greenwich, CT: Information Age Publishing.

THE PASTEURIZATION
OF EDUCATION [*]

David Williamson Shaffer and Kurt D. Squire

ABSTRACT

In his book Pasteur's Quadrant, Donald Stokes (1997) argued that research projects can be described by their contributions to theoretical understanding and the solution of practical problems. Building on this model, scholars have suggested that educational research should focus more or less exclusively on what Stokes called "use-inspired basic research." With this move has come a focus on projects with the potential to create systemic change – and the concurrent devaluation of naturalistic studies of learning in context and design research to develop innovative educational interventions. We argue that this current predilection is based on a fundamental misreading of the processes through which scientific investigation addresses practical problems, and (more important) is counter-productive for the field of educational technology. To make this

[*]The research reported in this chapter was supported in part by a Spencer Foundation/ National Academy of Education Postdoctoral Fellowship, a grant from the Wisconsin Alumni Research Foundation, a National Science Foundation Faculty Early Career Development Award (REC-0347000), the Academic Advanced Distributed Learning CoLaboratory, and by the Wisconsin Center for Education Research, School of Education, University of Wisconsin–Madison. Any opinions, findings, or conclusions expressed in this paper are those of the authors and do not necessarily reflect the views of the funding agencies, WCER, or cooperating institutions.

Technology and Education: Issues in Administration, Policy, and Applications in K12 Schools
Advances in Educational Administration, Volume 8, 43–55
ISSN: 1479-3660/doi:10.1016/S1479-3660(05)08004-2

case, we look more closely at the operationalization of Stokes' quadrant model in the field of education, suggesting that its short-term focus on systemic change is based on a misunderstanding of history. We use Latour's (1983) study of Pasteur to suggest an alternative lever model for the research-based transformation of educational practices through educational technologies. By way of illustration, we use a brief example of a research project in educational technology to ground a discussion of the broader implications of this alternative conceptualization of the process of education research.

For decades educational technologists have struggled with the problem of how to transform school systems to meet the needs of post-industrial, knowledge-based economy and society. In recent years, reformers have looked to Donald Stokes' *Pasteur's Quadrant* (1997) as a framework for reorganizing research on educational technology in order to create more lasting impacts on the practice of education.

Stokes argues that research can be described by its contribution to theoretical understanding and contribution to the solution of practical problems. His model maps the landscape of inquiry into four "quadrants:"

1. Bors' Quadrant of pure basic research: lots of theory but little practical application;
2. Edison's Quadrant of pure applied research: lots of practical application but little theoretical contribution;
3. Pasteur's Quadrant of use-inspired basic research: contributions to theory and practical applications; and
4. the ignominious, unnamed quadrant of research for its own sake: little contribution to anything at all.[1]

Perhaps in response to those who suggest with thinly veiled contempt that all of the contemporary education research is in the unnamed, useless fourth quadrant, scholars in recent years have argued that studies should focus more on Pasteur's Quadrant of "use-inspired basic research" (Sabelli & Dede, 2001). With this move has come an emphasis on projects driven by "use-inspired" questions with the potential to create systemic changes, and a reliance on randomized controlled trials as the preeminent method of investigation – and a consequent devaluation of naturalistic studies of learning in context and design research developing innovative educational interventions, as well as the methods of inquiry that support them.

We argue that this current predilection is both counter-productive and based on a misreading of the processes through which scientific investigation addresses practical problems. To make this case, we look more closely at the operationalization of Stokes' *quadrant model* in the field of education, suggesting that its short-term focus on systemic change is based on a misunderstanding of history. Based on Latour's (1983) study of Pasteur, we then suggest an alternative *lever model* that emphasizes the transformation of educational practices through technological innovation. We argue that the renewed focus on use inspired research in education, while important, has placed undue emphasis on tinkering around the edges of existing educational systems without seriously reconsidering the fundamental values or organizing structures behind schooling. In short, it has led to a privileging of research programs that work within the current constraints of schooling rather than those that have the potential to change it.

INHABITING PASTEUR'S QUADRANT

Over the past decade, Pasteur's Quadrant has been taken up as a rallying cry for the reform of educational research, particularly among researchers in the learning sciences working on developing innovative learning technologies (Sabelli & Dede, 2001). Stokes, who was a political scientist before his death in 1997, argued that policy makers have long held an oversimplified view of science. Too many people in the public and in policy-making communities, he suggested, believe that innovation is simply the result of doing "basic" research, generating results, and then applying them outside the laboratory. In practice, Stokes pointed out, the distinction between "basic" and "applied" science is messy: each overlaps and informs the other. Writing for policy makers, Stokes argued that rather than exclusively funding "basic" research, the government (particularly the National Science Foundation) should also fund research projects driven by pragmatic questions, such as those faced by educators and educational technologists. He describes Pasteur's work as a prototype for this kind of use-driven research, and the National Institutes of Health as a grant-giving agency that exemplifies this commitment to solving problems while furthering fundamental understandings (Sabelli & Dede, 2001; Stokes, 1997).

Building on Stokes' argument, some scholars have suggested that "use-inspired" research – research in Pasteur's Quadrantmight rescue the "awful" reputation of educational research by simultaneously creating successful interventions and developing fundamental understandings about educational practice (Kaestle, 1997). Sabelli and Dede (2001), for example, argue: "now that the causes underlying educational dysfunctions are better understood, practitioners and policy makers are asking researchers to focus on applied larger studies that improve practice in a sustainable, affordable, and scaleable manner" (p. 12). In suggesting this application of the concept of Pasteur's Quadrant, educational researchers have often interpreted "use-driven research" as meaning *research that addresses the everyday questions of teachers and principals in typical – or more often, "problem" – schools.* Sabelli and Dede explain: use-driven problems are problems "stemming from issues in curriculum, pedagogy, assessment, professional development, etc." (p. 4).

In this model, in other words, researchers should focus on what Sabelli and Dede call *scholarship of practice*: questions that speak to practitioners' concerns – "curriculum, pedagogy, assessment, professional development, etc." – with an eye toward improving extant practices. One can only assume that conference sessions, such as "Evidence-based motivation-related outcomes of mathematics improvement interventions: Collaborative adventures in Pasteur's quadrant" (a collection of papers at the 2005 American Educational Research Association annual meeting reporting on projects in the National Science Foundation Math and Science Partnership Program) would be part of such a scholarship of practice– asking use-inspired questions about programs or policies that work within the existing grammar of schooling (Tyack & Tobin, 1994).

The goal of such work is interventions that can be disseminated beyond specific research contexts. Fishman, Soloway, Krajcik, Marx, and Blumenfeld (2001), for example, describe the current conundrum facing educational researchers as one of the developing innovations that "scale." The problem with technological innovations, from this perspective, is that design experiments that show what might be accomplished with new learning technologies too often die off when they are taken out of the original research context and integrated into school settings. As Fishman et al. (2001) suggest:

> This form of research has been and will continue to be essential to developing both new technologies and refined understanding of the learning process. But it is insufficient for ensuring that the lessons learned about how to foster increased student learning find a foothold in everyday practice in classrooms that do not enjoy the same focused attention and support. The result is that the most valuable uses of technology are not achieving meaningful *scale*, and more importantly, are not becoming a part of the everyday or *systemic* practices of schools or school reform. [Emphasis in the original]

The metaphor of "scaling up" is core to this approach, which focuses on creating interventions that can be deployed beyond the context in which they are developed. The *quadrant model*, as interpreted by these researchers, is thus to answer use-inspired questions by developing scaleable, sustainable interventions that operate with the current assumptions and under the current conditions of schooling. And, of course, the way to evaluate such interventions, from this point of view, is with randomized controlled experiments, which provide policy makers the data they need to decide, which programs work best. As Feuer, Towne, and Shavelson (2002) explain: randomized, controlled experiments are "still the single best methodological route to ferreting out systematic relations between actions and outcomes" (p. 8) – and thus for deciding what interventions are worth bringing to scale and what programs are scaling successfully.

INHABITING L'ECOLE NORMALE SUPÉRIEURE

Unfortunately, this view of educational reform as "scaling up research in Pasteur's Quadrant through randomized controlled experiments" is problematic, both practically and metaphorically, because it is based on a misreading of the processes of change and innovation. While Stokes accurately described Pasteur's interest in basic research that addresses applied problems, his presentation of Pasteur's work – and thus the image on which the quadrant model is built – did not describe the *mechanisms* by which Pasteur connected the two. A more careful analysis of how Pasteur's "basic" research methods were "applied" to real-world problems suggests that the metaphor of "scaling up" is not the only (and perhaps not the best) way to conceptualize technological innovation in education.

In his studies of the history of science, for example, Latour (1983) recounts in some detail the process by which Pasteur isolated the anthrax bacillus in his laboratory at L'Ecole Normale Supérieure and developed a vaccine for the disease that was endemic to French farms in the late 19th Century. Anthrax had already been the subject of much study, of course, but outbreaks did not appear to follow any regular pattern. Veterinarians had concluded that local conditions played a large role in determining when and where anthrax appeared, and were suspicious that the disease could be linked to any single organism.

Pasteur's approach to the challenge of anthrax was to take his laboratory apparatus into the field – to start working with the natural conditions in which the problem occurred, trying to isolate as precisely as possible the conditions under which outbreaks took place. Pasteur's team systematically studied the natural history of the disease, and the life cycle of the organism they hypothesized as its cause.

Once a prospective organism was identified based on this naturalistic inquiry, Pasteur and his team returned to L'Ecole Normale Supérieure to grow the bacillus in culture. Under controlled conditions they were able to demonstrate that the organism was a critical agent in the spread of the disease. By designing systems for breeding the bacillus under a range of conditions, Pasteur was able to attenuate and strengthen strains of the organism, mimicking the variation observed in the disease in its natural setting. More important, by creating attenuated strains of the bacillus, Pasteur was able to produce, in his laboratory, the first ever artificial vaccine: a vaccination for anthrax. As Latour suggests, Pasteur was able to "do inside his laboratory what everyone tries to do outside but, where everyone fails because the scale is too large, Pasteur succeeds because he works on a small scale" (p. 149).

Having developed a vaccination in his laboratory, Pasteur moved to a field trial at Pouilly le Fort. But moving the vaccine back into the applied setting did not mean adapting the vaccine for use in the more complex and less controlled setting of French agriculture. Rather, it meant extending the practices of Pasteur's laboratory into the field. The conditions of the trial at Pouilly le Fort were carefully negotiated so as to recreate in a farm setting the conditions of Pasteur's laboratory that were essential to the success of the vaccination. The success of the field trial appeared "miraculous" to the public because Pasteur was able to show that all the vaccinated animals survived and all the unvaccinated animals contracted the disease and died. But as Latour is quick to point out, the trial was really a "staged" experiment, repeating results that Latour had already achieved in his laboratory, and the "dissemination" of the vaccine was not so much a process of scaling up as it was a transformation of farming practices to mimic the conditions of Pasteur's research. As Latour explains, Pasteur's achievement was that "on the condition that you respect a limited set of laboratory practices – disinfection, cleanliness, conservation, inoculation gesture, timing, and recording – you can extend to every French farm a laboratory product made at Pasteur's lab" (p. 152).

Latour describes Pasteur's method as a series of "translations" between farm and laboratory: the initial naturalistic inquiry that isolates the bacillus for study in the laboratory; the subsequent designed strains of the bacillus and controlled "outbreaks" within the laboratory setting; the transformation of pathogen into vaccine; the recreation of the conditions of the laboratory in the field at Pouilly le Fort; and finally the reorganization of French agriculture to accommodate the scientific practices that make inoculation effective.

In 1881, when Pasteur developed the first artificial vaccine, it was possible for a single scientist to undertake this process of naturalistic inquiry, laboratory research, and transformation of practice. But as problems – and the social and technological systems in which they arise – become more complex, progress comes rather from researchers working at various stages in this process, with each research program gaining leverage on the problems it tackles by building on the work of those focusing on other stages: naturalistic investigations provide the basis for laboratory research, which in turn provide models for the transformation of practice. Pasteur's own practice was, as Latour suggests, not merely "use-inspired basic research;" it was a series of levers by which problems and contexts were more deeply understood, tools and techniques were developed, and systems and practices were reorganized in light of the resulting process of inquiry.

We thus argue that this *lever model* of Pasteur's work is a more appropriate "translation" of Pasteur's methods to education research than the quadrant model described above. The lever model suggests that we need to support systematic naturalistic inquiries into the mechanisms by which learning takes place, in both exemplary and problematic situations. We need to support systematic, experimental, and design research into understanding these mechanisms more deeply and developing "ideal" practices and contexts, which show how students can learn effectively. And we need to reconceptualize the process of "dissemination" as one of the "transformation," in which practices developed in controlled settings become images that drive the reorganization of schooling in fundamental ways.

In the next section we describe an example of this process, showing how the lever model implies a different and powerful way of thinking about both education research and educational reform.

THE LEVER MODEL IN ACTION

One-hundred-and-twenty-three years after Pasteur used the new science of microbiology to defeat anthrax at Pouilly le Fort, 10 middle school students in Madison, Wisconsin were writing about cutting-edge research to cure Alzheimer's disease using stem cells. These students were participating in *Science.Net*, a role-playing game in which they became science journalists, reporting on scientific developments and discoveries and their impact for an online science newsmagazine.

As in a real newsroom, these cub reporters attended news meetings where they pitched stories for the health and medicine, technology, and environment sections of the magazine. Working with desk editors for each section, the cub reporters interviewed sources, submitted stories for copyediting, and copy-edited each other's work. To produce finished stories they learned to write leads and headlines, to use the neutral journalistic "voice of the newspaper," to source their stories using AP style, to include art and captions, to format their work for distribution on the web, and to prioritize copy on the section front. In a 3-week summer outreach program at the University of Wisconsin-Madison, these students collectively reported and produced some 50 news articles about science and technology.

Along the way, not surprisingly, students who play a game like *Science.Net* learn a lot about journalism. In a shorter pilot version of the study[2] in which we interviewed students before and after the role-playing game, students' use of journalism terms went up by 188% (mean before $= 3.5$, after $= 10$, $p < 0.01$), and more than twice as many students (9/12 compared to 4/12) said they thought journalism is about informing the public. For example, before playing the game one student said: "A journalist is someone who would write because they want to but they get paid to do it, so [journalists] bring stories that they're interested in and write something about it." After the game, the same student said: "To be a journalist [is] to inform people about current events by writing them."

Also not surprisingly, these students learned a lot about science. To be sure, they learned scientific facts and theories related to their stories, whether about nanotechnology ("Small Technology Goes to War"), ecology ("Study: Phosphorus Threatens Mendota"), or information technology ("Can games really help children?"). Perhaps more significant, writing about science and learning about science in the context of science journalism – and thus in the context of informing the public about events that impact their lives – helped to expand these students' understanding of what science is and why it matters. Before playing the game one student said:

> I think science is ... things that include electricity or the human body or ... I just, like, do science ... I don't really think about what science is.

After role-playing as a science journalist, the same student explained:

> I think science can be a lot of different things. Science can be technology, environment, health and medicine. Football fields can be considered science. Someone had to like help like make things up, inventing things. How to grow the grass ... . Like how long the yards are going to be ... . I didn't know science could be health and medicine. Things like environment ... before I just thought they were what they were ... [but I think about them differently after] picking the articles and finding stories about them and writing about them.

Overall, as shown in Fig. 1, students came to describe science less in terms of school subjects and topics ("electricity or the human body") and more in terms of the impact of science on society. (The changes in both categories of the graph are significant with $p < 0.05$.)

Our research on *Science.Net* suggests that what makes this role-playing game effective is that students are participating in an authentic recreation of the practices of journalists – or, more precisely, a recreation of the professional practicum through which journalists are trained (Shaffer, 2004). That is, students are learning about science by learning to work as – and thus think like – reporters. A role-playing game like *Science.Net* is based on the practices by which journalists are trained, and creating *Science.Net* meant conducting careful ethnographic observations of journalists in training – naturalistic study of the context in which reporters learn to think like journalists.

Elsewhere, we have described this kind of game based on the practices of real-world professionals as an *epistemic game* (Shaffer, 2005, in press; Shaffer, Squire, Halverson, & Gee, 2005). We raise the example here to ask: Where does an intervention such as this fit in our understanding of technology-based

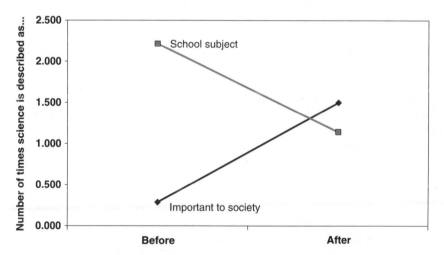

Fig. 1. Change in Students' Description of Science before and after Role-Playing as Science Journalists. Points Represent the Mean Number of Times Students Refer to Science as a School Subject or Topic and as something Important to Society. Both Changes are Statistically Significant with $p < 0.05$.

educational reform? Is this better conceived as a point in (or out) of Pasteur's Quadrant, or as an example of Pasteur's Lever?

QUADRANT vs LEVER

Is *Science.Net* in Pasteur's Quadrant as interpreted by educational researchers? It certainly addresses a real, persistent, and continuing educational problem: getting students deeply engaged in scientific issues, and in this sense might qualify as "use-inspired research" similar to Pasteur's laboratory study of the anthrax bacillus. However, *Science.Net* is not focused on scientific thinking in the context of schools as currently constituted. Indeed, we deliberately work *outside* of school settings because the structures of school – mandated curricula and assessments, 50-min periods, permissions for field trips, and large class sizes – make it difficult to simulate the conditions of journalistic practice. *Science.Net* is not driven by issues of "curriculum, pedagogy, assessment, professional development, etc." as currently constituted within our schools; rather, it is a deliberate attempt to reconsider such issues in light of the affordances of new technologies. As such, it is not a *scholarship of practice* as described by Sabelli and Dede (2001) but quite deliberately *scholarship of the possible*.

On the other hand, *Science.Net* is an excellent example of the lever model applied to education. In *Science.Net*, naturalistic study of a context in which learning takes place is the basis for a design experiment in a controlled setting. Methods from the naturalistic study are refined through successive iterations under "laboratory" conditions until an effective curricular model is developed. *Science.Net* is surely not yet as refined as Pasteur's final anthrax vaccine – and whether it will ever be is an open empirical question. However, the basic processes are similar: studying a real world context, simulating its essential elements within a laboratory setting, and developing a potentially powerful intervention through design and experimental research.

The reason that it matters whether we think of *Science.Net* as a good example of Pasteur's Lever or a poor exemplar of research in Pasteur's Quadrant is that each of these models has a different implication for the question: What next?

In the quadrant model, *Science.Net* would need to "scale up" – to be implemented in a large number of classrooms and compared to traditional instruction in randomized controlled trials. To make that possible, it would have to be re-adapted to the existing conditions of practice – rescaled to the class sizes, periods, content, and assessments of middle school science instruction. We have not done those experiments, but even without empirical data, it is easy to see that reworking an intervention based on the authentic simulation of real world practices to fit the existing structures of school would be about as likely to succeed as handing Pasteur's vaccine to a 19th Century farmer and asking him to inject it into his cows without changing anything else about the organization of his farm.

But, of course, that is precisely *not* what Pasteur did. Latour's point is that successful implementation of the vaccination, Pasteur developed at L'Ecole Normale Supérieure, meant adapting the conditions of practice to recreate the features of the laboratory essential to the success of the intervention. The *quadrant model* for educational research argues that design experiments under laboratory conditions are not useful because they "are not becoming part of the everyday or systemic practices of schools or school reform" (Fishman et al., 2001). But the point of the *lever model* is that the role of such experiments is not to adapt to existing practices but rather to provide guidelines for the transformation of practice. Following the lever model, the pathway would be to develop more and larger contexts that can accommodate *Science.Net* and other epistemic games of its kind – thus providing an engine for improving schools in fundamental ways rather than tinkering within the constraints of what is clearly a complex and very stable system.

CONCLUSION

We argue, then, that the Stokes' concept of Pasteur's Quadrant may not be the most productive metaphor for thinking about educational reform in the context of new technologies. A more careful reading of the practices by which Pasteur used the new technologies of microbiology and experimental science to transform 19th Century animal husbandry suggests that educational research needs to abandon the notion that successful "scaling up" in the rough-and-tumble world of extant schools is the only meaningful test of an intervention. There is, of course, a place for research that directly addresses the needs of practitioners. But not all research can or should be conceived in that way, particularly research with and about new technologies, which have the potential to transform practice in more radical ways.

Rather, we should conceive of the role of research on educational technology as also being about finding ways to reorganize schools in more fundamental ways. To this end, we suggest adopting the concept of Pasteur's

Lever. In the lever model, naturalistic study of extant contexts provides the foundation for design-based laboratory research. This design research leads to new and powerful interventions that serve as models for large-scale transformation of schooling. That is, we suggest that rather than focusing on "scaling up" an intervention by adapting it more broadly to the conditions of practice, we emphasize "scaling up" the transformation of schools by adapting them more broadly to the conditions under which meaningful learning takes place. We suggest that in an age of technologies that have the power to expand the limits of our pedagogical imagination, we provide conceptual space for research that looks broadly at the possible future rather than narrowly at the here-and-now – scholarship that focuses deliberately on the ideal rather than doggedly on the practical.

NOTES

1. Although it is beyond the scope of this paper, we would suggest that the fourth quadrant might be more aptly thought of as Picasso's Quadrant: the realm of art, intended not to advance theory or to solve practical problems through scientific investigation, but to express the human condition.

2. As of the writing of this chapter, we are still collecting and analyzing data from *Science.Net*. Data presented here are from an earlier, shorter design experiment using the same tools and practices as *Science.Net*.

REFERENCES

Feuer, M. J., Towne, L., & Shavelson, R. J. (2002). Scientific culture and educational research. *Educational Researcher, 31*(8), 4–14.

Fishman, B., Soloway, E., Krajcik, J., Marx, R., & Blumenfeld, P. (2001). *Creating scalable and systemic technology innovations for urban education.* Paper presented at the American Educational Research Association Annual Meeting, Seattle, WA.

Kaestle, C. (1997). Improving the awful reputation of educational research. *Educational Researcher, 26*(7), 26–28.

Latour, B. (1983). Give me a laboratory and I will raise the world. In: K. Knorr-Cetina & M. Mulkay (Eds), *Science observed: Perspectives on the social study of science* (pp. 141–170). London: Sage.

Sabelli, N., & Dede, C. (2001). *Integrating educational research practice: Reconceptualizing goals and policies: How to make what works, work for us?* Retrieved July 17, 2005, from http://www.virtual.gmu.edu/ss_research/cdpapers/policy.pdf

Shaffer, D. W. (2004). Pedagogical praxis: The professions as models for post-industrial education. *Teachers College Record, 106*(7), 1401–1421.

Shaffer, D. W. (2005). Epistemic games. *Innovate, 1*(6).

Shaffer, D. W. (in press). Epistemic frames for epistemic games. *Computers & Education.*

Shaffer, D. W., Squire, K., Halverson, R., & Gee, J. P. (2005). Video games and the future of learning. *Phi Delta Kappan, 87*(2), 104–111.

Stokes, D. E. (1997). *Pasteur's quadrant: Basic science and technological innovation.* Washington, DC: Brookings Institution Press.

Tyack, D., & Tobin, W. (1994). The grammar of schooling: Why has it been so hard to change? *American Educational Research Journal, 31*(3), 453–479.

TEACHER AS BRAND: PURSUING PROFESSIONAL IDENTITIES IN A DIGITAL DOMAIN

John B. Keller and Matthew J. Stuve

ABSTRACT

With the advance of web portals, teacher portfolios, and other digital means for representing professional productivity, teachers have new strategies for demonstrating their effectiveness and instructional acumen. These external, predominantly norm-referenced methods resemble the concept of "brand" used in economic contexts. This chapter explores the construct of brand and how web presence technologies influence how teacher quality is cultivated for mutual benefit to teachers, schools, and society. We propose a framework for how the profession might respond productively to the demands for demonstrable teacher quality. We briefly discuss the impact on the profession from a teacher advocacy standpoint.

DEFINING TEACHER QUALITY

Teacher education reform and the No Child Left Behind Act (NCLBA) have accentuated the challenge of defining what makes a good, high-quality

Technology and Education: Issues in Administration, Policy, and Applications in K12 Schools
Advances in Educational Administration, Volume 8, 57–70
Copyright © 2006 by Elsevier Ltd.
ISSN: 1479-3660/doi:10.1016/S1479-3660(05)08005-4

teacher. This law requires that schools hire only highly qualified teachers beginning with the 2002–2003 school year and that by the 2005–2006 school year each classroom be staffed with a highly qualified teacher (Education Week, 2005) although there is some evidence that this requirement is being relaxed. The logic of the law highlights the critical relationship between teaching and learning but, in practical terms, achieving this threshold has not been as straightforward. For each state to attain this goal, the question of "who passes as a highly qualified teacher" must be answered. The challenges California has faced in establishing this definition are illustrated in a lawsuit brought against the state by Californians for Justice, an activist group, alleging a violation of NCLBA in awarding "highly qualified" status to teachers holding provisional licenses (in this case, teachers had demonstrated adequate subject knowledge but had not completed the full course of teacher preparation) (Gewertz, 2005). Each state must provide a plan to the federal government outlining how it is addressing the teacher quality mandates in the NCLBA. Doing so requires states to meet the technical letter and the broad spirit of the law using a strategy that is workable in the local policy context – a truly daunting task.

Measuring teacher quality has been vexing for the profession. On one hand, input models for determining teacher quality rest on what the teacher brings to the classroom (e.g., SAT and GRE scores, teaching credentials, subject matter major) (Wenglinsky, 2000). Under such models, schools and districts can certify the quality of their teacher force by showing that each teacher holds a degree and a teaching license aligned to the job assignment.

Output or value-added models (McCaffrey, Lockwood, Koretz, & Hamilton, 2003) that attempt to quantify the effect of particular teachers or schools on students are gaining attention in discussions about teacher compensation (Blair, 2004) and in quantifying academic progress that meets muster at the federal level (Olson, 2005). Under such models, student growth can be described from year to year as a factor of expected growth or as a percentage of normal progress. This practice is appealing in light of NCLBA's linear improvement model – that is to say, if schools can demonstrate that students are increasing their academic stature by at least one year, the school can claim that adequate yearly progress (AYP) has been achieved despite falling short of the line that targets 100% proficiency by 2013–2014 (McCall, Kingsbury, & Olson, 2004). The value-added approach can also be used to detect differences in effectiveness among teachers – i.e., through statistical modeling, teachers add more or less than a year of growth to their students.

Both models for measuring or certifying the quality of teachers have merits and drawbacks. Even if inputs and outputs were used in concert, one could argue that there is more to understanding and gauging the quality of teacher practice. In fact, the dimensions of interest in the teacher quality *answer* shift depending on the origin of the teacher quality *question*. For example, meeting the requirements of the NCLBA or other policy requirements by demonstrating teacher quality is fundamentally an effort to meet an acceptable albeit minimum threshold.

It is important to point out that another manifestation of the quality conundrum is that the profession of teaching is devoid of rank. In other words, if the quality of teachers could be easily measured, differences in levels of performance would be difficult to model in current compensation structures that focus on tenure and credentials to achieve increases in pay. Perhaps the explorations of pay-for-performance models that are receiving spotty attention across the nation hold some promise that measures of effective performance could influence compensation. However, in a profession that is egalitarian at its core, formal indexing of teacher quality may be far less welcome than minimum standards of quality such as credentials and test scores.

The aim of this chapter is not to offer a definitive algorithm pleasing to all audiences for determining teacher quality. Rather, our goal is to suggest that there are additional ways to demonstrate teacher quality and that the availability of these new means for demonstrating effective practice will shift the locus of the effort from institutions to the professional.

In the remainder of this chapter, we illustrate how the web is providing new opportunities for teachers to demonstrate their professional capacities. In light of these opportunities, we suggest that concepts from brand theory can be useful in framing an advocate response to the question of teacher quality. We outline a framework for how the profession can respond productively to the *teacher as brand* construct.

APPLYING BRAND THEORY TO TEACHER QUALITY

The concept of brand has been with humanity for millennia. Roman potters etched symbols in their products to create a cultural association of a mark with a person and a certain quality or style of work (Clifton & Simmons, 2004). Global brands such as Coca-Cola and Nike are widely recognized and associated with not only their distinctive products, but with a range of emotions and affective appeal that are carefully crafted and managed to increase sales and brand loyalty. According to Clifton and Simmons (2004), the postWorld War II era has witnessed a brand explosion aided by dramatic changes in mass communication.

Brands are not only the concern of multi-national corporations. Think of Oprah Winfrey, Dale Earnhart, and Michael Jordan as successful personal brands. McNally and Speak (2002), in their book *Be your own brand* advance the notion that everyone is a brand. Haig (2004) notes that individual brand management involves making oneself "attractive for a particular person or audience" (p. 146). Thinking about the concept of "brand" in this way may not be terribly revolutionary because, as social beings, to some degree, we have always managed the perceptions that others have about us.

So, what facets of brand theory are relevant to the current discussion? The new domains of digital presence (discussed later in this chapter) permit interplay between the notions of brand (in the economic and marketing sense) and need for the professional teacher force to demonstrate teacher quality. Just as in economics, we can think about *teacher as brand* in terms of producer, consumer, product, and market demand.

In the case of producer, we are referring to a teacher's work in relation to something larger than his or her own classroom and, to some degree, larger than a school improvement plan. The product (discussed later) in the sense of this chapter is not student learning directly, but teacher impact on the educational endeavor of their school and profession.

Likewise, the consumer is also not necessarily the student. The idea of *teacher as brand* brings together current notions of teacher quality and leaves room for a broader conception of this construct including the perceptions of other professionals, stakeholders, and consumers (including, yes, parents and the students as "consumers" of the brand).[1]

The main product, we argue, is the teacher's expertise. This is a relative commodity that has numerous components and is inclusive of historic measures. We advocate for harnessing the web's relational power to include more norm-referenced measures of comparative expertise. In other words, the web can showcase the quantity, breadth, and demand for the teaching expertise of a teacher by pulling together the evidence of a teacher's online contributions. Previous constructs of production, when examined in this context, can be used by teachers to cultivate a brand that has recognition and value at various levels (e.g., local, regional, national) and with a variety of professional communities (e.g., schools, districts, language arts teachers, instructors of autistic children, etc.). In addition to the input and output measures of teacher quality, there are techniques from other domains that could be useful in measuring teaching expertise. Goolge's relevance ranking method for search results is based on the construct that the sites people want to find are the ones most linked to from other sites. The parallel for *teacher as brand* is that exemplary practice can be singled out by tracking the relative frequency by which colleagues seek/consume a teacher's advice, wisdom, and artifacts of practice. Therefore, the demand for one's professional expertise, as the core "product" that we define in this market, can be an indication of the emergence of a teacher's brand.

Another indicator of the relevance of brand construct is in the consumer response to the intentions of teachers (i.e., market demand). Data engines that permit sharing of expertise (real or perceived) have an application to how teachers might establish a professional web presence. For example, Apple's popular iTunes product allows users to easily publish lists of favorite music. This highly exploited functionality is one testament to the notion that people like to display their work and their opinions, and will do so for as little reward as the satisfaction of making their work public. What are the iTunes-like tools for teachers? Perhaps it is an environment where artifacts and evidence of professional practice are easily displayed, such as "playlists" entitled "Top ten web links about the Revolutionary War" or "Five best strategies for teaching first grade North Carolina science standards." Teachers could also consume and rate "playlists" produced by their colleagues. The demand for access to playlists and the strength of the rating or ranking could contribute to a teacher's brand strength.

The tools and technologies that we describe point to a productive intersection of brand theory and digital presence in the next section where teachers can craft a holistic image of their professional relevance. This response introduces both market-driven forces (i.e., norm referencing) with the powerful and intentionally managed evidence-based productivity that an array of digital tools now permits.

WEB AS PROFESSIONAL CANVASS: TECHNIQUES AND TECHNOLOGIES

As the web and the Internet continue to evolve, more people are producing content in public spaces. In its infancy, the web effectively limited participation of most users to a passive or consuming role. As the means of production have become more accessible, the connected public tends to play both consumer and producer in the online ecosystem. With the increasing ease of web publication comes a ballooning of web-available content.

As this trend gains momentum, there are more and more points of reference about individuals, goods, and services available. When purchasing a car, for example, one can not only find manufacturer's specifications but also accounts of customer experiences at particular dealers and comments about user satisfaction with the product. Essentially, the web is connecting and coordinating data, making possible a more complete and multi-dimensional picture of just about anything.

What is true of the general public is also true of the teaching profession. Where once teachers went to the web to find information to support lessons, they now produce and share lessons, participate in professional dialogue, and conduct a portion of their teaching effort in digital work spaces. But again, these are commodities that have little economic value because their producers – teachers – do not have an economic market for their expertise.

In this section, we explore some illustrative web-based means of production that have already been exploited by teachers as well as web-based technologies with potential application to *teacher as brand*.

Professional Web Sites

More and more professionals – in any discipline – anchor their intentional web presence with a domain name that serves as their professional web site. This can serve as the launching point for all content but is not the sole source for the brand. The power of a short, identifiable domain name is the ultimate presence technique for which all web producers strive. There is value of membership within an institutional site (institution.edu/myname), while there is complementary (and competing) value to myname.com. Saving that topic for another time, the point here is that all teachers need to define and control their intentional web presence as the authoritative source for public brand content.

Web-Based Portfolios

Digital portfolios have become a widely accepted form of representing longitudinal teacher development in relation to professional standards. This movement was energized by teacher education reforms that made the creation and maintenance of teaching portfolios a condition of graduation. The self-promotional aspect of such a web presence finds natural resonance with the current generation of pre-service teachers. Web-based portfolios also play an essential role in the National Board certification process.

Portfolios act as pass keys to stages of the profession (e.g., licensure, first teaching position, admission to the guild of Board-certified teachers). Over time, portfolios evolve from a mere collection of artifacts to a point of presence for one's professional production. Since such professional web sites are dynamic and iterative, one's "brand identity" requires constant grooming and strengthening with new content, resources, and evidence of professional relevance. As we have seen with prominent professionals in other fields, the depth, range, and activity on one's domain name or web site help to promote and secure greater professional autonomy. This emergence of professional identity is a radical shift for the culture of teaching.

Blogs

Blogging has emerged as one of the more generative forms of web production. Blogs – short for web logs – is a technique and a set of technologies for quick publication of high-frequency web content. Blogs originated as online journals, but the technologies that enable quick production of daily entries have expanded in their usefulness to other publishing tasks. Blogs, especially those that permit easy multimedia publishing, multiple categorization of entries, and user participation, provide one method that a teacher might use for establishing a significant part of the online presence of their expertise.

Educational Portals

A portal is an authenticated web environment that permits a customized entry point to a collection of shared resources, multiple functional components, and other collaboration services. Portals reflect their community and enable professionals to build knowledge bases. Newer portals permit queries of all content associated with a particular member. These "portal strands," therefore, represent a "portfolio" of contributions to the community and/or discipline defined by the portal.

Digital Planbooks

New planning tools such as the digital planbook available through the Indiana Humanities Council's smartDESKTOP allow teachers to create, manage, and share their daily lesson plans through a portal framework. What once was an artifact of practice rarely seen by other professionals is now being published and shared. Again, this points to additional transparency and review driven by teachers. Such technologies allow the arena of professional practice to expand to like-minded professionals no matter where they are located geographically. As teachers use the digital planbook year-in and year-out, the digital plans become a repository of professional knowledge that show the enacted curriculum. These repositories also have potential for catalyzing professional growth since they can be searched, annotated, and refined.

Moodles and self-declared courseware

Countless tools already exist with which teachers can autonomously create an online course, or at least create a complementary component to their traditional class instruction. Moodle[2] is one example of a free web site that allows teachers to build their own online education infrastructure. Course management systems have had a strong presence in K-12 and higher education but in recent years, a teacher can facilitate the same kind of interactions even if his or her institution is not using a specified courseware package (or even if it is). Moodle and similar environments create the vehicle for freelance teaching online, which greatly threatens traditional, institution-based models, but certainly empowers the individual teacher.

As these means of production illustrate, educators are voluntarily utilizing the web for a variety of purposes. We expect that the web will evolve toward demand and that teachers will continue to find innovative uses for emerging technologies. With a greater quantity of teacher practice taking a digital form or being web enabled, there comes a need for intentionally grooming the sum of one's webpresence. We now turn to the intersection of brand theory and this increasing digital presence for teachers – a concept we call "teacher as brand."

A FRAMEWORK FOR TEACHER BRAND MANAGEMENT

As we examine the landscape of brand technologies and professional sites, we can begin to articulate a framework for how *teacher as brand* might be productively realized in the coming years. We argue for this framework to advance a productive discourse for what is, in one sense, an inevitable by-product of the ubiquitous and virtual nature of the web. The framework below outlines some of the dimensions and trajectories of change that, if framed from the position of advocacy, can influence how teachers might be viewed (and how they view themselves) in an era of teacher and school accountability.

Advocacy

Perhaps the starting point for a teacher's personal brand is that he or she needs to take ownership of the digital portrayal of their professional personas or brand. Taking ownership of one's professional brand means moving beyond the traditional markers of quality, value, and belonging (e.g., licensure documents, union memberships, and years of service) to an enlarged notion of "consumable" professional expertise that includes the traditional markers and the evidence of practice in the digital domain. This is not to diminish the worth or value of the traditional markers of professional identity, but rather to spur teachers and the profession toward a more nuanced and rich portrayal of value, contribution, and professional attainment. On one hand, this may seem like bald-faced self-promotion and indeed, this is one critical force in the process. Properly understood, taking ownership of one's professional brand is the thoughtful ownership of professional identity – a pattern of thought that is inversely proportional to mere self-promotion. Teachers already carry other collective brands (the school's, the union's, their alma mater's, their National Board Certification, etc.) – what we urge here is a thoughtful self-advocacy that reconciles and unifies *brand by association* and brand as a result of professional contribution and practice. Without a personal commitment to the branding management, there is no way for the teachers to defend and cultivate their brand.

Responsiveness

One essence of the web is the speed at which content ages. Teachers with a digital brand representation should seek high-frequency dissemination models and techniques to assure that their newest contributions, advice, and products are easily accessible. What this requires of teachers is a gardening mindset – a view toward professional representation that, like gardening, involves regular work at short intervals, taking into account environmental variables and opportunities. The well-manicured garden is achieved intentionally with diligent care, not in irregular spurts of frenzied activity. The same is true of the new environment for professional identity made possible by the web.

Engagement

Related to responsiveness is the degree that the teacher engages others in his or her web presence. In other words, teachers should provide the means for constituents and audiences to respond to and participate in or "consume" the brand. This creates a situation where on the one hand providing for engagement is critical to support the responsiveness demand of brand management, while on the other the richness of engagement around a teacher's brand is also an index of the brand strength. Soliciting input is important; the quality, duration, and frequency of input are also an indicators of brand demand.

Evidence

While web publishing and blogs foster easy ways for teachers to create and present content on the web, portals and search engines create easy ways to manage, associate, and find content. On the whole, teachers have countless ways to associate large corpi of productivity, expertise, and effectiveness in navigable ways. The production needs to have some sense of durability to it or, better yet (for the digital domain), longevity. The more evidence of professional action and contribution that a teacher can present in a navigable form, the better.

Originality

The *teacher as brand* construct needs to have individual and professional protections that are diligently pursued. The fluid nature of the web poses challenges to ascertaining the origin of ideas (Burbules & Bruce, 1995). As managers of a brand, teachers must disclose the origin of ideas to the best of their knowledge while taking special care to protect their original thinking and contributions. Whether it is copyright declaration (and recognition) or simply citing others' work, the brand concept falls short of its professional trajectory if the individual fails to account for the origin of the content of the brand.

Legitimacy

The evidence and content of the brand needs some aspect of peer review. This is different than market-based (norm-referenced) indices of value, for those are subject to the pragmatic variables of popularity and demand rather than careful vetting by a community of professionals. Professional agency is needed to provide relevance and assurance to consumers of brand. We encourage teacher professional organizations to find ways to recognize teachers' professional web sites in systematic ways. It is also possible to imagine a return to guilds where professionals band together according to common principles, adherence to certain methodologies, or based mutually held standards of quality. Whatever the case, the legitimacy of one's brand is strengthened when it is endorsed by some type of accrediting agency according to a published standard of excellence.

Frameworks

Frameworks are any set of "lenses" or criteria that can be used to relate, organize, and navigate content. Professional competencies, curriculum standards, and similar descriptors all become more meaningful when related evidence can accumulate. As the construct of *teacher as brand* matures, organizational schemes that have the most cross-context utility for the consumers and audiences of teacher brands will become de facto standards. These organizing frameworks will facilitate cross-brand comparisons.

BRAND AND THE FUTURE OF TEACHERS AND SCHOOLS

The notion of *teacher as brand* poses challenges for school districts, which have historically enjoyed a workforce with adequate supplies[3] of equally qualified applicants (as measured by a license) eager to fill vacant positions. The professional autonomy and growth/improvement-oriented mindset that will accompany the intentional management of a teacher's professional brand will be at cross-purposes with the cloistered culture that has typified schools for years. As a greater portion of teachers' work moves online, it will become increasingly possible to propel expertise out of the classroom and into a space for professional consideration. To be sure, the absence of this capability to date is not the only inhibitor to such work. The egalitarian nature of the profession makes it difficult to privilege and honor everyday excellence. As a rule, special honor is reserved for those who persevere (accolades for years) and for the superstars (teachers of the year).

Traditional notions of teaching and schooling are being challenged by home schools, virtual schools, charter schools, and other hybrid educational environments. With the emergence of easy web publishing and as market demand for teacher quality energizes professionals, there is a certain consumer-oriented inevitability to the notion of *teacher as brand*. Marketability will align with composite measures of teacher quality that include input and output measures as well as evidence that is more iterative, varied, and peer referenced. The results will be increased opportunities for teachers to leverage the digital supports and virtual work environments to amplify their professional contributions. *Teacher as brand* is a good idea for teachers because it promotes audience and constituent accessibility with concomitant responsiveness and serves to elevate the public perception of the teaching profession.

Advancing the Teacher

It should be quite clear by now that the undertone of this entire chapter alludes to the future free agency of teachers. This may indeed be an outcome exploring what free agency and its second-order effects mean for the educational future, go beyond the scope of this chapter. However, it could be argued (albeit briefly again) that the very tools and technologies for which we advocate in this chapter are the same ones that can be used to facilitate the work of teachers, without teachers. The sooner teachers and the profession as a whole understand the potentials that we discussed in this chapter, the sooner teachers and the profession of teaching can enjoy a reinvigorated and appropriately deserving esteem.

Effects on Schools

The implications of the notion of *teacher as brand* for schools range from full-scale paradigm shifts to very particular and perhaps short-term policy issues. *Teacher as brand* challenges long-standing notions of teaching and maintaining a teaching force. A productive resonance must be sought between the personal and school-based contexts of representing the quality of content. For example, how can a teacher represent his or her school-based content on a personal site and vice versa? This may be a policy issue within the school, the district, and perhaps even the union. Additionally, coming to grips with the idea of *teacher as brand* would require schools and districts to grapple with issues of professional autonomy and academic freedom that shade toward the model of university teaching.

A Virtual Speaking Engagement

As academics, we have both been invited to speaking engagements and offered honoraria for our time. We hope our words have justified the time and the payment. We view such opportunities as professional joys and as a chance to be listened to (if not a stroke of the professional ego). The classroom teacher – whether it is because of professional culture, educational level, and/or policy constraints – will rarely enjoy such an opportunity. With some exceptions or as a result of patronizing gestures like shuttle missions,[4] K-12 teachers have very little opportunity to demonstrate their professional competence beyond their classroom. The stakes of this disconnect are raised further when school accountability efforts rest on definitions of teacher quality that set the bar somewhat awkwardly at minimums that often fall short of excellence.

Will there be a day when teachers' blogs and/or portal strands become a source of identity beyond their faculty picture in the school yearbook and their important relationships with students? We think so. Not because we have articulated a road map or provided external motivation for teachers in this chapter. This will happen because it already is happening.

Our goal with this chapter has been to prime a mindset for both teachers and the public on how to form and view, respectively, the professional and public identity of teachers. More teachers deserve the honor we as a society give, say, Christa McAuliffe.[5] We have been and will continue to advocate that teachers should think of themselves as brands because they already are, because the opportunities for demonstrating teaching expertise have never been more accessible, and because of what the widespread embrace of this opportunity could mean for the state of the teaching profession. Rather than obviating teachers, technology presents teachers with the means to demonstrate their effectiveness, relevance, and professional contributions in powerful new ways that will ultimately provide very satisfying answers to education consumers regarding the question of teacher quality.

NOTES

1. One hallmark of the digital marketplace that has been created by the web is the amplified voice of the consumer. Consider web sites such as http://www.ratemy-teacher.com. While the constructive merit of such sites may be debated, the fact remains that the web is a bully pulpit for anyone with means of publication.

2. See http://www.moodle.org/ for more information.

3. While some districts struggle perennially to fill teaching positions, distribution of the teacher force is a problem that results in localized teacher shortages (Murphy, DeArmond, & Guin, 2003).

4. We beg the readers' permission to make this somewhat politicized reference to Christa McAuliffe. We do not wish to dishonor her memory and the intentions of her mission to space. Rather, we make this reference to remind the reader of the

awkward difficulty we demonstrate as a society when we attempt to elevate teachers with evocative yet ambitious (and, in hindsight, reckless) political gestures. We argue that such elevation of the profession must come from within to have true and lasting effect. It is a sad irony that Ms McAuliffe is remembered for her selfless sacrifice rather than the rigorous selection process that awarded her the opportunity to fly as a champion of her profession.

   5. See http://www.christa.org/ for more information.

REFERENCES

Blair, J. (2004). Denver performance-pay plan yields student progress. *Education Week, 23* (18), 10.
Burbules, N., & Bruce, B. (1995). This is not a paper. *Educational Researcher, 24*(8), 12–18.
Clifton, R., & Simmons, J. (Eds) (2004). *Brands and branding.* Princeton, NJ: Bloomberg Press.
Education Week. (2005). States given extra year on teachers. Retrieved November 14, 2005, from http://www.edweek.org/ew/articles/2005/11/oz/10reprieve.h25.html
Gewertz, C. (2005). Calif. Group sues over 'highly qualified' label. *Education Week, 24*(44), 6.
Haig, M. (2004). *Brand royalty: How the world's top 100 brands thrive and survive.* London: Kogan Page.
McCaffrey, D. F., Lockwood, J. R., Koretz, D. M., & Hamilton, L. S. (2003). *Evaluating value-added models for teacher accountability.* Santa Monica, CA: Rand Education.
McCall, M. S., Kingsbury, G. G., & Olson, A. (2004). *Individual growth and student success (technical report).* Lake Oswego, OR: Northwest Evaluation Association.
McNally, D., & Speak, K. D. (2002). *Be your own brand: A breakthrough formula for standing out from the crowd.* San Francisco, CA: Berrett-Koehler.
Murphy, P., DeArmond, M., & Guin, K. (2003). A national crisis or localized problems? Getting perspective on the scope and scale of the teacher shortage. *Education Policy Analysis Archives, 11*(23). Retrieved November 14, 2005 from http://epaa.asu.edu/epaa/v11n23/
Olson, L. (2005). Education department convenes working group on 'growth' models. *Education Week, 24*(42), 20–21.
Wenglinsky, H. (2000). *How teaching matters: Bringing the classroom back into discussions of teacher quality.* Princeton, NJ: Educational Testing Service A Policy Information Center Report.

PART II:
TECHNOLOGY, POLICY, AND PHILOSOPHY: WHAT ALL SCHOOL DISTRICTS SHOULD KNOW

COPYRIGHT, TECHNOLOGY, AND YOUR RIGHTS

David M. Marcovitz

ABSTRACT

Copyright can be confusing and intimidating for schools. Copyright is difficult enough to understand when dealing with paper, but as new technologies enter the mix, copyright is often ignored as obsolete or is so confusing that even beneficial and legal uses are avoided. While copyright places restrictions on some use of material, educators have many rights to use work created by others. This chapter helps guide educators through the issues relating to copyright and technology so copyright is not used as an automatic "no" to legitimate uses or an automatic "yes" for questionable uses.

INTRODUCTION

In many ways, copyright seems to be obsolete.[1] If you see a picture on the Web, it is yours for the taking. If you hear a song that you like, peer-to-peer file sharing can supply it to you for free. Have you seen the latest movie? It is waiting for you online. If your students can benefit from a chapter in a book, the copy machine is available. This is *The Culture of Yes*. If you can find it, it is yours for the taking. The music and movie industries would like

Technology and Education: Issues in Administration, Policy, and Applications in K12 Schools
Advances in Educational Administration, Volume 8, 73–84
Copyright © 2006 by Elsevier Ltd.
ISSN: 1479-3660/doi:10.1016/S1479-3660(05)08006-6

you to believe that The Culture of Yes is pure, unadulterated evil. This leads to *The Culture of No*: you may not use anything in any way without the copyright owner's permission. Most answers to copyright questions lead to a quick rebuke from The Culture of No.

> Culture of Yes: I bought that CD; I can do whatever I want with it.

> Culture of No: No, you don't own the music on the CD, just a license to play it. All you can do is play it.

The law, however, does not subscribe to either The Culture of Yes or The Culture of No. Particularly in an educational setting, it promotes *The Culture of Fair Use*. In The Culture of Fair Use, many educational uses of copyrighted material are legal and appropriate without first obtaining permission, and many uses are not. This chapter guides you through often fuzzy lines between what fair use allows and what it does not while using technology in an educational environment.

THE CULTURE OF FAIR USE

In a school, The Culture of Yes often pleads *I'm doing it for the children* and *I'm not making a profit off of this* and *It isn't hurting anyone*. These are all valid arguments and important points. Fortunately, fair use takes these into consideration allowing some use in some circumstances but not unlimited use.

Imagine that you are a book author, and you make your living selling books; if you do not sell books, you do not eat. Imagine you are a teacher who finds material online that will benefit your students. Imagine you are a musician who sells millions of albums. Perhaps, you are a struggling musician trying to eke a living out of a few album sales and appearances. Imagine you are a librarian trying to disseminate information to the public. Imagine you are a student who found some great pictures on the Internet for a school report.

These examples are just the tip of the iceberg of the many competing interests in using or limiting the use of information. When I asked my students to role play some of these roles, they took stands against libraries and used-book sales, in favor of unrestricted use of anything for students and educators, limiting use to reading books and talking about them, and in favor of a wide range of uses with very strict limitations on the amount of material that may be copied. They learned that copyright laws have to balance these competing interests. While a bookseller, might think that it is reasonable that you cannot even copy a page out of a book, the student, teacher, and librarian would find those restrictions inappropriate.

The law tries to balance the rights of the copyright holder with the rights of the public while maintaining its primary goal of promoting the creation of new works, but copyright law is very confusing, especially when applied to the classroom. Many educational applications of copyright law fall under the domain of *fair use*. This is good and bad. Fair use allows you, as educators, to use materials that might otherwise be illegal for you to use. On the other hand, the rules of fair use are complicated and dominated by ambiguous case law.

WHY SHOULD I CARE ABOUT COPYRIGHT?

With the laws being so confusing and chances of being caught being remote, you might wonder why you should care about copyright. Legally, you should care about copyright because violations can bring fines of thousands of dollars. Many classroom uses are unlikely to bring the wrath of the copyright holders, but as material is distributed beyond the classroom walls (including presentations at parent nights, distribution on the world wide web, or distribution for distance learning), the chances of your actions violating the law and being noticed increase greatly.

Ethically, you should care because copyrighted works belong to someone else, and the holder of the copyright has the right to control distribution of the work. Copyright law is designed to encourage the creation of new materials by protecting the creator's rights to those materials. You should respect those rights and not do anything that will diminish the value of the creator's rights.

Finally, you should care about setting a good example for your students. Finding worthwhile material is important, but it should not take place at the expense of showing your students the law and ethics do not matter.

"ALWAYS LOOK FOR THE UNION LABEL"?

Many copyrighted works have a copyright notice. It is usually in the following form:

© 2005 David M. Marcovitz.

That is, it contains the "c" in a circle (or a "p" in a circle for non-visual things such as sound recordings), the date, and the copyright owner, sometimes followed by the phrase "All Rights Reserved." However, a copyright notice is not necessary. As soon as you create a work, you have some copyright protection for that work. If the creator has included the © in the document, that person has thought about protecting it, but even without it, the document is protected. Note that this was a change to the copyright law in 1989 so some works without a copyright symbol that were created prior to that date might not be protected by copyright law, but you should assume that it is protected unless you know otherwise.

PUBLIC DOMAIN

Exceptions to works being granted automatic copyright relate to the issue of *public domain*. Works in the public domain are free for anyone to do as they please. Works enter the public domain in three ways:

(1) Older works eventually lose their copyright protection and fall into the public domain.
(2) Works created by the United States government are automatically in the public domain.
(3) The copyright owner may choose to place works in the public domain and forego any copyright protection.

Work is generally copyrighted until 70 years after the death of the author (a recent law extended this from 50 years). Work created by a corporation is generally copyrighted for 95 years after publication (recently extended from 75 years, coincidentally, just in time to save Mickey Mouse from entering the public domain). After the time limits, the work is in the public domain. An author might choose to place his or her work in the public domain. This means that the work can be used by anyone for any purpose. Ethically, you should still give credit to the author, but you may freely use the work.

As an educator, this means that you have unlimited rights to use old books in any way you choose. Theoretically, you have unlimited rights to use old movies as well, but this does not yet apply because most movies are not 90 years old.

What about songs? Songs are a special situation because a song has three potential copyrights: the music, the lyrics, and the performance. Each can be copyrighted separately and have separate copyright owners. Very old songs might be in the public domain, but the particular recording, that is the performance, might not be. If you want unlimited use of old songs, you have to either use an old recording, or you need to record the songs yourself.

As one final note on public domain, public domain grants unlimited rights to use, alter, sell, etc. works. If you want to rewrite, republish, sell, alter, advertise with, or otherwise use disrespectfully public domain works, you are free to do so. However, this means that others can do the same to any works that you place in the public domain. While you might have no desire to make a profit off the works you create, you might choose to give limited permission, such as for non-profit educational uses. Creative Commons (nd.) and the Free Software Foundation's (2001) "copyleft" model are good models for allowing limited use.

PERMISSION

We know that some things are in the public domain and free to use while other material can be used with limits under fair use (discussed in detail below). Another way to use works created by others is to get permission from the copyright holder. The copyright holder has the right to grant you permission. Sometimes this is easy to obtain and sometimes it is not. Many copyright holders are sympathetic to non-profit educational uses and will be happy to give you permission.

To request permission, first you must figure out who owns the copyright. This is easy for traditionally published media (such as books, movies, and musical recordings). It will be listed on the packaging. Beware when you find something on the Internet. Many things are posted on the Internet by someone other than the copyright holder.

Once you determine the copyright holder, you can simply send an email or write a letter. Be clear about exactly how you want to use the material. Copyright holders are unlikely to grant you unlimited permission, but they might be sympathetic to educational uses with limited distribution of the work. Be reasonable and request permission for what you need, not every possible use you could possibly want.

Do not be surprised if your request is denied, goes unanswered, or is granted for a fee. Copyright holders have no responsibility to grant you permission, even for your seemingly benign use. Furthermore, they do not even have a responsibility to respond to your request. Many requests for permission include a phrase like *If I don't hear from you within 30 days, I will assume that permission is granted.* While this is a creative tactic, it will not work. Your assumption of permission is not permission, and a failure to respond to such a request is not permission. Finally, you might find that copyright holders are willing to grant you permission for a fee. Several years ago, Ann Landers had a very nice column about the failings of computer spell checkers. It was cute, and I wanted to share it with my students, so I wrote to Ann Landers' publisher and requested permission. A quick reply came back announcing that permission was granted as soon as I sent them a $50 fee. It was cute but not *that* cute. Instead of distributing the article, I taped it to my office door.

PLANNING FOR COPYRIGHT

As you plan a project that includes copyrighted material, you must plan for copyright. As you will see below, fair use grants you some rights, but those rights are very limited and often too restrictive. For example, limiting use of a substantial multimedia project to two computers for two years might make the development effort more trouble than it is worth. For that reason, you should plan: plan to get permission, plan for alternatives if permission is not granted, and plan to use as much public domain, copyright-friendly (i.e., work that retains copyright but comes with a notice that many uses are permitted), and self-created material as possible. Seek permission early in the process of designing your project so you still have time to make alternative plans if permission is not granted.

FAIR USE

Section 107 of the United States Copyright Code of 1976 defines fair use in the following way:

> Notwithstanding the provisions of sections 106 and 106A, the fair use of a copyrighted work, including such use by reproduction in copies or phonorecords or by any other means specified by that section, for purposes such as criticism, comment, news reporting, teaching (including multiple copies for classroom use), scholarship, or research, is not an infringement of copyright. In determining whether the use made of a work in any particular case is a fair use the factors to be considered shall include –
>
> (1)   the purpose and character of the use, including whether such use is of a commercial nature or is for nonprofit educational purposes;
> (2)   the nature of the copyrighted work;
> (3)   the amount and substantiality of the portion used in relation to the copyrighted work as a whole; and
> (4)   the effect of the use upon the potential market for or value of the copyrighted work.
>
> The fact that a work is unpublished shall not itself bar a finding of fair use if such finding is made upon consideration of all the above factors.
>
> (Limitations on the Exclusive Rights: Fair Use, 1976)

This implies a four-part test for fair use. However, the law does not define how much weight to give to each factor. Generally the courts have ruled that if the majority of the factors lean toward fair use, the use is fair use. However, this is not always the case.

Factor (1) relates to the way the material will be used. Commercial uses tip the balance away from fair use, and educational or other non-profit uses tend to tip the balance in favor of fair use. Criticism, parody, and news reporting are strong factors in favor of fair use because the courts have recognized that some important uses of copyrighted works are unlikely to get permission (would you give permission to a critic who did not like your work?).

Factor (2) relates to what type of material is being used: factual or imaginative/creative works. If the material is largely factual, it tips the scale in favor of fair use. If the material is non-factual (works of art, poetry, and fiction stories), it tips the balance away from fair use.

Factor (3) relates to the amount of the work that is being used, especially as it relates to the whole work. A brief quote is generally fair use. An entire work or a large section of a work is generally leaning away from fair use. This factor relates to the idea that your use of the material is preventing or avoiding the purchase of a copy of the whole work. For example, you would not buy a book (or make a class full of students buy a book) so they could read three sentences from the book. On the other hand, you might require students to buy a book if they had to read one or more full chapters. Of course, this is a wide range. As with all the factors, if other factors lean more toward fair use, this factor can lean a little further from fair use.

Factor (4) relates to the idea that the owner of the copyright could potentially make money off the work. If your use prevents that in any way, this factor leans away from fair use. This includes the copyright owner's ability to sell the work or collect licensing fees for use of the work.

Factor (5) is the stealth factor. It is not listed in the law, but it is generally agreed that an issue of time of use is important. As a rule of thumb, fair use only applies to use for one semester for reproduction of material. Some guidelines allow for up to two years of use for work that is part of a project (such as a multimedia project) that you created. Generally, you cannot use the same copyrighted material over and over again without seeking permission from the copyright owner (if you have permission, fair use does not apply; your agreement with the copyright owner applies). In addition, the time test applies to spontaneous use of work. If you want to use something in the very near future, and you would not have a reasonable amount of time to seek permission, you have a greater case for fair use (copying a newspaper article from that day's newspaper is a good example of this).

FAIR USE AND EDUCATIONAL
MULTIMEDIA PROJECTS

The laws about fair use are confusing, and they become more confusing as technology is introduced. In the mid-1990s, the Conference on Fair Use (CONFU) attempted to form a consensus on fair use in educational multimedia projects (CONFU: The Conference on Fair Use, 1996). CONFU developed guidelines and published them in 1996. However, the participants in CONFU never achieved consensus, with representatives of copyright holders finding the guidelines too permissive, and representatives of copyright consumers finding the guidelines too restrictive. With that said, the CONFU guidelines are the best we have. Because these are guidelines, not law, they do not define fair use, but they give guidance on its application. This guidance is very important because of the *good faith fair use defense*. An educator who, in good faith, believes use of copyrighted works falls under fair use has very limited liability for use. Someone who intentionally violates copyright, and to a lesser degree someone who violates copyright out of ignorance of the law, can be sued for large amounts of money plus legal fees. How will the courts know you have made a good faith effort to follow the law? One way they will know is that you have followed accepted guidelines, such as the CONFU guidelines. The courts may still rule against your use, but if you have made a good faith effort, you are unlikely to be sued and unlikely to have to do more than stop using the material.

The CONFU guidelines place specific limits on the amount of a work you may use (*portion limitations*), the time for which you may use it (*time limitations*), and the ways you may distribute it (*distribution limitations*). The guidelines only address non-profit educational uses of lawfully acquired material by educators and students in multimedia projects. That is, these are uses of copyrighted material in an educational setting that are incorporated into a multimedia project. The following will summarize some of the limitations. For more details consult the resources listed at the end of this chapter (e.g., CONFU: The Conference on Fair Use, 1996; Davidson, 2002; University of St. Francis, 2004; University of Texas at Austin, 2001).

Time limitations and distribution limitations differ for students and teachers. Students may keep copies of their projects as part of a portfolio (such as for a cumulative demonstration of academic work and for job interviews) indefinitely, and they may present the work to the class for which it was created during the academic term. Teachers may keep copies of their work in a portfolio indefinitely, and they may use the work with their students for a period of up to two years after the first use. However, teachers are limited to use two copies, that is, copies that are to be used by students (plus an additional backup copy that may not be used except to replace a used copy). Additionally, teachers may present their projects to peers at workshops or conferences. These limits are fairly restrictive and might mean that if you are going to take the trouble to create something more than a simple PowerPoint presentation, you probably want to use works for which you have greater permission. I would not want to spend several weeks creating a multimedia project and not be allowed to put it on all the computers in a computer lab or use it at all after a couple of years.

Portion limitations are the same for students and teachers. Portion limitations apply cumulatively to all work used throughout an academic term. Sorry, you cannot just break that larger project into three parts in order to use larger portions of works. Portion limitations vary by the type of work being used (CONFU: The Conference on Fair Use, 1996).

- Any kind of motion media (movies, videos, etc.) is limited to 10% of the entire work or 3 minutes, whichever is less.
- Text is limited to 10% of the entire work or 1,000 words, whichever is less.
- Poetry is limited to 250 words. Poems shorter than 250 words may be used in their entirety. Poetry is further limited to use of no more than three poems by one poet or five poems from different poets in an anthology.
- Music, lyrics, and music video are limited to 10% of the entire work or 30 seconds, whichever is less. Putting your favorite song as the soundtrack of your PowerPoint presentation is not permitted unless it is a very short presentation.
- Pictures and illustrations may be used in their entirety (10% of a picture would not make sense), but no more than five pictures from a single artist and no more than 10% of the images or 15 images, whichever is less, from a collective work.
- Numerical data sets are limited to 10% of the database or 2,500 cell entries, whichever is less. Note that cell entries refer to individual pieces of information, such as a name or social security number.

These limitations are fairly restrictive. You may not post copyrighted work on your Web site. You may not make CDs and distribute your work to your entire class. You may not use the copyrighted work for commercial or non-curricular uses, so you may not use clips of popular songs (even if they are each less than 30 seconds) as the soundtrack for your video yearbook. These are guidelines, so you might be able to justify some additional use beyond them, but most use of copyrighted works beyond these limitations requires permission.

PIRATED COPIES AND DOWNLOADING FROM THE INTERNET

Fair use applies only to works to which you have some legal right. This can be a problem for work that is posted on the Internet because much of what was posted was posted without permission (and is, thus, illegal). If the copyright owner has not given permission for distribution, you do not have any right to the work. The primary offense is that of the person who illegally placed the work on the Internet, but you are liable as well if you use the work. Unfortunately, it is not always easy to tell what work on the Internet is there legally. The Internet can be a great source of media for multimedia projects, but much of it might be illegal.

VIDEOS IN THE CLASSROOM

If you have an instructional purpose, you may show a copyrighted video in your classroom. If you have an entertainment purpose, you may not without permission. Permission for videos usually comes in the form of a public performance license and usually costs more money than you want to spend simply to entertain your students. This is true regardless of whether you own the video or rent it because you never really own the movie; you just own a copy of the tape/DVD and limited rights to show it. If, for example, you are teaching Shakespeare, you might show Othello to your students, or if you are teaching plot, you might show a few movie clips that demonstrate your lesson's points. But if you want to reward your students for acing their last test, serve pizza because the movie is not allowed. With that said, many school districts and school media centers have obtained movies with greater permission for use, so check with your media specialist.

EXAMPLES AND ADDITIONAL RESOURCES

As fair use and copyright are complex subjects and laws change regularly, example cases and current resources are valuable tools in understanding copyright. University of St. Francis (2004), Consortium for Educational Technology for University Systems (1996) "illustrative scenarios," Davidson (2002), and Agnew, Kellerman, and Meyer (1996, pp. 114–115) all have some interesting cases to explore. The University of St. Francis cases are fairly straightforward applications of the educational multimedia guidelines (CONFU: The Conference on Fair Use, 1996). Davidson gives brief cases with descriptions of how fair use applies to each case. Note that the Davidson cases are not all straightforward, and Davidson's fair-use analysis leans toward The Culture of No at times; it is possible to be more permissive than Davidson allows. The Agnew, Kellerman, and Meyer cases are fairly open-ended and no analysis is given.

With copyright (the law and the interpretation of the law) changing and confusing, it is helpful to look for additional resources that explain different aspects of the law. The Web site of the United States Copyright Office (2005) includes a wide range of copyright information, including basic descriptions of copyright, the text of the law, and information about registering copyrights. The Free Software Foundation (2001) and Creative Commons (nd.) provide guides to protecting works and making them freely available. These are valuable tools for academics who are not seeking to profit from their work but do not want to put it into the public domain. Roberts (1998) provides some good information from the perspective of creators of copyrighted work. Legal Information Institute of Cornell University (nd.) includes detailed notes concerning reports, legislation, and guidelines for fair use. Stanford University Libraries' Copyright and Fair Use Web site (nd.) provides a wide range of current information and analysis about copyright and fair use.

Because the issue of fair use is so complex, some simplified discussions of fair use are helpful to get you started. University of Texas at Austin's (2001) Copyright Crash Course is a valuable tool to understanding copyright and fair use. McAnear (2005) is a special issue of *Learning & Leading With Technology* that summarizes important issues of copyright and fair use in schools. Tysver (2000) offers a very good and brief introduction to fair use.

CONCLUSION

Copyright is confusing and difficult. Its complexity leads many to follow The Culture of Yes, happy to copy anything for the good of the children, or to follow The Culture of No, afraid to copy anything. The Culture of Fair Use teaches us that we have certain rights. We cannot copy anything, but we can copy some things. If we understand the law as best we can and make a good faith effort to follow it, we can serve the children and give all due respect to those who create the things that we use.

NOTES

1. Disclaimer: I am not a lawyer. Any information contained in this chapter is for information purposes only. For important matters of law, contact appropriate legal consultants (your school's or school board's attorney, for example). Also note that this chapter discusses United States copyright law. Most countries have similar laws protecting intellectual property, but laws are different in different countries.

REFERENCES

Agnew, P., Kellerman, A., & Meyer, J. (1996). *Multimedia in the classroom.* Boston: Allyn and Bacon.

CONFU: The Conference on Fair Use. (1996). *Fair use guidelines for educational multimedia.* Retrieved June 27, 2005, from http://www.utsystem.edu/ogc/intellectualproperty/ccmcguid.htm

Consortium for Educational Technology for University Systems. (1996). *Fair use of copyrighted works: A crucial element in educating America.* Retrieved June 27, 2005, from http://www.cetus.org/fairindex.html

Creative Commons. (nd.). Retrieved June 27, 2005, from http://creativecommons.org/

Davidson, H. (2002). The educator's guide to copyright and fair use. *Technology & Learning Magazïne, 23*(3), 28–33. Retrieved June 27, 2005, from http://www.techlearning.com/db_area/archives/TL/2002/10/copyright.html

Free Software Foundation. (2001). *What is copyleft?* Retrieved June 27, 2005, from http://www.gnu.org/copyleft/

Legal Information Institute of Cornell University. (nd.). Title 17, Chapter 1, Section 107 Notes. Retrieved June 27, 2005, from http://straylight.law.cornell.edu/uscode/html/uscode17/usc_sec_17_00000107-‑-‑-000-notes.html

Limitations on Exclusive Rights: Fair Use. (1976). *Copyright law of the United States of America,* Chapter 1, Section 107. Retrieved June 27, 2005, from www.copyright.gov/title17/92chap1.html#107

McAnear, A. (Ed.). (2005). Navigating the copyright highway. *Learning & Leading With Technology, 32*(7), (Special issue).

Roberts, P. (1998). Knowing your rights. *Adobe Magazine, 4,* 24–29. Retrieved June 27, 2005, from http://www.adobe.com:80/products/adobemag/archive/pdfs/98wifepr.pdf

Stanford University Libraries. (nd.). *Copyright and fair use.* Retrieved June 27, 2005, from http://fairuse.stanford.edu/

Tysver, D. (2000). *Fair use in copyright.* Retrieved June 27, 2005, from http://www.bitlaw.com/copyright/fair_use.html

United States Copyright Office. (2005). Retrieved June 27, 2005, from http://www.copyright.gov/

University of St. Francis. (2004). *A visit to copyright bay.* Retrieved June 27, 2005, from http://www.stfrancis.edu/cid/copyrightbay/

University of Texas at Austin. (2001). *Copyright crash course.* Retrieved June 27, 2005, from http://www.utsystem.edu/OGC/IntellectualProperty/cprtindx.htm

BEYOND THE DIGITAL DIVIDE

Nicholas C. Burbules, Thomas A. Callister, Jr. and
Claudine Taaffe

ABSTRACT

*The handy alliterative language of a "digital divide" continues to dom-
inate discussions of access to information and communication technologies and their importance for educational, employment, and other life
opportunities. Certainly, it must be a topic of crucial public concern if a
resource so central to life chances is reinforcing other dimensions of social
advantage and disadvantage. And yet, almost as soon as the term gained
currency, with its metaphorical imagery of a gulf between technological
"haves" and "have nots," it began receiving criticism for conceptualizing
the nature of the problem of technological inequalities in a misleading
fashion. This essay reviews the debate over the meanings of the "digital
divide," various attempts to reconceptualize the issue, and why, in our
view, the discussion still by and large misses key aspects of the problem.*

CRITICISMS OF THE "DIGITAL DIVIDE"

In the course of this essay, we will review six significant limitations in the
debate over the meanings of the "digital divide" (a useful overview of the
genesis of the term can be found in Williams, 2005). The first of these is that
there is not just one divide, but many. The dyadic character of the "divide"

Technology and Education: Issues in Administration, Policy, and Applications in K12 Schools
Advances in Educational Administration, Volume 8, 85–99
Copyright © 2006 by Elsevier Ltd.
All rights of reproduction in any form reserved
ISSN: 1479-3660/doi:10.1016/S1479-3660(05)08007-8

metaphor, with its image of a gulf or gap, suggests a gap between just two groups (Jung, Qiu, & Kim, 2001). But there are many groups differentiated by varying degrees of access to information and communication technologies: differences affecting racial and ethnic minorities, rural as opposed to urban dwellers, seniors, disabled persons, women, and those with low family incomes or less educational background (Kuttan & Peters, 2003; Hargittai, 2003; Payton, 2003). These are not simply gaps of "haves" and "have nots" – what Burbules and Callister (2000) call "quantity of access" – but also degrees of "quality of access." Even people who have technical access may not have the means, the incentives, or the opportunities to use it effectively. Such comparisons are not dyadic, but relations of degree. Hence, there is not simply one divide but many digital divides – and people who are relatively advantaged along one dimension (for example, family income) may be relatively disadvantaged along other dimensions (for example, gender). This makes the policy issues much more complex than simply seeking parity by some quantifiable measure between two particular groups.

But another sense in which there are many digital divides grows out of rethinking the meanings of "access." This is the second serious limit in many previous discussions of the issue (Burbules & Callister, 2000). Originally, concerns about a divide pertained simply to questions of access to computers and to Internet connectivity (particularly for schools in disadvantaged neighborhoods). This was a serious problem, and policies like the E-Rate program under the Clinton administration were designed to remedy these inequalities of what might be called "technical access." While costly, technical access itself is a relatively straightforward "divide" to remedy. But it quickly became apparent that equalizing technical access was meaningless without attention to many other "divides" in access, many of which were much more difficult to remedy through social policy – access to knowledge and skills, access to socially supportive networks, access to free time, and so on:

> Rather, access to ICT [information and communication technologies] is embedded in a complex array of factors, encompassing physical, digital, human, and social resources and relationships. Content and language, literacy and education, and community and institutional changes must all be taken into account if meaningful access to new technologies is to be provided.
>
> (Warschauer, 2003, p. 6)[1]

This discussion points up not only complexities in the notion of what constitutes "access": Is mere provision of an opportunity sufficient to guarantee that it is a *meaningful* opportunity that can actually be taken up successfully by the target group? (Burbules, Lord, & Sherman, 1982; Burbules, 1990). It also points up confusions in what society is trying to provide access *to*: access to technical resources; access to meaningful, effective, and enjoyable technology use; access to actual learning opportunities; and so on. These are not the same sorts of things, and are not susceptible to the same sorts of policies. As with wider notions of access and opportunity, especially in education, there are minimalist and wider conceptions of what counts as access: for example, the fact that an opportunity is available and that there may be no overt barriers to taking advantage of it, is not the same thing as making that opportunity relevant and attractive to potential beneficiaries. Lacking such a deeper analysis, the danger has been that questions of a technological digital divide get abstracted from the many other divides that characterize society: economic, social, and political divides that directly influence the prospects for success at remedying any technological divide, but which society has a much more complacent attitude about trying to address. The error has been in thinking that the technological divide can be undertaken in isolation from addressing these other divides or – even more remarkably – the notion that remedying the technological divide alone can ameliorate those wider social and educational inequalities: "The digital divide debate is based on a technologically determinist assumption that closing gaps in access to computers will mitigate broader inequalities" (Light, 2001, pp. 722–723). Yet as Warschauer, Knobel, and Stone (2004) point out, the more typical pattern is to witness "technology's *amplification* of existing inequalities in school and society" (emphasis added).

More recently, diversification in what might be counted as "information and communication technologies" complicates the access debate, and questions of quantity and quality of access, even further. What is the optimal form of access (even if we are just talking about technical access) for the casual user: a desktop machine? a laptop? a cell phone? a personal digital assistant (PDA)? or the new generation of Blackberries and similar hand-held computers that combine multiple information and communication functions? What about the tradeoff of connectivity and portability: direct connections, dial-up service, wireless? This complexity pushes even further the question of what counts as access and raises interdependent questions such as *access for whom?* and *access for what purposes?* (Selwyn, 2005). Useful and effective access for me may not be the same as useful and effective access for you. Such discussions point up the importance of considering questions of technical access within wider contexts that Warschauer, Knobel, and Stone term "social embeddedness." Yet, ironically, as Jennifer Light points out, public policy debates about the "digital divide," especially in educational contexts, have been *less* attuned to social and contextual

factors than were earlier discussions about unequal educational opportunities during the "Great Society" era (Light, 2001).

In large measure, many of these limitations can be traced back to the
metaphor of a "divide" itself: dyadic, unidimensional, a gulf or gap between
"haves" and "have nots" that must be "bridged" or "closed." In our culture,
gaps or divides between people or groups are thought to be bad, bridges (real
or metaphorical) are thought to be good – a technological solution to a social
problem. But, as is clear from these preliminary analyses, the gap (inequality)
that may be manifested by differences in access to information and communication technologies, and the educational and employment possibilities
they open up, is often not *itself* a technological gap, but a gap of social and
economic advantages and disadvantages. Recognizing this point is central to
putting the problem of technological access into proper context.

REDEFINING THE "DIGITAL DIVIDE"

If you track the references for this essay, you will see numerous variations
on the title, "Rethinking the Digital Divide." And, indeed, the term no
sooner gained currency than people got busy trying to redefine it. Burbules
and Callister (2000) argued this point in 2000, but were not the only ones.
Several authors have sought to reframe the problem as one of *digital inequality* or *digital opportunity*, focusing especially on expanding the concept
of what constitutes access and multiplying the potential audiences of concern
in respect to digital inequalities (Kuttan & Peters, 2003; Jung et al., 2001;
Mossberger et al., 2003; Selwyn, Gorard, & Williams, 2001; DiMaggio,
Hargattai, Celeste, & Shafer, 2005). In the process, the language of a "digital
divide" is used less widely (without some sort of qualification, at least), and
is often appended with a plural: *divides.* These changes respond in large
measure to the first two limits we identified in this essay, but they also draw
attention to a third limit: the distributive justice orientation of these policy
frameworks (Hendrix, 2005).

A distributive justice framework begins with a concern for some scarce
personal or public good and asks (a) who receives this good, in what measure and (b) by what principles and criteria is this good distributed? The first
condition focuses on dimensions of equality or inequality; the second anal-
yzes the fairness of the procedures or criteria by which that presumed good
is distributed. Significant inequalities, particularly of so-called "basic"
goods, or questionable or irrelevant criteria by which that distribution is
achieved, can both trigger distributive justice concerns. So, for example,

with some goods a significant degree of inequality is accepted by society: for example, educational attainment, because it is presumed to arise largely from *relevant* merit-based criteria such as talent, ability, or effort. Where significant differences in educational attainment are deemed to arise from *irrelevant* criteria (such as race or gender), society has sought to intervene to achieve a more just distribution of that good. With regard to some goods (say, health care), many societies have deemed this too important a fundamental entitlement to tolerate a very wide disparity in access to that good, regardless of prevailing factors such as income or where one lives: so some base-level equality is guaranteed by public policies.

This framework guides nearly all discussions of the digital divide, even the more recently "redefined" versions: the language of access, opportunity, and equality or inequality in provision of this presumed "good" (for example, through schools) is the central policy focus. The only questions are how to provide greater access (technical and otherwise), or how much inequality society is prepared to accept, or which group differences are the prime focuses of concern: given scarce funding resources, *which* of many divides will receive highest priority?

Whatever the limits of this perspective, in a liberal democracy it is the language that gathers public attention and the support of legislators and administrators: newspaper headlines or magazine covers querying, "What Should We Do about the Digital Divide?" summarize complex problems in a manageable (if inadequate) popular language. As noted above, if there is a "divide" or "gap," *of course* it must be bridged, or closed:

> The Internet has the potential to empower its users with new skills, new perspectives, new freedoms, even new voices; those groups who remain sequestered from the technology will be further segregated into the periphery of public life.
>
> (Carvin, 2000)

This concern is legitimate and pressing: if access to effective and meaningful technology use is becoming increasingly important to educational, employment, social, and even political opportunities, then clearly those who are closed out from this sector will suffer greatly in the others. Even worse, once such a "gap" is established, it will become self-perpetuating and even self-exacerbating over time, creating more and greater disadvantages. Some of these disadvantages may become enduring and intractable: people with and without technological access will simply live in different worlds, even though they live within the same society. Burbules and Callister (2000) term this the danger of establishing of a "digital caste society."

So it is of no little consequence to be alarmed by the significant, and even growing differences in the social distribution of access to this particular good: effective and meaningful use of information and communication technologies. What to do about it, as we have argued, is a more complex question because it inevitably brings up distributive questions concerning *other* social goods and opportunities that society has been more unwilling, or unable, to remedy. Nevertheless, the U.S. and many other developed societies have aggressively pursued policies intended to ameliorate the unequal distribution of this presumed benefit, to much good effect (Kuttan & Peters, 2003; Servon, 2002).

Still, we find this overall policy approach limited because it frames the question in terms of the social distribution of something which is determinate, and unambiguously good. As a result, important questions about what we are providing access *to* are less likely to be asked. In the next section of this essay we want to focus in greater detail on the limitations of the distributive justice framework, on problematizing the notion of "using" technology, and ultimately on the limits of the language of "access" itself.

BEYOND THE "DIGITAL DIVIDE"

The most serious limitation of the distributive justice framework for thinking about the issue of digital quality and inequality is that it tends to focus remedies on questions of publicly disbursable resources and opportunities – of particular interest for us, resources and opportunities that can be distributed via public schooling (technical access to computers and networks, training and experience in their use, etc.). As we have noted, these are important goals for society to pursue; but they are insufficient to remedy the problems to which they are addressed. When these issues are reconceived as "socially embedded," the crucial dimensions of social support networks, institutional settings, communities, trust, comfort, and sense of purpose – without which technical access and skills are virtually meaningless – come to be seen as factors outside the framework of distributive justice. Some things can be given, some things cannot. Some problems can be addressed through school-based educational remedies, some problems must be addressed through social and community capacity-building. If marginalized communities *outside* the digital framework are simply given access to it, with no attention to these wider capacity-building efforts, there is no reason to think that their involvement *within* that framework will be any less limited – indeed, there are good reasons to expect, as we will discuss below, that their participation may *increase* their vulnerability.

Here and throughout this essay we are attempting to articulate a *critical* perspective on the issue of digital access: not "critique" in the sense of a rejection or attack on its worthiness, but as an acknowledgement of the problem's importance while also articulating a post-conventional reformulation of the nature of the problem – of going beyond the question of the "digital divide," not in the sense of abandoning the concern, but in the sense of questioning some of the partial and misleading ways in which it is ordinarily conceived. So while we acknowledge that there are distributive policies that can help – that have helped – in addressing the problem of inequalities of access to meaningful and effective use of information and communication technologies, within a suitably expanded notion of what goes into "access," we also question the limitations of that approach, and the need for community-based responses that may need public support, but which cannot be driven directly by public policy. Too many of the factors that go into meaningful and effective use of new technologies remain outside the framework of a redistributive system; and for this reason are less amenable to public policy solutions, however well-intended.

This critical perspective also calls into question the notions of "use" that operate within this discussion; this is the fourth limit we want to analyze. In earlier work, Burbules and Callister (2000) argue for the importance of a "post-technocratic" perspective: that is, one that takes seriously the limitations of any technology to do what we want, without simultaneously doing things we do not want. This perspective takes seriously the incidence of unintended consequences, double-effects, and self-defeating feedback loops (what Edward Tenner (1996) calls "revenge effects") as reasons to question the efficacy of *any* sort of tool or technology to simply operate as an instrument for our will. Of course, the use of technology is inevitable, and frequently beneficial; but the language of "use" suggests a much simpler and unidirectional cause-and-effect relation than is typically the case. The car that takes us to the forest also creates pollution that is helping to destroy the forest. The pesticide that kills off certain pests also gives rise to the emergence of more virulent adaptations which are resistant to it. The video cameras we post in stores to prevent illicit activity, like shoplifting, may actually do little to deter serious shoplifters, but may instead discourage all sorts of perfectly legitimate activities, like public displays of affection, or may be used for surveillance of employees during their break times.

Needless to say, for any of us who use information and communication technologies on a regular basis, such contradictory effects are easily recognized: we love email, but hate all the spam; we think the technology will save time, but it only seems to take up more and more time; we like being instantly available via email or instant messaging, except when this leads certain people to assume that we want to be instantly accessible to *them*; and so on. We talk about *using* the technology; but we understand the sense that *we* are being changed within a dynamic relation as well: our wants and needs, our expectations, our purposes, our ways of doing things. "Use" is a unidirectional descriptor of what is in fact a dialectical relation. As a result, concerns about digital access cannot be properly conceived as simply a matter of re-orienting patterns and rates of *use* of technology.[2]

One way to summarize this concern is "be careful what you ask for" (Callister & Burbules, 2001).[3] When policies succeed in expanding access to the online experience, one set of problems gets exchanged for another. Access to what? News, information, cultural resources, social networks of personal interaction and community building, games, entertaining diversions, vistas on a globalizing world. But also: pornography, hate mail, unsolicited product promotions, pop-up ads, viruses, fraudulent scams, and sometimes an overwhelming amount of what, in smaller measure, was exactly what we (thought we) wanted. We cannot evaluate the value of promoting greater access to the content of digital technologies without a skeptical assessment of what we are providing access to, *and* an assessment of how those particular harms and nuisances weigh upon the risks and vulnerabilities of particular users. For here is another paradox: it is precisely those new users to whom we are trying to provide greater access who are at the greatest risk of being abused or exploited by online content. A naïve user who is not familiar with pyramid schemes and similar scams might truly think, when they receive the first message that begins, "I request your assistance in transferring $35 million dollars from my account ... " that the message is meant for them personally. After they have received a thousand similar messages they will know to recognize them for what they are – but it may only take that first time to deceive them, especially if they might be less educated, innocent, or partly senile.

This inability to question the value of access as a good to be socially distributed is a fifth limitation to much of the work on the digital divide. It is far from clear that more access is always better than less: indeed, for many technology-intensive users, the goal is sometimes to limit access – to limit access to others, but especially to limit their access to *you*. And this is our next point: access always runs both ways. The greater one's online presence and usage, the greater one's online exposure and risk. Experience and some technical fixes (such as spam filters) can help, but they do not eliminate the problem.

For these sorts of reasons, several analysts have preferred the discourse of "literacy" to the discourse of "use." Literacy, or reading, emphasizes an active and interactive relation with the content to which one has access: often, in fact, a critical or skeptical orientation (Warschauer, 2002, 2003; Warschauer et al., 2004; see also Willinsky, 2005). Burbules and Callister (2000) term this "hyper-reading." This capacity is not a given (even for users who can read, this sort of critical literacy cannot be taken for granted): and it is not a simple matter of educational intervention either since, like other socially embedded traits, its development and exercise depend upon communities and local networks that value and support such critical capacities – not all do.

Yet there is another important and legitimate critical response: and that is to refrain from, or withdraw from, access to the online world, entirely or in part. This phenomenon is particularly problematic for the distributive justice framework: What about the opt-outs? What about those who rightly or wrongly do not believe in the benefits of an opportunity that society believes is beneficial, even essential? As Ralph Page (1976) has argued, the essence of an opportunity is that it can be passed up. People pass up opportunities for many sorts of reasons, some of which seem primarily the results of considered and autonomous decision-making, some of which seem the results of external pressures and influences, and many of which are impossible to judge as "considered and autonomous" from the outside at all. At what point do policies of distributive justice threaten to "blame the victims" by refusing to grant the legitimacy of decisions to opt-out from the "goods" being distributed, or to be subtly coercive in assuming that what society believes is good for you is in fact something *you* should believe is good for you (Selwyn et al., 2001; Crump & McIlroy, 2003)? (These concerns are amplified, of course, by questions of cultural and/or religious diversity, in which the very nature of certain traditions, values, and belief systems may be put at risk by participating in the "benefits" of online access.) The point, of course, is that non-users opt-out (or feel excluded or unwelcome or intimidated) for many reasons that have to do with the very content to which society and schools think it is beneficial for them to be exposed. Yet if opportunities can be passed up, then a distributive system can at most provide the *possibility* of access, not access itself.

From the critical perspective introduced earlier, what this means is that despite the ideal that providing educational and other sorts of opportunities to online access can ameliorate other dimensions of social disadvantage, in actual practice it is just as likely to underscore and even exaggerate those very disadvantages. Where the same conditions and differences that underlie a larger system of advantages and disadvantages also, at the same time, shape the likely responses to, and receptiveness to, those online opportunities, the very aim of increased access can have the effect of heightening some of those very effects. In this sense, the "digital divide" is a persistent *product* of wider social inequalities, not their remedy; indeed, well-intended distributive policies that do not take account of this fact can, for the reasons just mentioned, make some of those inequalities even worse.

"Well-intended distributive policies." Are there any other kind? Here it must be noted that much of the impetus for expanding access to the Internet among under-represented groups has been commercial in nature: opening up new audiences for online advertising; attracting more customers to online purchasing; and disseminating a wide range of licit and illicit marketing and promotional strategies (Hoffman, Novak, & Schlosser, 2000). The fact that many of these new potential customers may have less disposable income is counterbalanced by the sense that they may be more susceptible to the kind of aggressive, often intrusive marketing and promotional strategies typical of many online vendors. Here again we see the principle at work that giving people access to the Internet also gives other people access to them. This commercial incentive may not necessarily be ill-intended or exploitative in nature: online purchasing, like catalogue purchasing of a bygone era, can be a tremendous convenience and cost-savings for potential customers – but once again we see the two-sidedness of good intentions, because the very convenience and cost-savings made available by online purchasing can also be an incentive to over-purchasing (see also Home Shopping Network, Price Club-style megastores, etc).

Finally, a sixth limitation to many discussions of the digital divide: the lack of a global perspective. The most striking divide of technological haves and have nots is international, not domestic in nature (Molina, 2003; Norris, 2001; Behera, 2005). Indeed, on this scale a basically dyadic picture *is* emerging: one in which vast regions of the globe have little or no access to these new technologies at all (they do not even have electricity or phone service). It is beyond our concern here to explore this problem in depth, because our central focus has been on national policies, here in the U.S. and elsewhere, deriving fundamentally from liberal, distributive justice principles – there is no analogous framework, yet, on the global scale. But to the extent that the Internet is an intrinsically globalized and globalizing influence, these questions cannot be ignored even *within* a domestic context.

Two dimensions are pertinent to our present discussion, illustrating the bi-directionality, but also the asymmetry, of access questions. One example pertains to the commercial imperative just discussed: there is no doubt that, as things stand, the effects of the Internet on global commerce are in no way symmetrical or balanced; few of the benefits, and many of the costs, have an impact on underdeveloped regions of the world. To take one example: many developing countries are struggling under the additional handicap, on top of all their other disadvantages, that many of their best educational success stories, of trained professionals, medical personnel, and science and technical experts, are being enticed away from their countries to higher salaries and greater opportunities elsewhere. For these individuals, it is a prospect that they understandably find difficult to pass up: greater comfort, security, and opportunities for their own families. Yet the net effect of this "brain drain" for the home countries is that all their effort and investment in "growing their own" professional and scientific/technical class simply ends up subsidizing the well-being of countries that were better-off to begin with. The Internet is playing a central role in recruiting and facilitating the transfer of these home-grown professionals to pursue new opportunities in other countries, even as it is also a medium through which their advanced training (for example, through online graduate degrees or exchange programs) may have been provided. (Many graduate programs are expressly designed to "cherry pick" the best and the brightest international students for research and employment opportunities in the host country.)

A second example of this two-sidedness of benefits and costs is the spread of the English language as the language of globalization.[4] Certainly, today there are vast regions of the Internet in non-English languages: but the major international resources remain in English only, and the common "lingua Franca" of the Internet remains overwhelmingly English. Is this an unjust tilting toward the convenience of dominant national and cultural interests? Is this an avenue for advancing a distinctive "American" or "Western" thought-orientation and value system? Is it a natural convenience to have a shared language that one can generally presume in anyone one encounters on the Internet? Is it an engine and medium for capitalist hegemony? Is it enlarging educational and employment opportunities for those who now have an incentive (and a medium) through which they can learn and practice their English? Is it inevitable that there must emerge *some* language of the Internet for it to function fully *as* the Internet – and if not English, would not the same issues arise for any other language? Is it a volunteeristic process in which the creators of the Internet and a great deal of its valuable content, the things that make it so attractive as a shared space for living and learning and interacting, "happen to be" mostly English-speaking?

Well, it is all of the above, really, and more. The incentive to learn English, to partake of the undeniable benefits of the Internet (for example, for educational opportunities) is inseparable from the potentially coercive effects of forcing the usage of a second language upon people who have no choice but to use English in certain contexts, for certain purposes. This is not an issue of conscious policy, it seems to us, as much as it is an inevitable consequence of the kind of globally networked space the Internet has become.

NETWORKED THINKING

There is a basic problem that recurs with all of the six limitations discussed here: (1) the dyadic and unidimensional character of the "divide" metaphor; (2) the prioritizing of "technical access" over the many other crucial dimensions of access; (3) the distributive model of thinking about issues of online equality and inequality; (4) the reliance on a constrained sense of "use" as the basis for thinking about what online participation means; (5) the presumption that online "access" is a simple and unambiguous good; and (6) the lack of a global perspective. In each of these cases, the limitation is a failure to see the interconnectedness of things: of thinking linearly rather than in a networked fashion; of not seeing the inseparability of what we (think we) want from what we do not want; of thinking in terms of proximate effects rather than indirect, dispersed, and unintended effects. This is what is for us at the heart of a "post-technocratic" point of view.

The online environment connects people within a shared virtual space: it is not just a medium of point-to-point communication. It is not just a passive tool that people use, but an active influence that changes the user, in anticipated and unanticipated ways. And its complex and interconnected nature, especially on a global scale, continually puts people in contact with the strange, the unexpected – and often the unwanted.

As a result, equity policies arising in the context of remedying something called a "digital divide" need to be more nuanced in thinking through what Light (2001, p. 726) calls "the complex and even contradictory consequences of technological innovation." Specifically, we have argued, they need to be rethought with an awareness that the sources of digital inequality are not, in most cases, fundamentally technological questions and are not amenable to exclusively technological solutions. Put more strongly, distributive policies often mistake the effect for the cause; and put even more strongly, can sometimes make the very nature of the problem they intend to solve worse, rather than better.

In the end, social policy needs to think in more networked ways, not just in the context of technology access: about the dependence for the success of public policies on community organizations and social networks that cannot themselves be the product (or the mere instrument) of public policies; about the complex and sometimes frustrating dynamics between good intentions and unintended consequences; and about the growing interdependence of local, national, and global dynamics. If we keep thinking about the digital divide merely as a flawed distribution process between technological haves and have nots, we can never come up with policies that will help address the problem, because we have already misunderstood what the problem is.[5]

NOTES

1. See also Mossberger, Tolbert, and Stansbury (2003), who discuss four divides: access, skills, economic opportunities, and democratic participation; Payton (2003) who cites "limited access to a social network that helps young people succeed;" Van Dijk and Hacker (2003) who emphasize the relation of technical access to a wider distribution of life chances; Behera (2005) who cites 13 dimensions of access; as well as Kvasny (2005) and Carvin (2000) who offer different typologies.

2. An essay that largely does take this focus is Stewart and Gould (2004).

3. This paper summarizes several aspects of a "post-technocratic" perspective on the problem of a digital divide, and anticipates some of the objections we articulate here.

4. Taik Sup Auh (2005), "Language Divide and Knowledge Gap in Cyberspace: Beyond Digital Divide" [URL www.unesco.or.kr/cyberlang/auhtaeksup.htm Last accessed August 17, 2005]. Interestingly, this highly informative and useful article, like Behera's, is written in fairly broken English, certainly not by a native-speaker, and available only online. Such papers would have a difficult time making it through the review process of a serious English-language academic journal.

5. The authors greatly appreciate the contributions of Tracey Taylor, research assistant.

REFERENCES

Auh, T. S. (2005). *Language divide and knowledge gap in cyberspace: Beyond digital divide.* [URL www.unesco.or.kr/cyberlang/auhtaeksup.htm Last accessed August 17, 2005]

Behera, S. N. (2005). *E-readiness: The knowledge component of the digital divide.* [URL http://bihar.bih.nic.in/Conference/Papers/DigitalDivide.pdf Last accessed August 17, 2005]

Burbules, N. C. (1990). Equal opportunity or equal education? *Educational Theory, 40*(2), 221–226.

Burbules, N. C., & Callister Jr., T. A. (2000). *Watch IT: The promises and risks of information technologies for education.* Boulder, CO: Westview Press.

Burbules, N. C., Lord, B., & Sherman, A. (1982). Equity, equal opportunity, and education. *Educational Evaluation and Policy Analysis, 4*(2), 169–187.

Callister Jr., T. A., & Burbules, N. C. (2001). Be careful what you ask for: Paradoxes about the 'digital divide.' Presented at the American Educational Studies Association, Autumn 2001.

Carvin, A. (2000). Mind the gap: The digital divide as the civil rights issue of the new millennium. *Multimedia Schools*, (January/February), 56–58.

Crump, B., & McIlroy, A. (2003). The digital divide: Why the 'don't want to's' won't compute: Lessons from a New Zealand ICT project. *First Monday, 8*(12). [URL www.firstmonday.org/issues/issue8_12/crump/index.html Last accessed August 17, 2005]

DiMaggio, P., Hargattai, E., Celeste, C., & Shafer, S. (2005). *From unequal access to differentiated use: A literature review and agenda for research on digital inequality.* [URL www.eszter.com/research/pubs/dimaggio-etal-digitalinequality.pdf Last accessed August 17, 2005]

Hargittai, E. (2003). The digital divide and what to do about It. In: D. C. Jones (Ed.), *New economy handbook*. San Diego, CA: Academic Press.

Hendrix, E. (2005). Permanent injustice: Rawls' theory of justice and the digital divide. *Educational Technology and Society, 8*(1), 63–68.

Hoffman, D. L., Novak, T. P., & Schlosser, A. E. (2000). The evolution of the digital divide: How gaps in Internet access may impact electronic commerce. *JCMC, 5*(3). http://www.ascusc.org/jcmc/vol5/issue3/hoffman.html

Jung, J.-Y., Qiu, J. L., & Kim, Y.-C. (2001). Internet connectedness and inequality: Beyond the divide. *Communication Research, 28*(4), 507–535.

Kuttan, A., & Peters, L. (2003). *From digital divide to digital opportunity*. Lanham, MD: Scarecrow Press.

Kvasny, L. (2005). *A conceptual framework for examining digital inequality.* [URL http://aisel.isworld.org/Publications/AMCIS/2002/022802.pdf Last accessed August 17, 2005]

Light, J. (2001). Rethinking the digital divide. *Harvard Educational Review, 71*(4), 709–733.

Molina, A. (2003). The digital divide: The need for a global E-inclusion movement. *Technology Access and Strategic Management, 15*(1), 137–152.

Mossberger, K., Tolbert, C. J., & Stansbury, M. (2003). *Virtual inequality: Beyond the digital divide*. Washington, DC: Georgetown University Press.

Norris, P. (2001). *Digital divide: Civic engagement, information poverty, and the Internet.* New York: Cambridge.

Page, R. (1976). Opportunity and its willing requirement. In: K. Strike (Ed.), *Philosophy of education 1976*. Normal, IL: Philosophy of Education Society.

Payton, F. C. (2003). Rethinking the digital divide. *Communications of the ACM, 46*(6), 86–91.

Selwyn, N. (2005). *Defining the digital divide: Developing a theoretical understanding of inequalities in the information age.* [URL www.cf.ac.uk/socsi/ICT/definingdigitaldivide.pdf Last accessed August 17, 2005]

Selwyn, N., Gorard, S., & Williams, S. (2001). Digital divide or digital opportunity? The rise of technology in overcoming social exclusion in U.S. education. *Educational Policy, 15*(2), 258–277.

Servon, L. (2002). *Bridging the digital divide: Technology, community, and public policy.* New York: Blackwell.

Stewart, J., & Gould, N. (2004). The rise and fall of the digital divide. In: J. Graham, M. Jones & S. Hick (Eds), *Digital divide and back: Social welfare, technology, and the new economy.* Toronto: University of Toronto Press.

Tenner, E. (1996). *Why things bite back: Technology and the revenge of unintended consequences.* New York: Knopf.

Van Dijk, J., & Hacker, K. (2003). The digital divide as a complex and dynamic phenomenon. *The Information Society, 19,* 315–326.

Warschauer, M. (2002). Reconceptualizing the digital divide. *First Monday* 7(7). [URL www.firstmonday.dk/issues/issue7_7/warschauer/ Last accessed August 17, 2005]

Warschauer, M. (2003). *Technology and social inclusion: Rethinking the digital divide.* New York: Cambridge University Press.

Warschauer, M., Knobel, M., & Stone, L. (2004). Technology and equity in schooling: Deconstructing the digital divide. *Educational Policy, 18*(4), 562–588.

Williams, K. (2005). *What is the digital divide?* [URL www-personal.umich.edu/~katewill/kwd3workshop.pdf Last accessed August 17, 2005]

Willinsky, J. (2005). Open access: Reading (research) in the age of information. In: C.M. Fairbanks, J. Worthy, B. Maloch, J.V. Hoffman, & D.L. Schallert (Eds), *51st national reading conference yearbook* (pp. 32–46). Oak Creek, WI: National Reading Conference. [URL www.pkp.ubc.ca/publications/NRC%20Galley.pdf Last accessed August 17, 2005]

TECHNOLOGY AND URBAN YOUTH: EMERGENT ISSUES REGARDING ACCESS

Dawn G. Williams, Tawana L. Carr and Nicole S. Clifton

ABSTRACT

While numerous approaches have been suggested for the improvement of elementary and secondary education in American urban public schools, one common component of such plans is the more effective utilization of computers, networking, and other educational technologies. When making these considerations, leaders must look at information regarding demographic analysis, assessments, demand factors, and access. The Digital Divide shines a light on the role computers play in widening social gaps throughout our society, particularly between White students and students of color. By providing equitable and meaningful access to technology we can create a stronger assurance that all children step into the 21st century prepared. Home access to computer technology is a continuous area of inequality in American society. If society assumes that academic achievement is facilitated by access to computers both at school and in the home, the gap in access to computer technology is a cause for concern.

Technology and Education: Issues in Administration, Policy, and Applications in K12 Schools
Advances in Educational Administration, Volume 8, 101–113
ISSN: 1479-3660/doi:10.1016/S1479-3660(05)08008-X

INTRODUCTION

The initial interest in writing this chapter on technology access for urban youth came as a result of a dissertation topic advisement meeting with a doctoral student (also a contributing author to this chapter). She was discussing issues regarding the achievement gap in her local context and the role that technology may play in aiding and/or narrowing the gap. Although undefined, our conversation turned to technology access and its connection to student acquisition of cultural capital.

Familiar and shared stories of repeated occurrences in our familial context began to emerge during this discussion. We are often called upon from immediate and extended family members for various trouble shooting issues related to computer usage. Although our advanced degrees are in education and not in computer science or information technology, we are still seen as a helpful resource because of our regular and dependent use of computers. The most recent calls have been to come to the aid of school-aged cousins. These calls usually involve some type of homework or larger out of school assignment that requires the use of a computer and Internet access. Functions that are often taken for granted become frustrating tasks for these cousins. Normally after reading and explaining what the assignment entails, they still are puzzled on the steps to take to complete the computer-generated assignments. Therefore, while sitting at a home computer (in another state), we walk through the proper steps in accessing and researching information via the Internet, controlling the function keys, creating and revising word documents, etc.

This chapter will take a closer look at computer access at school and particularly in the homes of African American and Latino students. Additionally, the usage of computers by these student compared to their White counterparts will be discussed under the framework of cultural capital. Lastly, the infusion of assistive technology for students with special needs will be discussed as a rising area of concern.

THE NEGOTIATION OF CULTURAL CAPITAL

These cousins live in two parent households, but lack the general, technical and educational support at home that they may receive in school. This lack of support (or people resource) can aid in loss of additional learning and reinforcement opportunities that their White counterparts may experience more frequently. Wealth , which is an indicator of both financial and human capital, can affect academic achievement as well as help to explain the gap in black–white test scores. Analyses reveal that wealth affects achievement through its effect on the amount of cultural capital to which a child is exposed. Because blacks have substantially less wealth than do Whites, wealth can help to explain a portion of the racial achievement gap (Orr, 2003). Max Weber (1968) argued that elite status groups generate or appropriate cultural capital which works to gain privileged access to scarce resources for members of that group. According to Bourdieu and Passeron (1977) schools and educators communicate more easily with students who participate in elite status cultures, give them more attention, and, most importantly, perceive them as more intelligent and capable than students who lack this "cultural capital." Bourdieu (1977) also contends that cultural experiences of the higher social statuses facilitate a student's adjustment to school and influence academic achievement, thereby transforming cultural resources into cultural capital.

Cultural capital has long been a tool used by disadvantaged students to access higher social mobility pathways that are easily operationalized by their White peers. Many working-class minority youth are able to manage their difficult participation in multiple settings. Gaining cultural capital may mean overcoming various obstacles and developing supportive relationships to negotiate institutional agency. A few research studies have examined how students take advantage of distributed home computers and how it has affected their academic and social performance in school.

Kraut, Scherlis, Mukhopadhyay, Manning, and Kiesler (1996)reported a study of 48 families who were each given a computer, Internet access, and technical support for a little over a year. The studies found that many families had difficulty getting started despite having attended a training session, but individuals were more likely to learn to use the Internet if they had contact with more knowledgeable friends or family members. In another family study of first-time home computer use Giacquinta, Bauer, and Levin (1993) found little academic or educational use of computers by the families. Instead computers were used mostly for playing games. The researchers attributed this to the absence of social support and parental encouragement.

Parental support at home is a major factor in the overall educational process of all students. Therefore, educators and administrators in major urban areas must learn to genuinely value, solicit, and encourage parental involvement as it relates to the academic achievement of their student population. A significant body of research (Olmstead & Rubin, 1983;

Henderson, 1994) indicates that when parents participate in their children's educational process, the result is an increase in student achievement and an improvement in students' attitudes toward learning. In addition, family involvement has been proven to be associated with a multitude of stellar outcomes, including better standardized test scores, higher grades, improved attendance, enhanced social skills, and a greater probability of admission to postsecondary institutions (Henderson & Mapp, 2002).

As observed in the Family Tech Program, a program initiated by the South Florida Annenberg Challenge, computer knowledge afforded parents and families the opportunity to keep pace with their children (Bessell, Sinagub, Lee, & Schumm, 2003). Following the training, parents and students shared a common understanding of computer technology and parents were better able to assist their children with schoolwork on the computer and with computer-related problems. Instead of waiting for children to ask their parents for help with homework, parents were given computer activities during training sessions that were to be completed at home with their children. This study serves as an excellent example of the benefits of having a parent or individual in the household with computer knowledge and how this knowledge serves to reinforce student learning as it does when a parent is available to supervise or assist with homework.

TECHNOLOGY ACCESS

Because computers and the Internet are widely perceived as having educational and economic value, it is not surprising that they have become the subject of equity debates primarily concerning access. Access to technology is not only a matter of access to hardware and software, but as emerging issues are showing, access involves the use, training, experiences, and the exercise of varied applications. Computer and Internet use in the United States, both at home and school, has been far more available to middle and upper class White Americans, with much less participation from lower income groups and cultural minorities (Ebo, 1998; Education Week, 1998).

The national student to computer ratio dropped from 125 to 1 in 1984 to just 4 to 1 in 2003 (Market Data Retrieval, 2003). The Digital Divide in access to technology based on race or income are closing rapidly. Eighty nine percent of high minority schools have classroom Internet access and 93 percent of low minority schools have such access (National Center for Education Statistics, 2003). Despite this increase in school access, some indicators suggest a lingering and detrimental Digital Divide at home. For example, 28 percent of 4th-graders and 24 percent of 8th-graders who are eligible for free and reduced price lunch report not having a computer at home. In contrast to only 7 percent and 5 percent of wealthier 4th–graders and 8th-graders respectively, do not have home computers (National Assessment of Educational Progress, 2005).

African Americans and Latinos face even greater disparities in access to computers and the Internet at home than at school. They are about 20 percent less likely than White Americans, Asian Americans, or other minority groups to own a home computer (NTIA, 1998; Wenglinsky, 1998). Hoffman and Novak (1998) found an even larger gap of 40 percent in access to home computers between African American and White American high-school and college students. Exploring Digital Divide issues in the schools is not enough. This exploration must extend to the access and usage inquiries in the home as well.

Kupperman and Fishman (2001) highlight another critical issue regarding access. In general, people with higher incomes and education levels have more information technology in their home, but for some technologies there seems to be differences among ethnic and racial groups, even when adjusted for income. For example, compared to White Americans, a larger percentage of African Americans and Latinos are without basic telephone service, therefore, limiting access to home Internet service. Of course the information superhighway cannot reach people who do not have a home telephone.

These research findings mirror another conversation with an entering doctoral student, who is also an elementary school principal. She discussed her initial amazement of personal computers and dial up Internet access being distributed to students and teachers at an Edison School. To the later surprise and dismay of the administration, they learned that many of the students were not able to capitalize on the use of the free home computers because they were without home telephone service and could not access the Internet. Unfortunately, those with the least access to computers and the Internet in school are also least likely to have access outside school, in places such as the home, friends' and relatives' homes, libraries, churches, or community centers.

School systems should begin to explore the role of technology in their restructuring and how technology can help the student population that they serve. It is said that, "Today's technology offers powerful tools for transforming what we do, what our organizations look like, and even how we think about the world"(David, 1991). A school's effective use of data (demographic analysis, needs assessment, etc.) can enable the successful identification of appropriate strategies ultimately leading to standards attainment and the increase of student learning. However, many schools do not effectively use available data to promote increased student learning or standards implementation.

There have been many approaches introduced to assist school systems with understanding the population that it serves and evaluative questions relevant to educational stakeholders. Bernhardt (1998) summarizes a student-based database. In using Bernhardt's (1998) student-based database, administrators should try to quantify the education-relevant life of each student. This database would identify who each student is (demographics), the experiences of each student with respect to what schools are doing to help them learn (school processes), what they perceive about the learning environment (perceptions), and what the students know (student learning). School personnel should look at individual student information, summarize the results and recognize the information to understand results for different groups of students.

With the aid of this data, the school system can: (1) classify and cluster different data elements to understand the impact of standards implementation with respect to the results they are getting, (2) understand the continuum of learning being crafted for students, (3) predict scores, in order to prevent failure, (4) understand what changes are needed to get different results, and (5) work smarter, not harder to get their desired outcomes.

COMPUTER USAGE

Today, we must educate teachers and students to use the computer as a productivity tool as well as a tool for learning, research, networking, collaborating, telecommunications, and problem solving. The question is not whether computers belong in classrooms, but how they can be put to most effective use and how schools can ensure that all of their students are getting the same online opportunities (Education Week, 2003). Data from NAEP (2003) found that 28 percent of 4th-grade teachers reported not using computers at all in class. Among those who did use computers, the most common uses were playing math games and engaging in drill-and-practice activities. Tasks that promote higher order thinking skills were used much less frequently. Continually using drill-and-practice software does not allow students to participate in meaningful and engaging learning environments. Learning gains are maximized when software offers simulation activities. However, using the computer for drill and practice can potentially help African American and Hispanic students improve their achievement. There is a need for drill and practice, but it should not be the only exposure to computers that students have, as drill software minimizes the learning process and can lower test scores and kills creativity. The same can be said about the drill and practice administered to students in preparation for a standardized test. This prescriptive teaching creates a new form of discrimination as teaching to the fragmented and narrow information on the test comes to substitute for a substantive curriculum in the schools of poor and minority children, where their entire schooling experience becomes dominated by an attempt to raise their test scores at any cost (McNeil, 2000).

Simulation promotes active learning. Students construct, produce and become responsible for their own learning. Thus, educators must have the desire to foster high-order thinking skills with respect to using technology for all students. Consequently, the way a student uses computers in schools depends on the teacher's perception of that pupil's cognitive ability. Unfortunately, teachers of African American and Latino students often have low expectations and are therefore likely to regulate them to drill-and-practice programs rather than to computer programs that require problem solving and higher-order thinking skills (Chisolm, Carey, & Hernandez, 2002).

SCHOOL–HOME TECHNOLOGY ACCESS PARTNERSHIPS

In this type of relationship, schools or school districts provide computers or other resources to families for use at home. Apple Classrooms of Tomorrow (ACOT) began providing home and school computers to selected sites in 1986. Results included increased student engagement, improved achievement in some subjects, and more use of student-centered instructional approaches by teachers (Apple Computer, Inc., 1995). Since 1987, Indiana's Buddy System Project has supplied every student and teacher in chosen schools with computers, modems, printers, and software, both at home and school. The Buddy System Project is a technology-based program in which the state of Indiana purchased home computers for students in grades 4–6. The program currently operates in 58 schools statewide and serves approximately 7,000 students. The Buddy System Project is "an effort to use technology to enhance learning in the schools and extend learning beyond the school day and into the home" (Rockman, 1995).

Rockman (1995) reported results including improved student writing achievement, more engagement in academic tasks, increased professional development, greater parent involvement, and improved family climate.

Rockman also noted increased student interest and attention to mathematics, although that was not reflected in test scores. Rockman's recommendations included increased integration of the home and school activities, more professional development, expanded use of telecommunications to connect home and school, and use of Buddy System graduates as resources in the community. When African American children had access to home computers according to a 1996 survey, they were enthusiastic users, just as they were at school: 53 percent of African American 4th-graders used their home computers at least once a week, significantly more than the 36 percent of Asian Americans, 33 percent of Latinos, and 29 percent of White Americans who did so. Using a home computer does not ensure success at school; however, extremely high levels of use could even be counterproductive, particularly for elementary students (Wenglinsky, 1998).

Researchers have examined relationships between home computer use and student achievement. A study by Rocheleau (1995) used data from the National Science Foundation's Longitudinal Study of American Youth to study the relationships among home computer access, home computer use, and student achievement. Rocheleau found higher overall grades and higher grades in mathematics and English among students who had access to a computer at home, compared with those students without home access.

Among the students in Rocheleau's study who had a computer at home, there were significant differences between heavy and infrequent users of computers. Students who used technology at home more frequently had significantly higher mathematics grades, on average, than infrequent users of technology at home. By contrast, Wenglinsky's (1998) cross-sectional analysis found a negative association between home use of computers and mathematics scores on the 1996 National Assessment of Educational Progress among 4th-graders. Wenglinsky found a small positive association between home use and achievement among 8th-graders.

Computers and other technologies afford families greater ways to contribute to their children's educational process. Access to computers can also help to strengthen the partnership between the home and school as seen through the Family Tech Program. For non-native English speaking parents they can use tools such as spelling and grammar software to assist their children in writing school related papers. A large number of these software programs are available in multiple languages, which will help to facilitate the translation process (Bessell et al., 2003). Additionally, Bessell et al. suggest if families have equitable access to computers, the lines of communication between the home and school are more likely to be maintained regularly through the use of email and school-based web pages.

TECHNOLOGY OPPORTUNITIES FOR STUDENTS WITH SPECIAL NEEDS

With a growing number of African American and Latino students being labeled at-risk and placed in special education programs, computers and assistive technology have become the tools of choice for many of the nation's school systems. These tools should also be viewed as valuable resources to assist students placed at-risk with learning and passing standards-based exams. While assistive technology is acknowledged in the area of rehabilitations for persons with physical disabilities, it has gained interest as a tool for helping individuals with learning disabilities and other specific cognitive deficits (Day & Edwards, 1996; Raskind & Higgins, 1998; MacArthur, 2000). Urban schools must seek to conduct research in this area and focus on integrating more technology into their existing educational framework. While the introduction of technology alone will not improve the overall quality of the nation's education, it can be used as an influential tool in addressing the increased demands placed on students (i.e. Standardized Tests).

Educational technology offers students access to information in a variety of formats – text, video, and audio (David, 1991). These varying formats afford students an opportunity to use the tools most effective to facilitate their learning needs. Technology enables teachers to focus their energies on educating students with their individual growth as emphasized in their Individualized Education Plans. Technology also permits students to work independently or in small groups. It allows students to take advantage of access to vast sources of information and work with complex connections among varied disciplines both at home and at school.

Technology motivates students, especially those placed at risk, to become active learners. It places them in charge of controlling the pace and direction of content, questions, and responses. Assistive technologies can provide students and teachers equitable access to learning no matter the geographic location or limited resources of the school system. Learning technologies expand the opportunities of teachers, students, and parents to connect learning activities in school with those in homes, centers, and other institutions.

During the past decade, advances in technology have offered new opportunities for individuals placed at-risk or with diagnosed learning disabilities (Bryant & Seay, 1998). Assistive technology is an instrument that can make a learning situation more attainable and for enhancing students' output (Day & Edwards, 1996). Offering suitable technology to educators, students, and parents will cost a great deal of money, but the cost of not providing the technology may be greater. Initiatives that help low-income minority families to afford home computers and support technology programs in public schools can play an important part in equalizing access.

Examination of the E-Rate federal technology assistance is timely, given that the Enhancing Education through Technology Program (EdTech), established with the reauthorization of the Elementary and Secondary Education Act (ESEA) in January 2002, seeks in part "to assist every student in crossing the digital divide." Allowable uses of funds under EdTech focus on promoting innovative uses of technology to increase student achievement; increasing access to technology, especially for high-need schools; and improving and expanding teacher professional development in technology.

Through January 2000, the largest share of E-Rate discounts (58 percent) supported the acquisition of equipment and services for internal building connections, with the poorest districts receiving higher average discounts for this purpose (Puma, Chaplin, & Pape, 2000). This may reflect a greater need in these schools for the basic infrastructure required to support the effective use of telecommunications services. Currently most, urban districts get funding for most of their technology initiatives from federal funds, but grants and entitlement programs allow only limited or targeted students to be helped. Equal access and equity must be the ultimate goal of education in general and of urban education in particular (Walker, 1997).

CONCLUSION

Some districts and states are working to provide students and teachers with greater access to technology off campus by purchasing wireless laptops, personal digital assistants, and hand held-computers that students may take off school grounds (Education Week, 2003). Most American schools are finding it increasingly difficult to keep pace with the new wave of technology. This is particularly true for poorer urban schools highly populated with minority students. The Digital Divide between the haves and have nots is widening. While some well financed suburban schools have installed wireless computers and have trained teachers to use the new technologies, urban schools are lagging behind with outdated computers, insufficient Internet access, and lack of professional development. This gap has serious negative consequences for the future of the next generation. Those students from urban working-class families, largely racial and ethnic minorities, will be unable to compete with their wealthier, better educated, and more technologically advanced peers in the global marketplace (Garland & Wotton, 2001). These gaps in technology access also affect students in higher education. According to NSF

(1998), college bound minority students have less experience with all major computing applications than their White counterparts (Chisolm, et.al., 2002). New tools create new literacies, and these in turn can create new abilities and disabilities. When a tool becomes dominant, those who are skilled with that tool become privileged (Kupperman & Fishman, 2001).

To stimulate change, and move beyond isolated programs toward wide-spread integration of technology into learning; urban school leaders must commit themselves to strategies that promote growth: technology-planning at district levels, funding, ensuring equitable access to technology, human resource training and support, and developing technology-based assessment tools. In addition, urban schools leaders must adapt to long-term changes in technology, curriculum, teaching tools, and other needs impacted by a changing school environment. By doing this we will see a greater return on our assets, our children. Our society's growing dependence on technology for personal, social, and economic development have a tremendous potential for disenfranchising these technologically poor segments of society and placing them at a disadvantage.

REFERENCES

Apple Computer, Inc. (1995). *Apple education research reports.* Eugene, OR: International Society for Technology in Education.

Bernhardt, V. L. (1998). *Data analysis for comprehensive schoolwide improvement.* New York: Eye on Education.

Bessell, A. G., Sinagub, J. M., Lee, O., & Schumm, J. S. (2003). Engaging families with technology. *The Journal, 31*(5), 7.

Bourdieu, P. (1977). Cultural reproduction and social reproduction. In: J. Karabel & A. H. Halsey (Eds), *Power and Ideology in education.* New York: Oxford Press.

Bourdieu, P., & Passeron, J. C. (1977). *Reproduction in education, society, and culture.* New York: Wiley.

Bryant, B. R., & Seay, P. C. (1998). The technology related assistance to individuals with disabilities act: Relevance to individuals with Learning disabilities and their advocates. *Journal of Learning Diabilities, 31,* 4–15.

Chisolm, I., Carey, J., & Hernandez, A. (2002). Information technology skills for a pluralistic society: Is the playing field level? *Journal of Research on Technology in Education, 35*(1), 58–79.

David, J. L. (1991). Restructuring and technology: Partners in change. *Phi Delta Kappan, 37*(40), 72–82.

Day, S. L., & Edwards, B. J. (1996). Assistive technology for postsecondary students with learning disabilities. *Journal of Learning Disabilities, 29,* 486–492.

Ebo, B. (Ed.). (1998). Internet or outernet? In: *Cyberghetto or Cybertopia? Race Class and Gender on the Internet.* Westport, CT: Praeger.

Education Week. (1998). *Technology Counts* '98[Online]. Available: www.edweek.org/sreports/tc98/

Education Week. (2003). *Technology in education.* [Online]. Available: http://www.edweek.org/rc/issues/technology-in-education/

Garland, V., & Wotton, S. (2001). Bridging the digital divide in public schools. *Journal of Educational Technology Systems, 30*(2), 115–123.

Giacquinta, J. B., Bauer, J., & Levin, J. E. (1993). *Beyond technology's promise: An examination of children's educational computing at home.* Cambridge, England: Cambridge University Press.

Henderson, A. T. (1994). *A new generation of evidence: The family is critical to student achievement.* St. Louis: Danforth Foundation and Flint MI: Mott (C.S.) Foundation.

Henderson, A., & Mapp, K. (2002). A new wave of evidence: The impact of school, family and community connections on student achievement.*SEDL's national center for family and community connections with schools.* [Online]. Available: www.sedl.org/connections/resources/evidence.pdf

Hoffman, D., & Novak, T. (1998). Bridging the digital divide: The impact of race on computer access and internet use. *Science, 279.*

Kraut, R., Scherlis, W., Mukhopadhyay, T., Manning, J., & Kiesler, S. (1996). The HomeNet field trial of residential Internet services. *Communications of the ACM, 39*(12), 55–63.

Kupperman, J., & Fishman, B. (2001). Academic, social and personal uses of the Internet: Cases of students from an urban Latino classroom. *Journal of Research on Technology in Education, 34*(2), 189–215.

MacArthur, C. A. (2000). New tools for writing: Assistive technology for students with writing difficulties. *Topics in Language Disorders, 20,* 85–100.

Market Data Retrieval. (2003). *Technology in education,* Available [online]: http://www.school-data.com/mdrtechhilites.asp

McNeil, L. (2000). *Contradictions of school reform: Educational costs of standardized testing.* New York: Routledge.

National Assessment of Educational Progress. (2005). *Internet access in U.S. public schools and classrooms: 1994–2003.* Obtained from the world wide web on August 1, 2005 at http://nces.ed.gov/pubsearchpubsinfo.asp?pubid = 2005015

National Center for Education Statistics. (2003). *Internet access in U.S. public schools and classrooms: 1994–2002.* U.S. Department of Education.

National Science Foundation. (NSF) (1998). *Division of science resource studies: Science and engineering indicators,* Available [online]: www.nsf.gov/sbe/srs/seind98/

National Telecommunications and Information Administration (NTIA). (1998). *Falling through the Net: Defining the digital divide.* Washington, DC: U.S. Department of Commerce.

Olmstead, P. P., & Rubin, R. I. (1983). Linking parent behaviors to child achievement: Four evaluation studies from the parent education follow-through programs. *Studies in Educational Evaluation, 8,* 317–325.

Orr, A. (2003). Black–White differences in achievement: The importance of wealth. *Sociology of Education, 76*(4), 281–304.

Puma, M., Chaplin, D., & Pape, A. (2000). *E-rate and the digital divide: A preliminary analysis from the integrated studies of educational technology.* Washington, DC: U.S. Department of Education, Office of the Under Secretary, Planning and Evaluation Service, Elementary and Secondary Education Division.

Raskind, M. H., & Higgins, E. L. (1998). Assistive technology for postsecondary students with learning disabilities: An overview. *Journal of Learning Disabilities, 31,* 27–40.

Rocheleau, B. (1995). Computer use by school-age children: Trends, patterns, and predictors. *Journal of Educational Computing Research, 12,* 1–17.

Rockman, S. (1995). *Assessing the growth: The Buddy Project evaluation, 1994–1995.* San Francisco.

Walker, V. (1997). The great technology divide: How urban schools lose. *The Education Digest, 62,* 47–49.

Weber, M. (1968). *Economy and society.* New York: Bedminster Press.

Wenglinsky, H. (1998). *Does it compute? The relationship between educational technology and student achievement in mathematics.* Princeton, NJ: Educational Testing Service.

ACCEPTABLE USE POLICIES IN SCHOOL DISTRICTS: MYTH OR REALITY?

Kona Renee Taylor, Eun Won Whang and Sharon Y. Tettegah

ABSTRACT

Although "acceptable use" policy (AUP) constitutes a fairly straight-forward perspective in many school districts – students' ethical, legal, and personally responsible educational usage of electronic technologies – there is a more ambiguous area of which administrators need to be aware. For example, what constitutes an AUP and who is responsible for creating them and upholding their guidelines? Other issues that need to be thought about are what makes up "appropriate" (instructionally acceptable) standards of educational quality in terms of the content of web sites?

IMPORTANCE AND PROBLEMS WITH THE INTERNET IN EDUCATION

Technology, especially the technology and resources provided by the Internet, are vital to students for a variety of reasons including education, future career

Technology and Education: Issues in Administration, Policy, and Applications in K12 Schools
Advances in Educational Administration, Volume 8, 115–123
Copyright © 2006 by Elsevier Ltd.
All rights of reproduction in any form reserved
ISSN: 1479-3660/doi:10.1016/S1479-3660(05)08009-1

skills, and communication. Yet, there are also important safety issues that come along with the use of the Internet. Poftak (2002) found the following:

> The new opportunities for knowledge and communication offered by the Internet are undeniably exciting, but with them come a raft of concerns for adults. On the one hand, kids are discovering new avenues for finding information, for socializing, for experimenting with different personas, and for gaining important technology skills they'll need for their futures. At the same time, we've all heard the stories of inappropriate and sometimes even dangerous experiences the Net potentially opens up for children: pornography, hacking, copyright infringement, and online bullying, to name a few (p. 36).

Consequently, there is a balance of using yet not misusing the Internet that must be found to maximize the significant contributions of the Internet while still keeping our children safe from harm. This leads to the importance and use of acceptable use policies (AUP) in education.

WHAT ARE ACCEPTABLE USE POLICIES?

In general AUPs are, "strategies that allow school districts to notify technology users of expected behavior and set forth the consequences of misuse" (Conn, 2002, p. 91). Yet, this fairly straightforward definition leaves much open to interpretation. For example, depending on the school district, some AUPs are only listed in a handbook with other school policies of conduct, while other districts require their AUP to be signed by both parents and students. This is further illustrated by another definition of AUP given by the Virginia Department of Education, Division of Technology (2005), which states that an AUP is "a written agreement in the form of guidelines, signed by students, their parents and their teachers, outlining the terms and conditions of Internet use-rules of online behavior and access privileges" (http://www.pen.k12.va.us/go/VDOE/Technology/AUP/home.shtml).

Notice the significant difference between the first definition and the second? Both are definitions of what constitutes an AUP, yet there are vast differences in the implications of what they entail. Thus, an important question to ask is whether these policies should be included with other school policies such as dress codes and absences, or if they should be more of a legal document that requires parental and student signatures? Marcroft (1998) maintained,

> Acceptable Use Policy (AUP) clearly delineates how students are expected to make use of school-provided Internet access – and how not to. Definitions of acceptable Internet use vary not only from school to school, but from place to place, time to time, or user to user within a single school. Particularly when teachers use the same computers as their students, administrators must take users' varying needs into account when creating an AUP (p. 72).

This question of legality is important to understand when one is thinking about AUPs because with these differences the roles the AUP and Internet play in the school district might also be different. Accordingly, what makes up a good AUP?

Rader (2002) explains the AUP should clearly define the standards for acceptable use as well as outline the consequences for specific types of violations. These "standards" could mean different things for different school districts, thus Conn (2002) further describes in detail that an AUP should state:

- The district's expectation that district computing facilities will be used exclusively for educational purposes;
- The district's expectations that students and teachers will use educationally appropriate speech and expression when using the Internet and other technological tools;
- User's responsibilities to avoid copyright violations; Users' reasonable expectations (or lack of such expectations) of privacy in any and all uses of district technology resources; and
- Users' responsibilities to avoid substantial and material disruption of the educational process for the school community (p. 93).

Along with these standards, Conn (2002) notes that districts should also formulate policies to deal with students or employees who refuse to sign the AUP, or with students whose parents refuse to countersign. Yet, even though school districts AUPs should have the previous aspects provided within it, the actual content of AUPs differ quite a bit between school districts. The following examples show AUPs are applied in different districts and/or departments.

ACTUAL ACCEPTABLE USE POLICIES

This section describes how AUPs are used in different school districts. We will briefly discuss the following examples.[1] The comparisons are based on AUP standards, Conn (2002) suggested.

Carpenter Central School District, East Coast

The AUP of Carpenter Central School District (CCSD) was organized into five categories: acceptable use, unacceptable use, network access and accounts, Internet access, and electronic mail. Each section was followed by a detailed explanation in bulleted lists that fulfill the overall AUP standards

set forth by Conn (2002, see Table 1). The consent forms were separated into
high school level, middle school level, and elementary school level, each
summarizing the key contents of the AUP for the certain grade level. CCSD
only required students' agreement in their consent form.

Miller School District, West Coast

Miller District's AUP provided an organized and specific AUP for the students and staff. The AUP was categorized into an introduction, Net e-mail
access, Internet use, unacceptable use, privacy, web content, copyright and
plagiarism, and Internet guidelines committee. As illustrated in Table 1, the
contents of Miller's AUP completely cover Conn's (2002) AUP guidelines.
Also, some of the important topics or terminologies, such as "student rights
and responsibilities handbook," "school board policy," "Internet privacy
protections and considerations," and "copyright information" were hyper-
linked so the readers could easily look up more information on these topics
if they were not sure what they were or if they were interested in gaining
more information. The consent or denial form for the students' e-mail accounts were available on the Web, but the actual AUP agreement form was
not linked to the Web page.

Larim Public Schools, East Coast

The AUP for Larim Public Schools focused on students' Internet usage. It
was written in long sentences, similar to a legal document, without any
categorization and was followed by the consent form for the use of Internet.
A warning message was present that indicated the transfer of certain kinds
of materials was illegal; however, a clear indication of copyright issue was
missing (see Table 1). Since the AUP focused only on the Internet usage,
statements regarding "'user's responsibilities to avoid substantial and material disruption of the educational process for the school community'"
(Conn, 2002) were also absent.

Mue County Community School Corporation, Mid West

The students in Mue County Community School Corporation (MCCSC)
had an AUP that was organized into five categories: responsibility, rights

Table 1. Comparison of Different School District's AUP According to [3]Conn's (2002) Standards.

AUP Standard	Carpenter	Miller	Larim	Mue	Lineal	Ponext
Computing facilities will be used exclusively for educational purposes	X	X	X	X	—	X
Students and teachers will use educationally appropriate speech and expression when using the Internet	X	X	X	X	X	—
User's responsibilities to avoid copyright violations	X	X	—	X	X	X
User's reasonable expectations of privacy	X	X	X	X	X	—
User's responsibilities to avoid substantial and material disruption of the educational process for the school community	X	X	—	X	X	X

Note: An "X" indicates that the standard was met.

and privileges, restrictions, disclaimers, and sanctions. The student and parent agreement form was followed by AUP guidelines. Conn's (2002) AUP standards were all met by this AUP, and there was a clear indication that the teachers are an important part of the AUP. It first required staff's permission to let the students use the Internet, and then the student's and parent/guardian's agreement. The AUP also implied that the instructor was to read and discuss the summary of the AUP with students and sign the consent form before an Internet account could be issued to the students.

Lineal School District, West Coast

Lineal School District provides a brief telecommunications use agreement. The AUP was divided into elementary users' group and the sixth to eighth graders' group. Both groups' agreements provided similar contents such as: be

polite; use appropriate, respectful language; privacy; electronic mail; information; and vandalism. For the higher grades, they added software and copyright issues. The consent form, which required both student and parent or
guardian's signature, followed each agreement. One issue with the AUP was
that there was not enough description for each category, and the statement
"the school principal may determine other behavior to be inappropriate" may
not provide sufficient information for the students to understand what is
meant by "inappropriate." Also, following Conn's (2002) guidelines, there
was no mention of how the computers were to be used and for what purposes
(see Table 1).

Ponext Independent School District (K-5), South West

The AUP for Ponext Independent School District (PISD) was divided into
three categories: equipment, Internet, and responsibilities and ethical use. A
distinguishing feature was that the AUP only showed one policy at a time
with related graphics, and then proceeded to the next policy once the "next"
button was clicked. After reading through the AUP, the readers were re-
directed to the very first page, and saw a question that asked whether all
three acceptable use guidelines were covered or not. If the user clicked on
"yes," the page would then move to the acceptable use permission form and
let you download the form in either English or Spanish. Students and parents were both required to sign the form. Along with the helpful graphics,
the short and concise guidelines were much easier to read compared to other
AUPs that were written in long sentences and paragraphs. However, it did
not contain enough information such as guidance for students on how to use
educationally appropriate speech and expressions when using the Internet or
other technology tools. In addition, the guideline did not warn users' of their
reasonable expectations of privacy (Conn, 2002, see Table 1).

As illustrated in Table 1, six different district's AUPs were reviewed to see
if they first met all of Conn's (2002) standards, and then for their ease of use
and understanding for the reader. It was found that the content of the six
AUPs were basically analogous; however, they did differ on some important
aspects. For example, some of the AUPs were organized in a coherent and
easy to understand format, while others read like a law book and were very
complex and hard to comprehend. What is significant to note is that when
an AUP is represented in an organized manner, it is likely to encourage the
students, parents or guardians, and staff to read and understand the policy.
Kinnmann (1995) criticized that some schools and districts are providing

confusing and offensive guidelines that affect people's belief in the validity of the AUP. As a solution, her suggestion was to provide well-written, logical and internally consistent AUPs that would both appeal to the readers and would be better understanding. With these content and usability issues related to AUPs, one important question to bring up is who currently decides what is included in an AUP?

WHO DECIDES?

The content of AUPs vary from school district to school district, yet there is underlying backbone that appears to remain consistent throughout. The differences between school districts are an effect of the differences between who decides what is included in an AUP as well as the needs of that particular district. In some states, Indiana and Virginia for example, the department of education sets forth specific AUP requirements that all school districts must comply with as well as additional recommended information that should be included (see http://www.doe.state.in.us/olr/aup/aupreg.html). This allows each school district some discretion in what their AUP actually states, but still provides some framework for what must be included. Other states, such as Illinois, have no formal policy set forth for acceptable use and leave it up to the individual school districts to come up with their own. Ultimately in both situations, the actual school districts' AUP "reflects the circumstances unique to the school or division, the electronic system used, and clearly defines what constitutes local responsible use of information networks" (Virginia Department of Education, 2005).

Thus, as a whole AUPs in public schools have yet to be standardized in the United States. So who gets to decide what is acceptable and what is not? Results from Flowers and Rakes (2000) found that out of 85 respondents from different school districts across the United States, 73% indicated that committees wrote their school AUP, yet 16.5% indicated that individuals wrote theirs. Of the respondents who said that their schools AUP was done by an individual, most indicated that the individual was their technology coordinator or librarian. This is interesting in that while a majority of the respondents said their schools had formed committees to formulate their AUPs, some school's allowed individuals to formulate theirs.

Conversely, Chmielewski (1998) stated that to have an AUP that is appropriate for the entire school district and that covers all possible scenarios of Internet usage, "a school should involve teachers, school librarians, media specialists, administrators, parents, and students. A school should also consult with a technology staffer and legal counsel" (p. 28). This is important because there are many different legal issues that can arise when dealing with education and the Internet and after implementing comprehensive AUP policies, "districts have prospective mechanisms to deal with students or staff who sign AUPs and then misuse the district's technology resources" (Conn, 2002, p. 96). Yet, as illustrated previously with the AUPs from different school districts, the ease of understanding the AUP's mandates can often cause confusion and lead to unknowing misuse.

While changing the format or wording of the AUP may help with comprehension, there is also the option of training students and staff on what is acceptable and what is not (see Lawson & Comber, 2000).

> An AUP is an important first step in promoting ethical computer use, but it is not a solution in and of itself. Although their schools had such documents, awareness on the part of students, parents, and faculty was not widespread ... Teachers and librarians from schools with strong acceptable use policies felt that guidance for students was enhanced by the policies, if students were sufficiently aware of them.
>
> (Bell, 2002, p. 34)

Also important with this training is a clear understanding of who is monitoring the students while they are on the Internet. Some schools require that monitoring come from the teachers or librarians, while other schools provide constant monitoring of all Internet use via various computer programs designed to observe all computer activity. Hall and Kelly (2005) note that, "Student abuse most often occurs when they are unsupervised. (School personnel should)...be aware of where and when you provide the greatest level of unsupervised access to technology in your school" (p. 28). Thus, an AUP alone may not be enough to lower the rate of computer misuse, but by combining an AUP with training, discussion, and awareness of who is monitoring the students, it is possible to increase the effectiveness of these policies.

CONCLUSION

Acceptable use policys (AUP) are, "...a set of guidelines for student use of the Internet and other school-provided computer network services, such as E-mail" (Chmielewski, 1998, p. 27). AUPs are vital for school districts on a number of different levels, but especially for bridging the gap between educator's desire and hesitation for students use of technology. As further discussed by Marcroft (1998):

> If they bar students from Internet use altogether, they deprive them of an exciting, state-of-the-art learning tool. If they allow unrestricted Internet access, they place students' safety – and schools' liability – at risk (p. 71).

With the use of AUPs, school districts can regulate the use of the internet and other technologies, while allowing students usage of these tools. Key to this use is the formation of an AUP that is both easy to understand, specific and fully covers all of the different aspects that may arise with Internet usage (see Conn, 2002). To help create this type of policy it is important to utilize a committee consisting of school personnel, parents and students, within the school district that represents the many different ways in which technology will be used in the schools.

NOTES

1. All schools are represented under pseudonyms.

REFERENCES

Bell, M. A. (2002). Cyberethics in schools: What is going on? *Book Report, 21*(1), 33–35.

Chmielewski, C. M. (1998). Savvy about cybersmut. *NEA Today, 17*, 27–31.

Conn, K. (2002). *The internet and the law: What educators need to know.* Alexandria, Virginia: Association for Supervision and Curriculum Development.

Flowers, B. F., & Rakes, G. C. (2000). Analysis of acceptable use policies regarding the internet in selected K-12 schools. *Journal of Research on Computing in Education, 32*, 351–365.

Hall, D., & Kelly, P. (2005). Security code: Red or ready. *Learning and Leading with Technology, 32*(6), 28–30.

Kinnman, D. (1995, June). Critiquing acceptable use policies. Retrieved August 24, 2005. Located at: http://www.io.com/~kinnaman/aupessay.html

Lawson, T., & Comber, C. (2000). Censorship, the internet, and schools: A new moral panic? *The Curriculum Journal, 11*, 273–285.

Marcroft, T. (1998). Safety first: Managing the Internet in school. *T H E Journal, 26*, 71–74.

Poftak, A. (2002). Net-wise teens: Safety, ethics, and innovation. *Technology & Learning, 22*, 36–45.

Rader, M. H. (2002). Strategies for teaching internet ethics. *Delta Pi Epsilon Journal, 44*(2), 73–79.

Virginia Department of Education, Division of Technology. (2005). ACCEPTABLE USE POLICIES – A HANDBOOK. Retrieved August 16, 2005, from http://www.pen.k12.va.us/go/VDOE/Technology/AUP/home.shtml

KNOWING AND GETTING WHAT YOU PAY FOR: ADMINISTRATION, TECHNOLOGY, AND ACCOUNTABILITY IN K-12 SCHOOLS

Saran Donahoo and Michael Whitney

ABSTRACT

Spurred on by the global economy and greater public interests, technology is no longer a luxury reserved for or exclusively used in wealthy schools. Indeed, educational leaders now experience strong pressure to increase and improve the use of the technology in their schools. Utilizing current research, program models, and best practices, this chapter provides educational administrators with issues associated with the costs of school technology plans, instructional, management, and other topics to address in planning to add or change the use of technology in schools, and a list of basic tenets to assist in creating and operating school technology programs.

Technology and Education: Issues in Administration, Policy, and Applications in K12 Schools
Advances in Educational Administration, Volume 8, 125–142
Copyright © 2006 by Elsevier Ltd.
All rights of reproduction in any form reserved
ISSN: 1479-3660/doi:10.1016/S1479-3660(05)08010-8

INTRODUCTION

Educational technology is no longer luxury reserved for wealthy school districts. Every elementary and secondary school must provide their students with access and training on how to use technology. However, recognizing the need to teach and help students develop these schools does not make it any easier for school leaders to construct or execute effective instructional technology programs. To that end, this chapter uses data drawn from existing research and successful program model to provide educational administrators with information regarding the costs associated with establishing and maintaining school technology plans, insight into issues to consider in crafting these plans, and suggestions for maximizing the effectiveness technology within the school environment.

THE COSTS OF EDUCATIONAL TECHNOLOGY

Technology Variables and Expenditures

As technology becomes a more integral and integrated part of society, school administrators are faced with the task of keeping pace with an ever-moving technological target. Invariably, the percentage of resources devoted to technology will become a larger, permanent fixture within the budget. Yet, what is the technological bottom line? The answer varies greatly depending on which variables the technology plan includes and how school leaders execute that plan. To be certain, costs does not focus on hardware and software alone. Similar to purchasing a new bus, the expenditures-related educational technology begins with initial costs, but also carries on into the future with maintenance, upgrades, and other operating expenses (Fickes, 2004; Institute for the Advancement of Emerging Technologies in Education Development Center (IAETE), 2005). The following provides a review of many variables schools face when going high-tech and the influence that these variables have on the total costs of supporting educational technology.

Student–Computer Ratio

How many students need access to a computer? In a perfect world, every student would have access to a computer workstation for the duration of the school day. However, the reality lies below the idyllic goal of 100% as it relates to both availability and the opportunities students have to access educational technology. Recognizing that 100% computer access and usage would be difficult for most school districts to implement, the federal government offers some guidelines. In 1997, the President's Committee of Advisers on Science and Technology recommended a four to five student per school computer ratio for all schools (*Education Week on the Web*, 2000). With this ratio in mind, it becomes theoretically possible to provide one hour of daily access to every student throughout the school day as part of an efficient and effective rotating schedule. While the estimated savings varies from school to school, this more attainable student–computer ratio and usage target can help school leaders save money by offering a more affordable way to effectively serve the technology needs of their students.

Environmental Alterations

Easily overlooked, but critical in the planning and budget is the cost of converting an existing facility into one capable of supporting current and advanced technologies. Known as retrofitting, the price tag for such work can vary greatly depending on the condition of the building. Newer buildings will need fewer modifications to areas such as the electrical supply, heating and air conditioning, network wiring, security, and accessible workstations. Even so, almost all buildings will require some modifications. As reported in the McKinsey study (1995), an estimated 65% of schools are more than 35 years old and need some form of retrofitting to support current technology. Breaking down the anticipated modifications, 23% of schools need to upgrade their electrical systems and 4% need to work on their heating and air conditioning systems. Moreover, schools should also anticipate paying approximately $350 per room to secure their new technology as well as an estimated $355 per computer for furniture. While some schools find wireless connections more feasible and appropriate, an old school will have to pay a projected $65,000 to remove asbestos and improve the infrastructure to support a traditional, less-expensive hardwired network. These are just a few of the costs school leaders must consider and account for in updating and implementing educational technology plans.

Indeed, the negative experience of some school districts further highlights the importance of financial planning in implementing educational technology. In 1995, approximately 42% of all schools and 52% of urban schools reported that they had insufficient electrical wiring infrastructure to support computer technology (Riley, 1996). As such, educational administrators must be certain that the physical structure of their buildings can adequately support various forms of technology before investing funds into hardware and software that will not function within their facilities.

Hardware

Beyond the high-costs of retrofitting school facilities, purchasing and installing technological hardware also requires large upfront investments on the part of schools. Although costly, retrofitting such as upgrades in electrical and heating, ventilation, and air conditioning (HVAC) systems typically account for only 20% of the expenditures associated with school technology programs. On the other hand, computer hardware generally account for 55%, while peripherals such as printers, scanners, security, and furniture stations account for 25% of technology costs, respectively (McKinsey & Company, Inc., 1995).

Furthermore, technology costs do not end once a school is outfitted with the equipment necessary to support its technology plan. Basically, technology expenses are never-ending due to the need for maintenance and upkeep. Moreover, changes in technology generally mandate that schools update their old computers and other equipment on a five-year cycle, thus further increasing the overall expense of hardware. Despite continuing technological advances and increasing attention to providing students with access to technology in schools, Quality Education Data, Inc. (QED, 2005) found that trends in hardware spending shifted from $54.73 per student in 2003–2004 to $53.72 per student during the following school year. Even so, it is likely that this shift in spending is a result of more limited resources available to school districts rather than a reflection of changes in the overall costs of hardware.

Software

In addition to hardware, software and instructional programs also have an impact on the total costs of school technology programs. Various studies examine the influence software expenditures have on technology programs. In 1996, RAND found that software occupied 4–10% of technology costs with most schools devoting an average of 8% of their technology expenses to software. Conversely, McKinsey & Company, Inc. (1995) estimated that software costs ranged from 14% to 20% and predicted that these costs will eventually grow to a range of 21–26%. In a more recent study, QED (2005) determined that 22% of technology costs went to software with 10% covering the costs of administrative software and 12% for instructional software and programs during the 2004–2005 school year. In dollars, QED (2005) estimated that schools spent $14.23 for administrative and $17.42 for instructional software during that school year. Given the broad differential in the research results, it is important to note that each study accounted for different budgetary variables. For example, McKinsey & Company, Inc. (1995) included subscription fees while the QED (2005) study specifically separated the costs of administrative software from the funding spent on instructional software. Nevertheless, taken together, these studies indicate that software expenses are a growing area within school technology budgets, which educational administrators must plan to cover long before making any actual purchases.

Replacement Costs
Although costly at the outset, wires, furniture, and other elements of retrofitting are fairly cost-effective given that most of these expenditures have a 20-year life span. Conversely, computer hardware, software, and other forms of technology become outdated or obsolete within a much shorter time frame. Given the new developments and advances in technology, private businesses generally replace or update their hardware and software on three-year cycles. School districts, on the other hand, often find it necessary to stretch the replacement cycle to five years or more in order to extend the life of their initial investment (Fickes, 2004). Replacing computers can be expensive for school districts since new computers can costs more than schools paid for the same technology only a few years earlier. At the same time, operating older, outdated machines can also be just as expensive in the long run due to the costs of continuous repairs and labor needed to maintain these systems.

Besides the funds required to replace their broken or outmoded technology, schools must also determine what to do with this equipment once they are done using it. Recycling programs often provide schools with low-cost ways of disposing off their old hardware. For example, some schools choose to dispose off old computers by giving them to students and their families (Lynch, 2002). However, recycling old technology does have its drawbacks. While recycling programs do exist and can help reduce the costs of disposal, the actual expense of participating in such programs varies according to geographic areas and other factors since many programs require schools to deliver equipment to specified drop-off locations. Moreover, the fact that these programs focus primarily on donations and philanthropy means that recycling old technology generally fails to offer schools the type of financial benefit that private companies and citizens receive for performing the same service (Lynch, 2004).

Donated Computers

As previously discussed, recycling and donation programs offer educational administrators a relatively inexpensive way to remove old technology from their schools. Likewise, many school districts also find that becoming the recipients of recycled machinery serves as a good way of narrowing the student–computer ratio without requiring a large financial investment from their budgets. The 21st Century Classrooms Act for Private Technology Investment (1997) encourages private businesses and corporation to donate their old computers and other technology to schools by offering special tax incentives. At the same time, the act helps schools to update their technology and increase student access without diverting or devoting funds from their already tight budgets. Yet, despite the initial advantage, accepting donated computers is an act accompanied by some unique expenses and downsides of its own.

First, private businesses generally choose to donate computers for a tax deduction only after the technology becomes too slow or too old to run current software or perform other business operations. As such, the donated computers schools receive may be in need of repair or simply incapable of carrying out the teaching–learning functions students need to develop technology skills while in school (Lynch, 2002).

Second, the fact that donated computers are not always in working order when they arrive requires schools and school districts to divert personnel and resources into making this technology operational. Oftentimes, technical professionals must spend countless hours sifting through these donated computers in an attempt to bring some of them up to speed or simply prepare them to perform basic functions. Similarly, the advanced age of this equipment upon its arrival means that technology personnel must plan to devote considerable time and resources to continuously repairing these machines and keeping them operational thus increasing the indirect costs associated with such technology programs (Fickes, 2004; Lynch, 2002).

A third problem with this approach arises from the software and other licensing that may or may not accompany donated equipment. The structure of many technologies makes it impossible for schools to perform certain operations or run particular software on donated equipment without obtaining proper licensing. In addition, licensing also limits the number of computers, which may operate a specific piece of software thus forcing schools to either purchase more software or pay for additional licensing. In this way, donated computers may fail to produce the savings that attract many school districts to these programs (Lynch, 2002).

Educational administrators should carefully consider the potential drawbacks and unanticipated costs before building a technology program around donated equipment. Lynch (2002) offers a variety of issues schools should consider before choosing to accept donated technology. Likewise, school leaders should also think about adopting a donation policy similar to the Syracuse City School District Guidelines for Donated Equipment (2005) to ensure that donated computers will be capable of performing up to needs and expectations of the school.

Internet Access

Internet access is becoming more popular and available in schools. In 2001, 99% of public schools in the United States had access to the Internet with 85% of them using broadband connections (Kleiner & Farris, 2005). Faster connections benefit schools by allowing students and staff to achieve information rapidly without maintaining large, expensive collections in the school library. Moreover, using the Internet also gives teachers and students access to video and audio files that simply are not available at most schools. Enacted under the Telecommunications Act of 1996, the School and Libraries Universal Service Fund established the Education-Rate or E-Rate, which provides refunds and discounts to ensure that all schools and public libraries can obtain internet access. Even so, QED (2005) estimates that internet access still costs schools approximately $19.88 per student or 14% of their technology budgets. As technology takes advantage of more and more bandwidth, school districts may have to increase this segment of their technology budgets in order to upgrade and sustain adequate connectivity.

Technical Support

Whether technology comes to the school as new or recycled, districts have to supply technical support to help students, teachers, and staff utilize equipment and software effectively. To do so, some districts have added an additional staff position for an instructional technology specialist to oversee this process as well as implement replacement, donation, and technology policies (Northeast and the Islands Regional Technology in Education

Consortium (NEIRTEC), 2002). However, in districts where budgets do not allow for the maintenance of such a position, administrators must utilize other staff and devise different means of providing these services to their schools. Although budget-friendly, operating educational technology programs without adequate technical support can be costly in other ways since it diverts faculty and staff attention away from other duties. At the same time, asking staff who are not technically inclined to bare the burden for a significant portion of technical support also jeopardizes the overall effectiveness of school technology programs as personnel become frustrated by or simply refuse to use technology (Means, Penuel, & Padilla, 2001).

As researched by QED (2005), technical support costs schools and school districts an estimated $22.24 per student taking up an average of 16% of the total budget. Nevertheless, employing properly trained technology specialist to monitor, implement, train, and oversee educational technology is worth the investment. Besides maintaining equipment and allowing other staff members to focus on their duties, on-staff technology experts also assist administrators with developing and operating appropriate technology plans, selecting suitable and effective hardware and software, and addressing other issues that can help to soften the impact technology programs have on the school and district budgets.

Professional Development

As with technical support, professional development is an expenditure that has the potential to both save money and improve the overall effectiveness of educational technology programs. The challenge for school districts is to provide adequate training for the instructors enabling them to utilize the computer as an instructional tool that can improve academic achievement as a whole rather than as an additional subject added to the curriculum. Indeed, professional development is an essential element of any technology plan. If teachers do not know how to effectively incorporate the new technologies into their curriculum, then the investment will not produce the envisioned results (The CEO Forum, 1999). Unfortunately, this is not the current case in many schools. QED (2005) estimates that during the 2004–2005 school year only 9% of most schools budgets or $12.82 per student was spent on professional development and integrating technology into the curriculum. These numbers are consistent with the RAND (Keltner & Ross, 1996) study, which found that schools devoted 10% of their budgets to this type of support. In either case, the actual level of funding devoted to professional development in most schools is far lower than that suggested by the U.S. Department of Education, which recommends that school districts devote close to 30% of their budgets and nowhere near the 38% average allocated by highly technical schools (Riley, 1996). Highly technical schools would not devote such a large amount of their funds to professional development if these efforts did not help to improve their technology programs. As such, other schools seeking to offer truly effective technology programs should consider increasing the professional development provided to their faculty and other instructional staff.

Value of School Technology

As administrators work through a technology budget, the focus becomes one of financial investment. Yet, why are these investments necessary? What is the value of supporting school technology? Globalization and the spread of technology throughout society is one reason why it is both valuable and necessary to provide such training in schools. Schools cannot truly prepare students to function within society if the curriculum fails to cover the equipment and skills they will actually use in the real world. Moreover, schools cannot hope to improve either the academic achievement of their students or the overall value of their programs without sufficiently integrating technology (Honey, 2001). Essentially, technology is valuable and worth the investment simply because all schools must offer instruction and access in order to remain relevant in this millennium.

Beyond basic exposure and access, technology is also valuable to schools in that it allows them to offer programs and materials few school districts could ever afford to maintain. As previously mentioned, offering internet access allows schools to give their students access to resources and research materials that are both up-to-date and more expansive than most school media centers (NEIRTEC, 2002). Likewise, the increased availability of distance education courses for people of all educational levels has also elevated the value of technology. During the 2002–2003 school year, an estimated 328,000 students enrolled public school districts also participated in distance education courses (Setzer & Lewis, 2005). Distance education is especially attractive to rural and other school districts with limited resources that prevent these schools from offering many college preparatory courses (Hicks, 2002). In this way, technology allows schools to better serve their students without spending the even greater funds that traditional delivery methods would require to extend equivalent services. In addition to assisting with learning and instruction, technology also helps schools by creating more efficient pathways for communication. If a teacher utilizes a computer quiz or test, results become available at the end of the test versus the time it would ordinarily take for instructors to score each exam individually. At the same time, this method also saves time for teachers by recording grades automatically. Consequently, using technology as an assessment tool allows teachers to devote more time to instruction and working directly with students. At the same time, technology also enables schools to make homework assignments, school schedules, grades, and other information readily available to parents (NEIRTEC, 2002; Valdez et al., 2000). In doing so, technology serves as a valuable communications tool both within and outside of the school by helping students, teachers, and parents work together to monitor and improve student learning and performance.

SCHOOL SUCCESS

Inundated by No Child Left Behind (NCLB) and widespread interests in school effectiveness, many schools value technology as a potential tool for promoting school improvement and student success. Upon reaching that decision; however, educational administrators often find that it is more difficult to identify how technology will assist in reaching these goals or determine what issues to address in order to implement successful technology programs. The following examines these elements of technology programs by first discussing the legislative and research foundations, which encourage administrative attention to technology and then moves on to outline key issues school leaders should consider in adopting such programs.

Legislation and Research

Among its other guidelines and expectations, NCLB emphasizes the need for K-12 schools to use various forms of technology to improve student academic performance. The Enhancing Education Through Technology Act of 2001 (EETTA), Title II, Part D of the Elementary and Secondary Education Act reauthorization of the same year, describes the technology goals included under NCLB. The primary goal of this subsidiary act is to use technology to improve student achievement. Other goals set forth include addressing the digital divide by making sure that all students are technologically literate prior to entering high school regardless of their background, and developing research-based integrative instruction and curriculum resources (EETTA, 2001).

Yet, despite significant interest from those inside and outside of education, the full effect technology has on academic success has yet to be determined. Examined from a broad perspective, research has found that the use of computers improves student performance on activities related to skills, drills, and rote memorization such as basic math problems. Computers also help to enhance the educational experience by allowing each student to move at his/her own pace, providing immediate assessment of completed assignments, and promoting the development of higher-order thinking skills (Coley, 1997; Valdez et al., 2000).

In spite of some positive results, increasing the presence of technology in schools is not a guarantee of academic success. Since the mid-1990s, students in both impoverished and wealthy school districts have had virtually equal access to computers within their school buildings. Likewise, "over 77% of instructional rooms and 98% of schools have access to the Internet" (National Center for Education Statistics (NCES), 2001, as cited by NEIRTEC, 2002, p. 29). Even so, students in poorer schools continue to experience disparities by having older, more outdated equipment, limited opportunities to actually access the Internet themselves, and teachers who are less likely to utilize technology to go beyond more traditional forms of instruction (Anderson & Ronnkvist, 1999; Becker, 2000; Daniel, 2003; Dickard, 2002; Means, Penuel, & Padilla, 2001). Essentially, merely increasing the availability of technology in schools does not always have a positive impact on student or school performance.

Elements for Technology Success

As studies indicate, a variety of factors influences the success of technology programs in public schools. Illustrated by schools that have utilized technology to improve learning and academic achievement, addressing many of these elements will help make technology programs effective for all types of schools.

Leadership

Leadership serves as a key element and starting point to school technology success. Whether the curriculum provides computers to students or personal digital assistants (PDAs) to help teachers with attendance and recordkeeping, technology programs require committed and involved leadership to be effective (Anderson & Dexter, 2005; Wizer & McPherson, 2005). Administrators of schools and districts that use technology do more than simply implement new programs. Instead, the leaders of these programs empower teachers, students, parents, and their school communities to support and promote technology plans focused on improving academic achievement (Honey, 2001; Lemke, 2003; NEIRTEC, 2002). Moreover, schools that utilize technology do not limit leadership to school administrators. Rather these programs employ leadership teams that include teachers, technology personnel, and even other stakeholders who help to craft instructional technology systems that promote the interests shared by the students, school, and surrounding community (Branigan, 2001; Manchester, 2004). Initiated in 2002, the Maine Learning Technology Institute (MLTI) intends to provide laptops to every teacher and student in that state's secondary schools (grades 7–12). To better ensure program success, MLTI encourages teachers to serve as leaders in improving technology and academic programs. As such, MLTI establishes leadership networks allowing teachers and school leaders throughout the state to discuss their programs, mandates that teachers play a direct role in determining what and how schools implement technology, and provides training opportunities to ensure that teachers actually feel comfortable working with the technology their schools choose to adopt (Manchester, 2004).

Core Vision

In addition to leadership, school technology programs also require a clear, focused vision. Indeed, the lack of clear mission and goals is one of the primary reasons why teachers fail to fully implement technology plans into their classrooms and curricula (Means et al., 2001). As such, schools seeking to introduce and increase technology usage should establish and communicate how teachers and students will use the equipment, the goals for the programs, and indicators that will illustrate program success (Anderson & Dexter, 2005; Lemke, 2003; Manchester, 2004; Means et al., 2001; Valdez, 2004).

Similar to leadership, schools with effective technology programs operate under clear visions that are both teaching and learning centered. For example, the networking teams used under MLTI allow teachers to help establish the technology vision for their schools before the program begins. This helps to encourage teachers to implement the programs because it follows the format the school faculty and administrators helped to select (Manchester, 2004). Likewise, the New Technology High School in Napa, California allows students to have increased accountability and greater influence on their curricula by treating them like employees who must complete certain tasks in order remain in good standing and complete secondary education (Branigan, 2001). Moreover, including parents and other community members in crafting a school's technology vision not only increases support for changes taking place within the building, but also helps schools attain their stated learning goals by getting more people to participate in making the program a success (Valdez, 2004).

Training and Professional Development

Researchers have found that one of the reasons that technology programs fail is because teachers do not always feel at ease using the equipment themselves. On the other hand, teachers who feel comfortable with computers and other forms of technology are more likely to effectively utilize these items as instructional tools in working with their students (The CEO Forum, 1999; Lemke, 2003; Means et al., 2001; Wizer & McPherson, 2005). As such, effective technology programs include training and technical support that focus on providing opportunities for both teachers and students to learn how to use the equipment to achieve the academic and other goals set by the school. Specifically, offering teachers on-going professional development that focuses on using technology to improve academic achievement and reaching programmatic goals increases the overall school effectiveness (Honey, 2001; Manchester, 2004; NEIRTEC, 2002; Wizer & McPherson, 2005).

Time and Access

Time influences the effectiveness of school technology programs in two ways. First, school technology programs need time to work. Similar to other school reforms and curriculum changes, the influence technology has on student and teacher performance will not show up instantly. Schools have to give technology programs adequate time to take root before judging that the approach is ineffective (Means et al., 2001).

Secondly, teachers and students must be given time to access the technology schools want to integrate. The New Technology High School structures its entire curriculum around computers and technology. Rather than change courses to accommodate the equipment, the New Technology High School functions as a technology company that does not use bells or traditional classrooms to promote learning. Instead, each student receives an email account and website on the first day of class which serve as the primary means of communicating school expectations and skill assignments (Branigan, 2001). Following more of a traditional model, West High School in Columbus, Ohio chose to start immersing a segment of its student population into technology in the mid-1990s by providing computer access both at home and at school. As a result of these efforts, 90% of the students who participated in the technology program went on to attend college compared to only 15% of their peers (Lemke, 2003). Similarly, the MLTI focuses on maximizing student and teacher access to technology by giving laptops to the students, thus promoting virtually unlimited access and universal computer ownership for all Maine families who have students attending public secondary schools (Manchester, 2004). Utilizing different structures, each of these programs have improved student performance and achieved success in their technology programs by allowing students and faculty sufficient time to learn and operate the equipment.

Assessment

The limited amount of conclusive data on the influence technology has on academic achievement mandates the need for assessment. Although the climate of accountability requires schools to prove the effectiveness of their programs, schools with successful technology programs experience an even greater imperative to generate data on their own rather than relying on limited outside research (Lemke, 2003; NEIRTEC, 2002). Reinforcing the core vision of the program, schools should adopt assessment and evaluation measures that monitor teacher and student progress toward reaching the goals set for the program (Anderson & Dexter, 2005; Lemke, 2003; Means et al., 2001). Besides examining curriculum effectiveness, accurate assessment of technology programs can also help to improve stakeholder support and attract new sources of funding (Branigan, 2001; Lemke, 2003; NEIRTEC, 2002). Moreover, accurate and adequate assessment can also assist school leaders by monitoring technology and programs based on their ability to achieve the goals set forth in by the school rather than those relayed by outside interests who are less likely to be familiar with the programs.

TECHNOLOGY RECOMMENDATIONS FOR EDUCATIONAL ADMINISTRATORS

The increased use of technology in all areas of society makes it necessary for schools to provide a technological education to all of their students. As such, educational administrators need to know what technologies will best help them to educate their children and achieve their school improvement goals. The following are some things school leaders should consider when choosing, implementing, or altering technology programs:

- *Know what you want to accomplish.* Implementing and updating school technology programs require a large investment of funds, personnel, and other resources. Clearly stating your goals before choosing technology will help to ensure that the plan you implement matches with the needs of your school.

- *Clearly identify what and how technology will help you reach your goals.* Bombarded by ever-increasing accountability expectations, schools and school districts have to be prepared to demonstrate why they need the items they ask states, school boards, and other stakeholders to support. As such, school administrators should always be able to articulate and justify the technology they request and desire to use before, during, and after the implementation process. In the short run, currying stakeholder approval will assist in the successful adoption of school technology programs. In the long run, establishing a pattern of regularly updating and communicating with stakeholders about changes taking place within the schools can help make improvements easier and more effective.

- *Communicate goals and plans with stakeholders.* Like other school improvement initiatives, technology programs need support from teachers, parents, community leaders, and other stakeholders in order to be successful. The public is now much more interested in knowing what schools are doing than ever before. Keeping stakeholders informed of your plans for improving their schools can help to minimize the negative impact of rumors and bad publicity. Moreover, informed stakeholders are more likely to both politically and financially support the changes taking place at their schools if they know more about them and genuinely feel that these developments are focused on achieving positive outcomes for the students and the community.

- *Include others in the development and implementation process.* Although school leaders are ultimately responsible for what goes on in their buildings, administrative decisions cannot succeed without the participation of teachers, students, and others. Many people are hesitant and resistant to change even when their current methods are found to be ineffective. Allowing teachers and others who will be directly involved with and affected by technology implementation will increase the probability for success by getting school personnel to uphold and promote the program and its vision.

- *Carefully plot the implementation of your program.* Developing a vision, communicating it, and including others in the planning process will help your school technology plan take shape. However, this will all prove to be wasted effort if you do not devise a practical way of putting the plan into operation. As you prepare to structure or restructure the way your school uses technology, be sure to pay close attention to how your plan will actually look and work in the classrooms and buildings where you intend to use it. Consider possible uses and flaws students, teachers, and technology personnel may encounter as they work to realize your vision. Attempt to prevent problems before they begin to slowly progress toward your goals.

- *Choose appropriate, accurate evaluation and assessment measures.* Although the basic approach may be similar, each school ultimately uses technology differently. As such, it is crucial that educational administrators select and adapt assessment methods that actually measure the content areas and skills addressed by the specific technology program operated in their schools. Utilizing appropriate evaluation tools will give school leaders the accurate data on technology program performance that national research really cannot provide.

- *Know when to change programs and update technology.* Appropriate assessment and monitoring will allow school leaders to gather the data needed to accurately judge the impact technology programs have on their students, teachers, and schools. Having access to this data will also enable educational administrators to identify and address shortcomings before the problems escalate or have a significant impact on either academic achievement or school performance. At the same time, school leaders also need to know when to replace and update the technology used in their schools. Compared to textbooks and many other scholastic materials, technology changes rapidly. For that reason, the Texas School Technology and Readiness (Texas STaR) suggests that schools and districts replace computers every three years to ensure that students and teachers have access to effective and adequate equipment (NEIRTEC, 2002). Although a three-year update schedule might be too concrete for many schools to commit to, educational administrators should recognize and prepare for the necessity of updating their equipment and technology programs according to a plan and schedule that fits their needs.

CONCLUSION

Despite the large investment required, school technology programs are worth the expense because of their potential to expand curricula, enhance learning, and enrich teaching all while working to improve student academic achievement. Yet, in implementing such activities, school leaders should always be mindful of the accountability that affects instructional technology and other school operations. By establishing reasonable goals, allowing various stakeholders to participate in the development and implementation process, and carefully monitoring the progress of technology programs, educational administrators can help to ensure that these programs will promote rather than inhibit school progress and student achievement. Exhibiting clear awareness and good judgment in implementing educational technology plans will help school leaders maximize the benefits of operating these programs.

REFERENCES

21st Century Classrooms Act for Private Technology Investment of 1997 (1997). *Internal revenue code.* Retrieved July 3, 2005, from http://thomas.loc.gov/cgi-bin/query/z?c105:H.R.1153

Anderson, R. E., & Dexter, S. (2005). School technology leadership: An empirical investigation of prevalence and effect. *Educational Administration Quarterly, 41*(1), 49–82.

Anderson, R. E., & Ronnkvist, A. (1999). *The presence of computers in American schools.* Irvine, CA: Center for Research on Information Technology and Organizations.

Becker, H. J. (2000). Who's wired and who's not: Children's access to and use of computer technology. *The Future of Children, 10,* 44–75.

Branigan, C. (2001, February 1). New 'high-tech' high schools aim to transform learning. *eSchool news online.* Retrieved June 23, 2005, from http://www.eschoolnews.com/news/showStory.cfm?ArticleID=2245

Coley, R. J. (1997, September). Technology's impact. *Electronic school online.* Retrieved June 27, 2005, from http://www.electronic-school.com/0997f3.html

Daniel, P. T. K. (2003). The digital divide in America's public schools. In: R. C. Hunter & F. Brown (Eds), *Challenges of urban education and efficacy of school reform* (pp. 145–164). Oxford, England: Elsevier.

Dickard, N. (2002, March 18). *Federal retrenchment on the digital divide: Potential national impact.* Washington, DC: Benton Foundation. Retrieved June 2, 2005, from http://www.benton.org/publibrary/policybriefs/brief01.html

Education Week on the Web. (2000). *New challenges: Overview of state data tables.* Retrieved July 5, 2005, from http://counts.edweek.org/sreports/tc01/tc01article.cfm?slug=35challenges.h20

Enhancing Education Through Technology Act of 2001 (EETTA) (2001). *Title II, Part D of Elementary and Secondary Education Act, 2001.* Retrieved June 2, 2005, from http://www.ed.gov/policy/elsec/leg/esea02/pg34.html

Fickes, M. (2004, May). How much does technology really cost? *School planning & management* [On-line]. Retrieved July 8, 2005, from http://www.peterli.com/archive/spm/669.shtm

Hicks, J. L. (2002, March). Distance education in rural public schools. *USDLA Journal, 16*(3). Retrieved July 2, 2005, from http://www.usdla.org/html/journal/MAR02_Issue/article04.html

Honey, M. (2001). *Issues to support local school change.* Newton, MA: Education Development Center, Inc. Retrieved June 3, 2005, from http://www.pt3.org/VQ/html/honey.html

Institute for the Advancement of Emerging Technologies in Education Development Center (IAETE). (2005). *Publications and tools.* Retrieved July 5, 2005 from http://classroom-tco.cosn.org/publications.html

Keltner, B., & Ross, R. (1996). *The cost of school-based educational technology programs.* Santa Monica, CA: RAND.

Kleiner, A., & Farris, E. (2005). *Internet access in US public schools and classrooms: 1994–2001*. Washington, DC: National Center for Education Statistics (NCES). Retrieved July 6, 2005, from http://nces.ed.gov/pubs2002/internet/3.asp

Lemke, C. L. (2003). Technology solutions that work. *Principal Leadership*, *3*(6), 54–58.

Lynch, J. (2002, December). Acquiring donated computer equipment. *The school administrator web edition*. Retrieved July 3, 2005, from http://www.aasa.org/publications/sa/2002_12/focLynch.htm

Lynch, J. (2004, January 13). Computer recycling and reuse FAQ. *TechSoup* [On-line]. Retrieved July 3, 2005, from http://www.techsoup.org/howto/articlepage.cfm?ArticleId = 537

Manchester, B. (2004). 'Maine learns': The four keys to success of the first statewide leaning with laptop initiative. *T. H. E. Journal*, *31*(12), 14–16.

McKinsey & Company, Inc. (1995). *Connecting K-12 schools to the information superhighway*. Palo Alto, CA: McKinsey & Company, Inc. Retrieved July 4, 2005, from http://www.uark.edu/mckinsey/

Means, B., Penuel, W. R., & Padilla, C. (2001). *The connected school: Technology and learning in high school*. San Francisco: Jossey-Bass.

Northeast and the Islands Regional Technology in Education Consortium (NEIRTEC). (2002). *Technology briefs for no child left behind planners*. Newton, MA: NEIRTEC, Education Development Center, Inc. Retrieved May 31, 2005, from http://tpesc.esc12.net/docs/technology_briefs.pdf

Quality Education Data, Inc. (QED). (2005). *Trends in ed tech across the nation 2004–2005*. Retrieved July 6, 2005, from http://www.k12schoolnetworking.org/2005/presentations/t301_hayes.ppt

Riley, R. W. (1996, June 29). *Getting America's students ready for the 21st century – Meeting the technology literacy challenge, a report to the nation on technology and education*. Washington, DC: US Department of Education. Retrieved July 6, 2005, from http://www.ed.gov/about/offices/list/os/technology/plan/national/index.html

Setzer, J. C., & Lewis, L. (2005). *Distance education courses for public elementary and secondary school students: 2002–03*. Washington, DC: National Center for Education Statistics (NCES). Retrieved July 6, 2005, from http://nces.ed.gov/pubs2005/2005010.pdf

Syracuse City School District Board of Education. (2005). *Syracuse City School District guidelines for donated equipment*. Retrieved July 6, 2005, from http://www.syracusecity-schools.com/donation.htm

The CEO Forum. (1999). School technology and readiness report. *Professional development: A link to better learning*. Retrieved July 7, 2005, from http://www.ceoforum.org/downloads/99report.pdf

Valdez, G. (2004, July). Technology leadership: Enhancing positive educational change. *Pathways* [On-line]. Naperville, IL: North Central Regional Educational Laboratory. Retrieved June 23, 2005, from http://www.ncrel.org/sdrs/areas/issues/educatrs/leadrshp/le700.htm#goals

Valdez, G., McNabb, M., Foertsch, M., Anderson, M., Hawkes, M., & Raack, L. (2000). *Computer-based technology and learning: Evolving uses and expectations*. Naperville, IL: North Central Regional Educational Laboratory. Retrieved June 2, 2005, from http://www.ncrel.org/tplan/cbtl/toc.htm

Wizer, D. R., & McPherson, S. J. (2005). The administrator's role: Strategies for fostering staff development. *Learning and Leading with Technology*, *32*(5), 14–17.

A HERMENEUTIC APPROACH TOWARDS INTEGRATING TECHNOLOGY INTO SCHOOLS: POLICY AND PRACTICE

Mustafa Yunus Eryaman

ABSTRACT

This chapter is an attempt at designing a post-positivist way of understanding policy evaluation and practices while exploring a hermeneutic approach toward integrating technology into schools. In this chapter, the author mainly focuses on three central themes on understanding policy making and evaluation: (a) type of practice (b) nature of knowledge, and (c) issue of evaluation. For each of the themes, the author compares a technical-positivist model of understanding policy making and evaluation with a way of understanding drawn from a hermeneutic approach. The former model is committed to and realized by means of an instrumental and objective knowledge for integration; the latter is connected to human existence, who we already are, and who we want to become. In the chapter, the author designs a practical policy and integration unit to partially describe the ethical, political, practical, and deliberative dimensions of the hermeneutic approach toward integrating technology into classroom practices.

Technology and Education: Issues in Administration, Policy, and Applications in K12 Schools
Advances in Educational Administration, Volume 8, 143–160
Copyright © 2006 by Elsevier Ltd.
ISSN: 1479-3660/doi:10.1016/S1479-3660(05)08011-X

INTRODUCTION

We have entered a new millennium in which human beings encounter one of the most dramatic technological revolutions in history, one that is changing everything from the ways that we work, communicate, and spend our spare time. The technological transformation centers on information and communication technologies is often seen as the beginning of a post-industrial or postmodern information age (Kellner, 2000, 2003; Kerr, 1996; Luke, 1998; Simpson, 1995). In this age, teachers are asked to prepare students for a future world whose citizens will have to combine old and new skills and knowledge in ways we cannot fully envision (Feenberg, 1991; Labbo & Kuhn, 1998; Webster, 1995). Policy makers debate how computer technologies should be integrated into schools, and search for new ways to evaluate the effectiveness of that integration (Burniske & Monke, 2001; Kellner, 2003; Kinzer & Leu, 1997; Lemke, 1998; Luke, 1998).

As a response to this search, a new discourse has emerged among policy makers against the traditional positivist view of policy making and evaluation. For decades, proponents of the traditional positivist[1] model believed that the only way to create an intellectual and scientific progress in society was to find some overarching ahistorical framework, some neutral descriptive language, and some permanent standards for policy making and evaluation (Wagenaar & Cook, 2003). However, proponents of the emerging new discourse aim to replace the traditional positivist view with an alternative post-positivist model of policy making and evaluation which identifies policy practices as political, ideological, gendered, sexual, racial, transformative, social, discursive, and performed Praxis. In this approach, the distinction between ontology and epistemology seen in positivism and neo-positivism gives way to a view that what can be known is intertwined with the interaction between a particular policy maker and a particular school community. This transactional and subjective epistemology and ontology that is value mediated and value dependent leads educational policy makers to conduct policy studies in a manner that emphasize dialogue with the members of local school communities. This interaction is dialectical, transforming historically mediated and distorted structures into a view of how the structures might be changed.

This chapter is an attempt at designing a post-positivist[2] way of understanding policy evaluation and practices while exploring a hermeneutic approach toward integrating technology into schools. The chapter mainly focuses on three central themes on understanding policy making and evaluation: (a) type of practice (b) nature of knowledge, and (c) issue of evaluation. For each of the themes, I compare a technical and procedural model of understanding policy making and evaluation with a way of understanding drawn from a hermeneutic approach. The former model is committed to and realized by means of an instrumental knowledge for integration; the latter is connected to human existence, who we already are, and who we want to become. In the chapter, I also design a practical policy and integration unit to partially describe the ethical, political, practical and deliberative dimensions of the hermeneutic approach toward integrating technology into classroom practices.

POLICY MAKING AND EVALUATION AS TECHNICAL-PROCEDURAL ACTIVITY

In this traditional positivist model, the process of integrating technology into schools and evaluating that integration are seen as a kind of technical-procedural activity. The job of an evaluator or policy maker in the integration process is to apply the technical, objective, and instrumental knowledge to the process in order to gradually remove human error in the activity. The aim of this technical activity is to generate a body of scientific and objective generalizations capable of explaining policy practices across socio-cultural and historical contexts independently of specific times, places, or circumstances.

It is also usual to hear policy and evaluation practices in this model as the activity of an expert consultant. Policy makers or evaluators as expert consultants in the integration process possess a special set of tools and competencies that enable them to deliver a particular kind of service to members of local school communities (Carr, 1995). And, the purpose of reflection for the members of the community, such as teachers, students, school administrators, etc., is to decide how to proceed in integration by making a selection from the bodies of scientific knowledge provided by the expert consultant, policy maker. In this light, policy practices and integration processes are understood as a matter of technical rationality, a problem-solving based on scientific knowledge of how to achieve ends (Wagenaar & Cook, 2003).

Knowledge which is used as an instrument or methodology, or produced as a result of the integration process, in this model, has some unique characteristics. First, it is propositional; that is, it comprises a set of statements that can be packaged, scrutinized, and transmitted. Second, it is objective knowledge; that is, it is something outside integration process that educators draw upon in order to legitimate process. Furthermore, the knowledge produced in the activity can be stored, applied, coded, and quantified.

Our dominant ways of talking about the integration demonstrates the main characteristics of this model: a state or district *chooses* an appropriate educational setting, *establish* objective standards, *provide* computers with the internet and install software programs without consideration of what these might be used for, and *assess* the effectiveness of the integration by using the quantitative results of the standardized tests.

In this way of looking at integration, the process of integration is limited to enacting a given set of technical skills or strategies, and understanding and evaluating the integration means having objective, scientific, instrumental knowledge about it. What makes the process of integration and evaluation objective or scientific is that it is the outcome of the application of methods that serve as an instrumental tool to protect the process from the contamination of local discourses and socio-politic and economic expectations of members of the local community (Gadamer, 1989; Carr, 1997; Taylor, 2002). The attitude of technical rationality condenses the process of integration to problem-solving. "A problem is something that can be totally objectified and resolved in objective terms because the person confronting the problem can completely detach himself from it and view it externally" (Gallagher, 1992, p. 152). Ontological issues – our "being" in the world as moral–political, social agents – are not part of this model. Ethical concerns in this model only play an objective-procedural role as professional ethic in which detachment, disinterest, and neutrality are the major virtues of policy makers and evaluators' ethical consciousness (Carr, 1997; Schwandt, 2002).

Today, with the No Child Left Behind Act (NCLB) (2001), calls for more scientifically based standards and procedural evaluation in education studies have gained a new momentum in Washington policy circles. The NCLB policy seeks neutral, universally applicable principles of validity for educational policy and evaluation studies, which would exclude considerations of individuals' and groups' place in history and society. The NCLB Act of 2001 now requires school leaders who depend on federal funding to be aware that educational policies and practices must be grounded in the results of "scientifically based" research and evaluation studies. This technical and instrumental way of looking at the policy making and evaluation develops a positivist conception of policy and evaluation science designed to eliminate the multidimensional complexity of social and educational reality.

A HERMENEUTIC APPROACH TOWARD POLICY MAKING AND EVALUATION

Hermeneutics can be defined as the art (or science) of interpretation, or the study of human understanding. It is the study of interpreting and understanding the moral, political, and historical relationships between humans and their world. Therefore, a hermeneutic approach toward understanding the integration processes tends to place moral, historical, and political questions and issues of selfhood and human agency at center stage. Moral–political dimensions of human agency in the hermeneutic approach include: (a) human beings are self-interpreting beings, (b) the self is linguistically, socially, politically, and historically constructed, (c) the self is dialogic in nature, and (d) to know is not separate from to be; a self both functions and interprets (Taylor, 1991). However, placing moral and political issues of human agency at center stage does not mean that technical knowledge per se does not matter, but that scientific, technical, and procedural knowledge and practices should not be the ultimate way of understanding and evaluating the process of integrating technology into schools. From the hermeneutic approach, the main concepts of the positivist-procedural model, which are technical expertise, methodological conformity, instrumental rationality, and ethical neutrality, may only play a secondary role in the practice of integration.

The main issue in the hermeneutic approach is that we as evaluators and policy makers need to primarily come to an understanding of our "being" in the world as moral–political, gendered, self-interpreting, and meaning-making human agents (Taylor, 1991). We need to realize that the process of integrating technology into schools is not just a technical activity but also a political, ideological, gendered, sexual, and racial practice. We need to know that race, gender, ethnicity, socio-economic status, social justice, and equality matter when we make any kind of decision in the integration process. For decades, the research studies proved that schools with higher percentages of poor and minority students generally either provide students less access to educational technology or only use technology for remediation (Sutton, 1991; Trotter, 1997; Chen & Wellman, 2004). Furthermore, generally girls have had only word-processing experience with computers, whereas boys have used computers to solve math or science problems (Brunner, 1997; Holzberg, 1997; Bimber, 2000; Chen & Wellman, 2004). Bromley (1997) also argues that because technical resources in our society are typically concentrated in the hands of men, a "culture of exclusivity" has developed at places where those resources are used. Therefore, new technologies can most likely be appropriated for continued male use. As the results of these research studies indicate, it is very important and crucial to take ontological (race, gender, ethnicity, etc.) issues of selfhood and human agency into consideration to generate genuine policies and practices of technology integration in order to eliminate the digital divides and inequalities in society.

The hermeneutic approach also describes the process of integration as a way of generating both local and public knowledge about the integration – that is, knowledge developed by and useful to members of local communities themselves as well as knowledge useful to the larger district and other local communities. This way of approaching policy making and evaluation takes into account teachers, students, parents, administrators, and other school members' complex and competing discourses and beliefs, identities and voices, and fears and anxieties at both macro and micro level.

But, what all do these hermeneutic considerations practically mean for integrating technology into schools? In the following section, I describe a practical and imaginary case of a policy and integration unit that partially emphasizes on ethical, political, practical, and deliberative dimensions of the hermeneutic approach toward integrating technology into classroom practices.

PLANNING THE PRACTICAL POLICY AND INTEGRATION UNIT

This practical policy and integration case is designed for a classroom of students who are 12–13 years of age in the school in Istanbul, Turkey. The school is located in Alibeykoy, one of the poorest regions of Istanbul. More than 80% of the student body has a Kurdish ethnic background, and others identify themselves as Turks. Almost every student has a working class socio-economic status, and lives in "Gecekondu," illegally constructed one-bedroom shelters, in Alibeykoy. More than 1,500 people in this region (the biggest number among the regions of Istanbul) lost their lives in the 1999 Marmara Earthquake because of their insecure and broken shelters, the "Gecekondu."

The classroom in which I designed its integration unit in this school has 30 wireless laptop computers, 10 printers, two CD-ROM drives, two televisions, and a video recorder, video camera, laser disc player, modem, telephone, and scanner provided by the government. The school employed a full-time technician who installed software and repairs all types of equipment.

Each student in the classroom has a personal laptop computer on his/her table as well as access to a multimedia workstation which contains a scanner, multimedia encyclopedias, CD-ROMs, instructional games, and software applications. This is an alternative school selected by the government which provides all technical equipment to the school in order to eliminate digital divide in the region.

Process of designing the integration unit begins by eliciting questions the students, parents, and other members of the local community have about themselves (micro level) and the world (macro level). Since the first of these requires initial thinking about themselves, the opening request is this:

> Who are you? What are your interests, problems, needs? Make a list of themes or cases you would like to investigate!

After answering to these questions, they explore a macro question as follows:

> Please, look outside yourself at the world you live in. That world could be close to you – your culture, your community, or could be distant – your state, your nation, all the way to the global world. Think about that world and list questions or concerns you have about that world. What questions or concerns do you have about the world you live in?

The next step in the planning involves a search for common or shared questions and concerns in both the self and world dimensions. At this point, all students would come together, brainstorm, and decide on a possible theme to study.

During the planning, the policy maker, teachers, parents, and other members of the community would play a secondary role. This meant posing questions, clarifying ideas, and encouraging reflection. However, as the study unfolds, they may play a more active and visible role in helping to find resources, facilitating group work, and coordinating the schedule. On some occasions they could also take time to introduce or explain ideas and alternative views related to the study.

CARRYING OUT THE INTEGRATION UNIT

Let us assume that after the deliberation, the students chose the theme "Earthquake: Preparation and Prevention" from the several they have identified. And, they decided to create a project to analyze and identify the potential hazards of an earthquake ahead of time and develop an advance plan to reduce the dangers of the earthquakes in both micro and macro level, and inform their community, other schools in Istanbul, the governor, and the members of the house of representatives about their advance plan which may introduce possible solutions to the concerns and problems of their community and the world that suffers from the earthquakes.

To do this project, the students first would brainstorm specific planning areas and then divide into groups focusing on the following issues: preparation, prevention, planning, webpage design, performance and role playing, creating earthquake animations, broadcasting, and presentation. Each group would be responsible for researching their area, creating an online message board and sharing their data and information on the board, and making recommendations to the whole group. The latter activity involves several rounds of discussion and debate as the whole group tried to integrate the work of smaller groups. As a culminating activity for the project, the students would also invite a city planner, politicians, and professors from the Istanbul University to listen to them and give them information about the project.

A second activity would involve finding out what other people in the other parts of the world are doing in order to prevent themselves from the earthquakes. In order to do this, the students would go to the school library and find information from books, videotapes, magazines, and CD-ROM encyclopedias. They would return to the classroom and find more information from the Web, laser discs, and multimedia encyclopedias.

Each group would use "mindtools," computer application programs, to engage in constructive, higher-order, critical thinking about the themes they are studying in this classroom (Jonassen, 2000). Examples of mindtools are:

- *Databases*: such as Microsoft Access to create a population density database and explain if people avoid living in areas at high risk for earthquakes.
- *Spreadsheets*: such as Microsoft Excel to create a dataset to show the seismic hazards of the earthquakes in history of the region, develop graphs to compare the results with other regions of Istanbul and Turkey.
- *Semantic networks (concept maps)*: such as Inspiration, Kidspiration SemNet, Learning Tool, and Mind Mapper to show the relationships among government, civic education, environment, accommodation, economy, social justice, and earthquakes.
- *Computer conferencing*: such as Microsoft Netmeeting, Online conferencing tools such as Chats, MOOs, and MUDs, and asynchronous discussions, including electronic mail, listservs, and bulletin boards to inform the residents and politicians of the risk areas and the risks of living in these areas and prevention methods from the earthquakes.

- *Hypermedia construction*: such as Microsoft FrontPage, Netscape Composer, Macromedia Dreamwaiver, Flash to design a webpage about the project, and create animations to show how continental plates shift to illustrate what causes an earthquake.
- *Microworld environments*: such as MathWorlds, SimCity to create interactive learning environments on earthquakes.

The students would use the mindtools for following purposes in their project:

- support for individual learning,
- group learning,
- instructional management, and
- communication.

Applications to individual learning include engaging students in critical thinking about the project, using CD-ROMs or the Internet to find resources not available in the school, communicating with specialists such as the city planner, politicians or professors, and demonstrating simulations of the project, creating visual stories about earthquakes by using Flash and Microsoft Power Point. Group learning applications include using e-mail to support group communication, using presentation software to allow group presentations on the classroom project, and providing collaboration in collecting related texts, sounds, and visual effects. Applications to instructional management include integrating standards and assessments, and managing student portfolios. Communication applications include communicating to remote locations such as schools in other regions of Istanbul or another city, even in a different country, and improving communication among students, teachers, parents, and people who live in the region to share their project through their web pages, and e-mail listserv. Finally, applications to executive functions include supporting attendance and accountability functions. Clearly, using technology in all of these ways would result in the implementation of technology into every aspect of the school day.

Finally, after working on this project for two weeks and meeting with team members at several times, the students would meet a final time to discuss their presentations and final report. The students would also write a play on the theme "Earthquake: Preparation and Prevention," and would perform it in front of the people and politicians of the region to inform them about this issue. They would also videotape their performance (and their project report and animations) and place it to their website as .mpeg and .avi format to let other people from different regions and countries know about the issue.

EVALUATION OF THE UNIT

At the end of the project, the policy maker, teacher, parents, and students would deal with the issue of evaluation at two levels. One is the evaluation of the unit of integration policy itself. The other is evaluation of student work, including identifying letter grades for each student.

Throughout the course of the integration unit, the students would do some journal writing aiming at reflecting on their own work and that of the group.

In the end, the teacher and policy maker would deliver a survey form that includes questions about what the students, parents, and other members of the local community liked best and least about the integration unit and project, how this educational experience compared to others they had, and what recommendations they would make for other units in the future. Each student would also be asked to write about the activities he/she have been involved in and what each has learned. Finally, the students would be asked to say what letter grade they deserved and why. This self-evaluation then will serve as the basis for assigning grades. While this method may be un-popular in some places, it is consistent with the general philosophy of con-structing meaning and empowering young people that lay behind the hermeneutic approach toward policy and integration practices.

But, what makes this practical policy and integration unit a genuine and effective example of the hermeneutic model, and what are our criteria to decide whether the practical policy and integration unit represented the basic characteristics and notions of hermeneutics?

In the following section, I explore two central themes of understanding policy making and evaluation from the hermeneutic perspective in order to answer to the questions: (a) nature of knowledge and (b) issue of criteria. Then, I provide four "existential" criteria and seven critical questions toward development of a view for what needs to be captured and represented about understanding a genuine and effective integration of technology into school.

UNDERSTANDING THE NATURE OF KNOWLEDGE AND CRITERIA IN THE HERMENEUTIC APPROACH

The hermeneutic way of understanding the process of integrating technology into schools generates a different conception of the notions *knowledge* and *criteria* than the traditional positivist model does. In the hermeneutic approach, knowledge is not a product of a mere cognitive and metacognitive activity which can be stored, applied, or quantified, but it is experience itself which is always improvisational, incomplete, and open to change based on the expectations of local communities. Furthermore, the process of integration in this model is more like a *critical and existential experience*, which defines the process as an existential accomplishment, than a mere technical, cognitive activity. This is a view in which integration process is considered as a fundamentally social, moral, and political process. In this sense, integration activities and their meanings are always under the influence of a particular context; they embody and transform particular ways of thinking, acting, and knowing within specific communities as indicated in the practical policy and integration unit.

The way of talking about the issue and nature of criteria in the hermeneutic approach is also very different from the traditional positivist model. Success in this approach is not measured in terms of the one best solution, or quantitative results of standardized tests.

Evaluation criteria in the hermeneutic approach are not a procedure or a product, which can be stored, applied, or quantified. But they are *existential experience*, an unfinished, incomplete language which breaks the artificial language that disengages us from our direct contingency to being. Criterion in this approach is ethical knowledge that "is...not knowledge that we possess in the sense that we can decide whether to apply it or even decide whether we are ethically skilled enough to apply it. Rather...we are always applying our ethical knowledge, whether adequate or not, in acting as we do" (Warnke, 2002, p. 84). That is, there is something about the criteria as ethical knowledge that is not detachable from our being but mainly determined by and determinate of it. Moreover, the application of the criteria is not straightforward; in other words, we do not simply apply them to reach an end. Furthermore, descriptive nature of the criteria in this hermeneutic approach is both mutable and relative. First, the criteria in this approach are mutable because their definitions change overtime. Therefore, they are always unfinished and temporal in nature. Second, the criteria are value rational and contextually relative, because they can only be defined within a particular context.

In general, an existential criterion is a kind of criteria, which is both universal and flexible. It is a kind of knowledge that is neither global, nor local. It is both global and local, which means it is a "glocal"[3] knowledge (Eryaman, 2004).

But, what are these existential criteria, and what do they practically mean for evaluating the processes and practices of integrating technology into schools? The following section, in this chapter, provides the four existential criteria toward development of a view for what needs to be represented about understanding a genuine and effective integration of technology into school.

FOUR EXISTENTIAL CRITERIA FOR A GENUINE
AND EFFECTIVE INTEGRATION

1. *Ethics*: Genuine integration and evaluation are first about ethics of judgment. They are about making good judgment relevant to every instance of human activities. Practical knowledge of a genuine integration and evaluation is not acquired in making some kind of product, or solving some kind of problem, disconnected from our way of being in the world. Rather it is existential accomplishment that involves a genuine understanding that is not required in technical know-how. Technique requires clever application of skills; a genuine evaluation requires understanding. The genuine integration and evaluation are not a cognitive capacity that one can use at one's choosing, but a way of knowing bound up with who we are and what we want to become (Schwandt, 1994, 2002). It is particularly related to expectations of the members of local communities. For example, the Turkish government's attempt in the practical policy and integration unit to provide computer technologies and technical equipments with a full-time technician and policy expert to a school in one of the poorest communities of Istanbul in order to eliminate digital divide in the area could be seen as an excellent example of understanding "ethical" dimension of policy making as existential criteria. This ethical and deliberative policy judgment to provide the service to the local community took into account the expectations of the members of the local community.

2. *Deliberative excellence*: Deliberative excellence is one of the most important components of an effective and genuine integration of technology into schools. It can be characterized as "ethical know-how" (Bernstein, 1983, p. 147) . According to Schwandt,

> Even so, it does not simply mean knowledge of ethical behavior. It points to a union of ethics and politics. It is a kind of knowledge that is embedded in praxis and distinguishable from technical knowledge guaranteed by method. Deliberation means choosing a course of action and defending one's choice by means of a practical argument that is concrete, temporal, and refers to actual events (p. 50).

Deliberative excellence therefore requires a different approach toward relationship between means and ends than that found in technical know-how. In deliberative excellence, "there can be no prior knowledge of the right means by which we realize the end in a particular situation. For the end itself is only concretely specified in deliberating about the means appropriate to a particular situation" (Bernstein, 1983, p. 147). Furthermore, in the genuine evaluation and integration, understanding is always application. To have such way of knowing about the world is bound up with one's being and becoming. Deliberative excellence is not detached from the policy maker or evaluator who has such knowledge, rather that knowledge becomes constitutive of her or his practice (Bernstein, 1983).

Deliberative excellence is not a monological act; it is interactive in nature. The rule in the deliberative conversation is that the other person might be right, and that one takes the reasoning of the other person seriously. The possibility that one might be wrong, or might learn something new from a conversation, is not a risk but a gain. But one must be open to the Other in conversation. This is what Gadamer (1989) and Dewey (1938) called "openness." It is an ethics of rightly understanding a topic or a situation and working to change it if it is wrong. In this light, policy makers and evaluators should be open to listen to and dialogue with teachers, students, parents, administrators, and other school members to learn their complex and competing discourses and beliefs, fears and anxieties about the policy and evaluation practices of integrating technology into the schools. The practical integration unit described above provided a genuine and practical example for the policy makers and evaluators to achieve the kind of openness, which the hermeneutic approach requires based on the expectations of the members of the school community in both macro and micro level. In the case, the policy maker did not impose his/her own vision of what the integration must look like, in contrast, he/she developed the unit with the members of the community and based on their practical needs. And, the policy maker just played a secondary role in the planning process while helping the students find resources, facilitating group work, and coordinating the schedule.

3. *Aesthetic*: This artistic ability of making good policy and evaluation decisions can be identified as the aesthetic of practical decision making and evaluation. This artistic ability invokes images of a creative, inventive, and imaginative mind. According to Schwandt (2002) , the use of the term artistry is intended to signal a sharp distinction with the technical and procedural model of policy making and evaluation. It indicates that practical decision making is "more art than science"(p. 53).

Dewey also argues that "the arts do more than provide us with fleeting moments of elation and delight. They expand our horizons. They contribute meaning and value to future experience. They modify our ways of perceiving the world, thus leaving us and the world itself irrevocably changed" (Jackson, 1998: p. 33). Art, Dewey (1938) tells us, "quickens us from the slackness of routine and enables us to forget ourselves by finding ourselves in the delight of experiencing the world about us in its varied qualities and forms"

(p. 110). The practical policy and integration unit provided earlier illustrated a genuine and practical example of how the students with low socio-economic status used the multiple and advanced computer technologies to create the artistic performances and presentations to make a difference in their lives for themselves and for their community.

4. *Rhetoric*: Traditionally, the relationship between policy making and evaluation and rhetoric has been articulated in terms of deliberation. From one perspective, scholars articulate rhetoric as a means for transmitting the deliberations of the practically wise policy maker to an audience. From this angle, the policy making and evaluation/rhetoric relationship is negotiated by addressing the practical question of how well the policy expert might share his excellent deliberations and lead the public through rhetoric. Rhetoric refers to the art of persuasion, the ability to move an audience to action. From another perspective, rhetoric promotes, rather than merely transmits, good deliberation. As Johnstone (1980) puts it, "Since rhetoric aims properly at facilitating reasoned judgment about such matters, we can say that it aims at excellence in practical deliberation" (p. 11).

The practical policy and integration unit described above indicated following five shared characteristics of rhetoric and making wise policy judgments in order to create genuine and effective integration policies and practices: (1) rhetoric and making wise policy judgments in the integration were both deliberative processes, in search of making right judgments about integration practices; (2) both made their particular conclusions presumptively, not necessarily; (3) both generated local and global conclusions based on problems of the moment experienced by the policy makers or evaluators with the members of the communities in the particular place and time; (4) for both rhetoric and wise policy making in the integration, the aim was to persuade people about the rightness of the decisions about the technology integration; and (5) both were "embodied;" they were both linguistically and socially negotiated (Schwandt, 2002).

On the other hand, the hermeneutic approach toward policy making and evaluation in the integration process without the regulative ideas of emancipation and social justice is blind; and the critique of ideology and rhetoric without a concrete content from our practical interest in communicative decision making is empty. It is, therefore, policy makers and evaluators task to show how an understanding of policy analysis and integration practices is guided by both a recovery of shared tradition and a projection of an emancipated inquiry. The following seven critical questions are essential for the policy makers and evaluators to be successful to accomplish the task.

SEVEN CRITICAL QUESTIONS FOR AN EFFECTIVE INTEGRATION AND EVALUATION

1. *Ontological*: How does classroom discourse and use of computer technology shape and construct teachers and students' practices and identities, their way of being in the world?

2. *Political*: Who shall control the selection and distribution of knowledge and technological goods? Through what discursive practices?

3. *Economic*: How is the control of language and discursive practices linked to the existing and unequal distribution of power, technological goods, and technological services in school?

4. *Ideological*: What knowledge and what kind of software and hardware are of most worth? Whose knowledge and technology is it?

5. *Technical*: How shall local–practical knowledge and technology be made accessible to students?

6. *Ethical*: How shall we treat others responsibly and justly in the integration? How shall we eliminate the digital divide between "haves" and "haves-not"? What is the link between moral responsibilities and discursive practices of students and teachers in using technology in their classroom practices?

7. *Historical*: What ongoing and historical discourses on the issues of integrating technology into classroom instruction already exist to help us answer these questions? What other resources do we need to go further? (Beyer & Apple, 1998)

For Dewey, this kind of hermeneutic and critical evaluation may develop a "growth" in teachers, policy makers, evaluators, administrators, and students' moral–political consciousness. However, this "growth" is not a "… progress towards anything like Truth in the Platonic, realist, sense. Rather, it is progress towards new possibilities for humanity – new ways in which men can think of one another and do things for one another (Rorty, 1997, p. 529)."

CONCLUSION

This chapter was an attempt to explore a hermeneutic approach of talking about issues of integrating technology into schools, and nature of evaluation practice and criteria in the process of integration. In the article, I broadly compared a positivist and a hermeneutic approach for understanding the experience of the technology integration and evaluation. I argued that the process of integrating technology into education, and evaluation of the process is an existential experience which cannot be detached from who we already are, and who we want to become. It is an existential accomplishment in which we break old sense of community and develop new possibilities for humanity. It is not a technical enterprise, which aims to eliminate uncertainty, ambiguity, and unpredictability of the everyday life by using general, systematic foundational knowledge, methods. It negotiates with the ambiguous and unpredictable world by acting upon it, or interacting with it. And, the discussion of the issue of criteria in the article was more a moral–political analysis than a technical one. This does not mean that I aim to develop a binary opposition between the technical issues and moral–political issues of the policy making and evaluation, or that I underscore the importance of technical and scientific analysis of the nature of criteria; instead, my aim is to remind evaluation practitioners and policy makers about the importance of hermeneutic analysis of the process of integration. This approach considers the social, political, cultural, economic, ethnic, and gender factors which shape the structures that are taken as "real" and immutable in the integration process.

The hermeneutic approach toward policy making and evaluation is premised on the assumption that the implementation of educational technologies in schools can be best understood by exploring the multiple interacting contexts which shape the lives of classrooms. By entering into the complicated intersections of students, teachers, and classroom and school culture, and by perceiving an educational technology as an object for change in subject matter, we can deepen our understanding of the process of implementing educational technologies within classrooms.

I also believe that the hermeneutic way of looking at issues of criteria, evaluation, and experience can give new insights to educators, policy makers, program evaluators, politicians, researchers about their understanding and conceptualization of reform, public policy, justice, education, cross-cultural evaluation, and communication.

NOTES

1. Positivism bases its premises on the idea that the world is governed by laws and rules that are quite independent of human beliefs, values, desires, and interpretations. Knowledge must mirror or correspond to the objective world; and our methods must also be objective, i.e., unbiased and context independent, in order to guarantee this result. According to positivism, claims not capable of being described in the language of science, and any method that is not totally person free, and interest neutral, are meaningless and must be discarded.

2. Post-positivism rejects the modern scientific outlook, which is rooted in the belief in God and in an absolute, objective perspective on the universe. Post-positivism

emphasizes the importance of power relationships, subjectivity and moral–political discourse in the "construction" of truth and world views.

3. Glocal: This term is derived from terms of "*G*lobalization" and "*Locali*zation."

REFERENCES

Bernstein, R. J. (1983). Part three: From hermeneutics to praxis. In: R. J. Berstein (Ed.), *Beyond objectivism and relativism* (pp. 109–169). Philadelphia: University of Pennsylvania Press.

Beyer, L. E., & Apple, M. W. (1998). Values and politics in the curriculum. In: L. E. Beyer & M. W. Apple (Eds), *The curriculum: Problems, politics, and possibilities* (2nd ed.) (pp. 3–16). Albany, NY: State University of New York Press.

Bimber, B. (2000). The gender gap on the internet. *Social Science Quarterly, 81*, 868–876.

Bromley, H. (1997). The social chicken and the technological egg. *Educational Theory, 47*(1), 51–65.

Brunner, C. (1997). Opening technology to girls: The approach computer-using teachers take may make the difference. *Electronic Learning, 16*(4), 55.

Burniske, R. W., & Monke, L. (2001). *Breaking down the digital walls: Learning to teach in a post-modem world.* Albany, NY: SUNY Press.

Carr, W. (1995). What is an educational practice? In: W. Carr (Ed.), *For education* (pp. 60–73). Philadelphia: Open University Press.

Carr, W. (1997). Philosophy and method in educational research. *Cambridge Journal of Education, 27*(2), 203–209.

Chen, W., & Wellman, B. (2004). In: W. Dutton, B. Kahin, R. O'Callaghan, & A. Wyckoff (Eds), *Charting digital divides: Comparing socioeconomic, gender, life stage, and rural-urban internet access and use in five countries in transforming enterprise.* Cambridge, MA: MIT Press.

Dewey, J. (1938). *Experience and education.* New York: The Macmillan Company.

Eryaman, M. Y. (2004). Truth, method and writing: Towards an existential pedagogy. *The paper presented at 2004 Annual Meeting of the Ohio Valley Philosophy of Education Society.* Bergamo Conference Center, Dayton, OH, 31st September.

Feenberg, A. (1991). *Critical theory of technology.* New York: Oxford University Press.

Gadamer, H. -G. (1989). In: J. Weinsheimer, & D. G. Marshal (Eds), *Truth and method* (2nd rev. ed.) (Trans.) New York: Crossroad.

Gallagher, S. (1992). *Hermeneutics and education.* New York: State University Press.

Holzberg, C. (1997). Computer technology – it's a girl thing. *Technology & Learning, 17*(8), 42–48.

Jackson, P. W. (1998). *John Dewey and the lessons of art.* New Heaven, CT: Yale University Press.

Johnstone, C. L. (1980). An Aristotelian trilogy: Ethics, rhetoric, politics, and the search for moral truth. *Philosophy and Rhetoric, 13*, 1–24.

Jonassen, D. H. (2000). *Computers as mindtools in schools: Engaging critical thinking.* Columbus, OH: Prentice-Hall.

Kellner, D. (2000). Globalization and new social movements: Lessons for critical theory and pedagogy. In: N. Burbules & C. Torre (Eds), *Globalization and education.* New York: Routledge.

Kellner, D. (2003). Toward a critical theory of education. *Democracy and Nature, 9*(1), 51–64.

Kerr, S. (1996). Visions of sugarplums: The future of technology, education, and the schools. In: S. Kerr (Ed.), *Technology and the future of schooling* (pp. 1–27). Chicago: University of Chicago Press.

Kinzer, C. K., & Leu, D. J. (1997). The challenge of change: Exploring literacy and learning in electronic environments. *Language Arts, 74*, 126–136.

Labbo, L., & Kuhn, M. (1998). Electronic symbol making: Young children's computer-related emerging concepts about literacy. In: D. Reinking, M. McKenna, L. D. Labbo & R. Kieffer (Eds), *Handbook of literacy and technology: Transformations in a post-typographic world* (pp. 79–92). Mahwah, NJ: Erlbaum.

Lemke, J. L. (1998). Metamedia literacy: Transforming meanings and media. In: D. Reinking, M. McKenna, L. D. Labbo & R. Kieffer (Eds), *Handbook of literacy and technology: Transformations in a post-typographic world* (pp. 283–302). Mahwah, NJ: Erlbaum.

Luke, A. (1998). Getting over method: Literacy teaching as work in new times. *Language Arts, 75*(4), 305–313.

Rorty, R. (1997). Hermeneutics, general studies, and teaching. In: S. M. Cahn (Ed.), *Classic and contemporary readings in the philosophy of education* (pp. 522–536). New York: The McGraw-Hill Companies, Inc.

Schwandt, T. A. (1994). Constructivist, interpretivist approaches to human inquiry. In: N. K. Denzin & Y. S. Lincoln (Eds), *Handbook of Qualitative Research* (pp. 118–137). Thousand Oaks, CA: Sage Publications.

Schwandt, T. A. (2002). *Evaluation practice reconsidered.* New York: Peter Lang.

Simpson, L. (1995). *Technology, time, and the conversations of modernity.* New York: Routledge.

Sutton, R. E. (1991). Equity and computers in the schools: A decade of research. *Review of Educational Research, 61*(4), 475–503.

Taylor, C. (1991). The dialogical self. In: D. R. Hiley, J. Bowman, & R. Shusterman (Eds), *The interpretive turn* (pp. 304–314). Cornell University Press.

Taylor, C. (2002). Gadamer on the human sciences. In: R. J. Dostal (Ed.), *The Cambridge companion to Gadamer* (pp. 126–142). Cambridge, UK: Cambridge University Press.

Trotter, A. (1997). Taking technology's measure. *Education Week, 17*(11), 6–11.

Wagenaar, H., & Cook, N. S. D. (2003). Understanding policy practices: action, dialectic and deliberation in policy analysis. In: M. Hajer & H. Wagenaar (Eds), *Deliberative policy analysis: Understanding governance in the network society.* Cambridge, UK: Cambridge University Press.

Warnke, G. (2002). Hermeneutics, ethics, and politics. In: R. J. Dostal (Ed.), *The Cambridge companion to Gadamer* (pp. 79–101). Cambridge, UK: Cambridge University Press.

Webster, F. (1995). *Theories of the information society.* London and New York: Routledge.

PART III:
TECHNOLOGY, APPLICATIONS, AND PRACTICE: ACTIONS AND STRATEGIES

EDUCATIONAL DIGITAL LIBRARIES: PLATFORMS FOR INNOVATION AND EQUITY

Marcia A. Mardis and Ellen S. Hoffman

ABSTRACT

Digital libraries (DLs) are currently in place or being developed for a variety of educational applications. These resources offer support for instructional innovation, traditional curricula, and equitable access to learning resources. Yet, the carrot of instructional innovation is often overwhelmed by the stick of conflicting educational policy priorities. This chapter will define and situate the term "educational digital libraries," and discuss the ways in which sustained use through school libraries and lessons learned from exemplary projects can transform the contemporary educational policy, reform, and learning landscape.

Throughout the world, digital libraries have proven to be an important technology in promoting human development by providing information about health, agriculture, nutrition, and governmental policy and through cultural expression and preservation (Witten, Loots, Trujillo, & Bainbridge, 2002). In higher education, this powerful technology has made its impact through the pervasive use of electronic repositories and because of the

Technology and Education: Issues in Administration, Policy, and Applications in K12 Schools
Advances in Educational Administration, Volume 8, 163–180
Copyright © 2006 by Elsevier Ltd.
All rights of reproduction in any form reserved
ISSN: 1479-3660/doi:10.1016/S1479-3660(05)08012-1

increasing digitization of rare and special applications (Falk, 2003). Educators at all levels can greatly benefit from the ease of access to and variety of materials found in digital libraries.

A digital library (DL) is a computer-based system for acquiring, storing, organizing, searching, and distributing digital materials for end-user access (Sharma & Vishwanathan, 2001). Gunn (2002) uses the related term, "virtual libraries." Gunn emphasizes that these collections are different from information located through search engines like Google because they incorporate a variety of formats and are designed with tools and scaffolds to serve a specific user community.

Educational digital libraries are a subset of this group with a focus on providing materials and services to instructors and students in both formal and informal learning environments. Digital libraries for education remain an emergent technology, with many still in various stages of development. Earlier versions disappear as when new technologies and content become technically and economically feasible. DLs for education encompass both freely available and commercial offerings.

K-12 users are a distinctive subgroup of educational users having unique and challenging requirements for educational digital libraries in terms of content, description, and user assistance. Because of the complexities of existing DL technologies accompanied by the less-developed reading levels of young children, most digital libraries have been developed for older children and adults both within and beyond schools. Further, as a subset of educational technologies, K-12 digital libraries have the additional challenges of adoption and sustainability within school systems faced by any new instructional system. Widespread adoption of digital libraries shares the barriers inherent in technology integration generally in schools, such as the need for leadership, planning, professional development, support, access, and improved infrastructure (Cuban, 2001; Jukes & McCain, 2000; Schofield & Davidson, 2002; Tomei, 2002). Further, digital library challenges include systemic implementation, sustainable inclusion in classroom teaching, methods of resource discovery, and adequate levels of user support (Mardis, 2003).

In this article, we explore the unique affordances and challenges that digital libraries bring to the K-12 environment within the contexts of competing legislative, social, and educational demands. School systems, and particularly school libraries, can embrace digital library innovations as tools that can enhance their missions rather viewing such technologies as competitors that threaten their existence. Digital library resources can be used to transcend the limitations of traditional learning settings and to foster media and subsequently, critical, literacies by children. But there remain multiple challenges representing a divide in vision, technologies, and organization still to be overcome to ensure the success of continuing digital library efforts.

Using a case study approach to examine the policy landscape and educational considerations that surround the National Science Foundation's (NSF's) National Science, Technology, Engineering, and Mathematics (STEM) Education Digital Library (NSDL), and select exemplary NSDL projects, this article is a review of the potentials and implications of digital library used in elementary and secondary education. Further, through an exploration of the potential for school libraries and their information professionals to support digital library integration into the learning process and to counter prevailing obstacles, the authors suggest directions for the sustainable adoption of these vital educational resources.

FEDERAL POLICY FOUNDATIONS AND INFLUENCE

With the prominence of the federal "No Child Left Behind" (NCLB) legislation dominating the policy environment of K-12 schools, other federal policy actions aimed at impacting teaching and learning can easily be masked. While mandates and major school funding as incorporated into NCLB directly impact school curricula, other change efforts arise through research and development funds that work through a "carrot" and "sermon" approach to reform [Vedung, 1998, p. 90]. Federal dollars and services are offered to schools and classrooms with incentives for implementation that may be as concrete as direct grant funding for participating schools (carrots) or as intangible as dissemination through conferences and publications (sermons) that are encouraging educators to consider and adopt promising practices. The growth of the Internet and electronic forums have made the potential for small-scale experiments to be more widely disseminated than in the past, so that a curriculum development from a single school or project initially spurred by federal funds can receive national and even international distribution.

Science and Math from the National Science Foundation

The focal point for most pre-K-12 curriculum policy and reform is the U.S. Department of Education, today the center for implementation of NCLB. But curricular efforts arise in other federal agencies, from the National

Institutes of Health (NIH), the National Endowment for the Humanities (NEH), the National Aeronautics and Space Administration (NASA), and the National Science Foundation (NSF). NSF has been a key in both large- and small-scale curricular development for math and science in K-12 schools. This work includes development of full disciplinary curricula, grant funding for experiments in more narrow topic areas or grade levels, support for standards efforts, research on learning and cognition, and development of materials, professional development seminars, and workshops to support the improvement of teaching.

The role of NSF as the center of science and math curriculum efforts emerged during the Cold War with the launch of Sputnik in 1957. Responding to calls for renewed focus on science and math, massive funding was channeled into NSF for curriculum research and development that took the agency beyond its more traditional audience of higher education and advanced research centers that had been its base from NSF's founding in 1950. With the National Defense Education Act of 1958, Congress mandated that NSF expand its science and math curriculum programs for K-12. Large-scale curriculum development funding led to an innovative Physical Science Study Committee (PSSC) high school physics curriculum, in the late 1950s. The success of the PSSC program led to expansion of curriculum development for other K-12 math and science subject areas. During the next 20 years, NSF spent $500 million on elementary and secondary school curricula and teacher development. In a 1977 survey, NSF found that 41 percent of the nation's secondary schools were using at least one form of the science curricula developed with NSF funds (National Science Foundation, 2000). Vinovskis (1999) calls this broad adoption of science curricula one of the major educational innovations of the 1950s and 1960s.

As with many school innovations that have not achieved massive outcome effects and vociferous public acclaim, Congress decreased support for the NSF curriculum efforts by the late 1970s. Efforts continued with a shift toward smaller, shorter-term curricular efforts. However, new larger-scale programs were again funded following the 1983 release of the federal report, *A Nation at Risk*, with its emphasis on the needs for a future workforce skilled in science, technology, engineering, and math.

Conception and Development of NSDL

Within the context of curricular programs, the NSF today is a center for impacting schools through incentives by encouraging the widespread distribution of innovative classroom teaching and learning materials. One of these efforts designed to impact math and science education is the NSDL. The NSDL, which officially debuted in 2002, is still an emerging resource. As one of the major tool initiatives of NSF, the digital library is promoted as a way of strengthening STEM education. Such tools are part of a larger NSF strategy "to invest in a wide range of instrumentation, multi-user facilities, distributed networks, digital libraries, and computational infrastructure that add unique value to research and are accessible and widely shared" (National Science Foundation, 2005, p. 8).

Like many federal programs (Vedung, 1998), NSDL has multiple purposes and goals as implemented by NSF, and even more when viewed from the perspectives of multiple grantees who have been funded to provide resources, services, and research within this grant program. In early studies from the mid-1990s, NSF viewed a digital library as a way to disseminate the many products, resources, and reports that emerged as a result the agency's funding programs. NSF recognized that many good efforts were funded but those often failed to propagate in part because of insufficient funds for continuation and scaling, as well as lack of marketing and national distribution. Within this context, a digital library developed by NSF could be a primary vehicle for both preserving and making widely available the results of NSF funded projects. NSF also recognized that once an infrastructure and stable technology were developed for its own resources, the research and development effort had the potential to create the basis for a larger national digital library to serve other agencies and disciplines, much as the earlier NSFNet project had been the basis for today's ubiquitous Internet technology and infrastructure.

As envisioned in a 2001 white paper by the NSDL community, the library is to become "a gateway to diverse digital collections of quality SMET (science, mathematics, engineering, and technology) educational content and services developed by a rich array of SMET educators" (Manduca, McMartin, & Mogk, 2001). The initial basis for digital library is the result of multiple funded projects representing collections and services developed through formal and informal partnerships among universities, K-12 schools, professional organizations, government agencies, non-profit organizations, and corporations. Other NSF programs, non-NSF government agencies, and private foundations have also provided initial collections. The library is tied together through an infrastructure developed by a consortium funded through a Core Integration grant with broad responsibilities for outreach, technical systems, and collection and service coherence. When the NSDL opened its virtual doors in December 2002, it was the culmination of over a decade of research and collaboration among librarians, technologists, and educators in the public and private sectors.

NSDL and Education Reform

While a digital library can be seen simply as a repository for content, the NSDL's goals far exceed collection and distribution of STEM materials. The NSDL program has an additional objective to enhance and reform of math and science education, both within the traditional arena of higher education of NSF as well as K-12 education. As noted by NSF program officer, Lee Zia, "By enabling broad access to reliable and authoritative learning and teaching materials and associated services in a digital environment, the National Science Digital Library expects to promote continual improvements in the quality of formal STEM education, and also to serve as a resource for informal and lifelong learning" (Zia, 2005).

From the earliest planning, NSDL was seen by its architects as becoming a key national resource in improving math and science teaching. The 1997 National Research Council workshop, *Developing a Digital National Library for Undergraduate Science, Mathematics, Engineering, and Technology Education (SMETE)*, raised important reform issues that a digital library could address: faculty who want to change their method of teaching, but have no single point of contact to search for useful ideas; journals that often do not discuss classroom implementation; and educational change efforts that need an easily accessible and searchable database of successful and evaluated programs and resources. Participants in the SMETE Library Workshop held at the National Science Foundation in July1998, reported that "the educational benefits and national impact of the SMETE Library will be both to improve the quality of education and to improve access to information" (National Science Foundation, 1998, p. 2).

The use of digital libraries to promote educational reform are intended for both higher and K-12 education. In the 1999 report Serving the Needs of Pre-College Science and Mathematics Education: Impact of a Digital National Library on Teacher Education and Practice, workshop participants emphasized that a digital library would need to be "constructed, collected and organized by groups of users.... The community should define what needs to be in the library and what services it provides." One of the most important of the identified communities were teachers and teacher educators. The report proposes that practicing teachers "can keep in touch with the cutting edge in science and mathematics education" (National Research Council, 1999, p. 18).

The workshop participants noted that teachers reported that they are pressed for adequate time to plan innovations in the classroom. Workshop participants also continually stated concerns over the requirements for educators' initial and continuing use of a digital collection. Concurrently, participants indicated "people need to dream about how information technology might transform teaching and learning and allow technology to develop in parallel to those visions." Among issues raised were that searching be easy and quick, materials be categorized by the amount of review they have received users be able to contribute to the content of the collections, the collection supports the training of new teachers, any charging mechanism would discourage use, and the library go beyond simply being a collection by creating a sense of community. This sense of community and innovation are repeated in current NSDL materials, with the web site noting "NSDL is emerging as a center of innovation in digital libraries as applied to education, and a community center for groups focused on digital-library-enabled science education" (National Science Foundation, 2005).

NEW CONTENT FOR NEW-LEARNING PARADIGMS

More than just a collection of resources, educational digital libraries are seen as incorporating novel content that will enhance learning through visualization, inquiry, problem-solving, interactivity, communication, and individualization for students with differential learning modes. Digital libraries for education typically contain a range of media types including images, video, audio, text, and applets that can support K-12 teaching and learning. In many instances, these media types can be combined to create powerful learning materials for use by teachers in instruction or by students who use it to enhance their own understanding of materials and concepts. One of the most commonly cited new capabilities of digital libraries is the ability for educators and students to also be contributors, so that there is a blurring of the "user" and "provider" role not typical of brick-and-mortar libraries.

NSDL follows this paradigm by providing a center for organizing resources that allow visualization, interaction, and participation in community that moves learning beyond the classroom. Digital libraries allow massive distribution, permitting easy access so the capability to experiment with new teaching is possible without high entry cost; and promoting equity through open availability of high quality learning objects that allow repurposing, so that students and teachers have new capabilities to construct learning. NSDL supports teaching and learning at all levels with materials ranging from journal articles and lesson plans to interactive animations, and from real-time data sets and technology-based tools to ask-an-expert services.

The examples below exemplify the range and diversity of NSDL-funded projects for K-12 students, and provide an illustration of the affordances of these new technologies for K-12 teaching and learning.

Teachers' Domain

Studies of the influence of electronic resources on higher education have shown that the availability of digital media types like images and data sets positively affect the depth and impact of student learning (Friedlander, 2003). Digital libraries like NSDL, then, can affect the direction of curriculum reform in K-12 education by promoting inquiry-based learning, increased visualization of concepts, and real-world application. A powerful example of these learning affordances for teachers and secondary students in the NSDL is Teachers' Domain (http://teachersdomain.org). Teachers' Domain is an effort by the WGBH Education Foundation to deliver their broadcast programming linked to supporting educational content to increase its value and usability for teachers and students. This ever-expanding multimedia digital library includes high-quality video digitalized from NOVA, American Experience, and other public television productions and partners in the content areas of Life Science, Physical Science, and Engineering, with more recent additions representing the social sciences including the Civil Rights Movement and *Brown v. Board of Education*.

In each subject area, teachers and students can access online clips from broadcast programs, extended interview segments, interactive Web-based activities, photographs, animations, still images, text translations of original source documents, graphic representations, audio interviews, and outtake footage from WGBH programs. Each resource also includes explanatory background articles.

While Teachers' Domain provides diverse, rich, and high-quality content resources for multimodal learning, it also employs many features that enable teachers to quickly and effectively integrate the digital library resources into their classrooms. The collection is accessed via a login that enables resources to be automatically correlated to national and state curriculum standards. Resources are accompanied by media-rich lesson plans created by curriculum experts that undergo an extensive peer-review process by content experts and teachers. Management tools allow users to create a "My Resources" list of items from the collection that can be organized into units, lessons, or student assignments. The Custom Resource folder feature allows users to gather resources to a particular folder along with submitted student work and notes on the resources. This organizing device enables exchange of annotated and compiled content from teacher to student, student to student, or student to teacher.

Teachers' Domain is an important digital library for educators in a number of ways. First, it couples widely recognized and validated content seamlessly with state and national curriculum standards. Second, its ancillary content is generated and reviewed by experts and practitioners (Blumenthal, 2003). The quality and diversity of the resources and rigorous vetting process combined with a small level of granularity ensure that teachers can deliver instructional materials that will help them to immediately target curriculum objectives for their students. Third, and most importantly, Teachers' Domain is a learning environment that couples its repository with workspace and tools that allow teachers to contextualize and customize resources.

Digital Library for Earth System Education (DLESE)

The DLESE, founded in 1998, is a mature but extremely progressive educational digital library that was initially aimed at higher education, but has increasingly expanded and prioritized its mission to encompass K-12 needs. DLESE involves educators, students, and scientists in working together to improve the quality, quantity, and efficiency of teaching and learning about Earth systems at all levels. Collection activities include identification of electronic materials for both teachers and learners such as lesson plans, maps, images, data sets, visualizations, assessment activities, curriculum, and online courses. DLESE provides access to data sets and imagery in the earth sciences, including the tools, interfaces, and user documentation that enable their effective use in educational settings. This combination of resources and supportive structures for teachers and learners is complemented by its evaluation activities that inform its own and other digital library developers about the behaviors and needs of users. Evaluation activities encourage a dynamic, iterative approach to operation of DLESE to continually improve quality and usability.

DLESE's vitality as a digital library is not just due to the variety of resources and user services it provides. This digital library intentionally cultivates community involvement by the recognition of user-as-contributor. Digital libraries enable an environment where users can share materials that they create for their own classroom environments; DLESE has fostered this sharing and gathered these resources. The blurring of the line between reader and author allows the dissemination of practitioner-generated activities that has previously not been possible beyond buildings or geographic locations (Gunn, 2002). The project is also sustained by the tireless work of the DLESE organization that is always engaging new user groups, undertaking technological improvements, and scanning the environment for educational changes. Through the constant community renewal and invitation, DLESE respects and encourages a strong human component in its activities. Rather than viewing the digital library as a unidirectional location for information retrieval, DLESE can credit its progress and wide acceptance to the community of interactive users it has built, serving as a model for other developing digital library efforts because of its success.

AskNSDL

While a number of fully functioning libraries are already making an impact on teaching and learning, the power of the digital world resides in the possibility of creating new structures and functions that will enhance what is possible in the digital library realm. Beyond established discrete collections such as DLESE or Teachers Domain, a number of digital library services exist to help users to locate, organize, and present information on the open Web, particularly for children who have unique information-seeking needs. Two example areas are virtual reference services that represent enhancements to traditional user services, and object location and presentation tools that present an emerging area to more powerfully support the use of digital libraries for instruction.

Building on the power and user familiarity with human-mediated information-seeking assistance, Digital reference, or "AskA," services are Internet-based question-and-answer services that connect users with experts and subject expertise, thus enhancing traditional reference services by expanding the range of expertise. Digital reference services use the Internet to connect people with people who can answer questions and support the development of skills, particularly by providing knowledgeable support that can add capabilities to a school. Access to human expertise in a range of topics is beyond what a traditional school library can offer (Gunn, 2002).

Query formation is often the most challenging part of students' information seeking process (Bilal, 2002; Fidel, 1999), and projects like AskNSDL (https://ask.nsdl.org/), help learners at all levels to negotiate their questions.

The AskNSDL project coordinates a collaborative Internet-based question and answer service comprised of archived questions and a network of science and mathematics experts willing to field new questions. As part of the Virtual Reference Desk Network, AskNSDL is linked to Ask-an-Expert (or AskA) services by including their experts in question triage. When the AskNSDL service receives questions beyond its scope, it can forward those questions to the VRD Network for assistance as well.

Although virtual reference services are widely available and many of them are for children, Silverstein (2003) points out that these services are built upon structures designed for adults and often cannot meet the unique information needs and query difficulties of children. As a result, these services are still evolving to fully meet K-12 needs. Silverstein calls for custom-designed architecture with developmentally appropriate question negotiation methods, adapted and facilitated interactions with experts, and increased use of images in navigation and communication as steps in this emerging area. Until these "next-generation" reference services are deployed, current virtual reference services have the best effect when they are used by children and adults together. Nonetheless, projects like AskNSDL enable users to create their own collections of authoritative information through interactions with experts and the review of previously asked questions and responses.

The Instructional Architect

Another promising digital library technology assists users, particularly teachers, with the presentation and contextualization of information. The Instructional Architect (http://ia.usu.edu), a project of Utah State University and also a part of the NSDL, allows the dynamic location and combination of learning objects from different digital library collections into personalized collections for learning and instruction. The software is open source and free to download. The Instructional Architect allows users to discover learning objects through its search and retrieval function, organize them into folders, plug resources into ready-made attractive templates, and create immediately published Web pages that sequence and display learning objects (e.g., activities, simulations, or virtual manipulatives) along with user-generated narrative text. The Web pages structure the materials selected by an individual teacher who can then use them in the classroom or as student tutorials. Case studies of mathematics teachers who used the Instructional Architect revealed that the tool aided their classroom practice and encouraged the use of dynamically generated collections of learning objects in the classroom (Recker, Dorward, & Reinke, 2003).

THE SCHOOL LIBRARY: CONTEXT FOR SUSTAINABLE ADOPTION

One possible way to begin to address the variety of systemic and cultural barriers to digital library adoption and integration is to cultivate a powerful and sustainable context for adoption. School libraries, situated in most schools and facing their own challenges of reestablishing relevance in the current educational climate and widespread layoffs and retirements (Miller & Shontz, 2003) can be renewed and enhanced as vehicles for the provision of digital library resources and venues for using these resources to build meaningful and relevant student media and critical literacies.

Digital libraries are already having an impact on school media practices as students increasingly favor online over traditional print materials (Bell-South Foundation, 2003; Corporation for Public Broadcasting, 2003; Levin & Arafeh, 2002; NetDay, 2004). Most schools have used CD-ROM and/or Web-based subscription services for enhancing their print collections for many years. As the Web became an increasingly rich source of freely available content, school media centers were often the first place in schools with computers connected to the Internet and remain one of the higher technology instructional areas in many school buildings (Lance, 2001). As a result, the school media center is increasingly not just a discrete and organized collection of information resource materials physically located in space, but the framework for a collection of "digital libraries." These newly added digital libraries dramatically increase the richness of the information sources by expanding the knowledge base beyond the school walls. At the same time, the expansion increases the complexity of managing the multiple information resources now part of the school media center collection, as well as the need to manage the physical and technical environment to serve a school's population (Gunn, 2002).

As detailed in the profiles of exemplary projects above, digital libraries, and the NSDL in particular, offer resources and tools that are more complex than text alone but also offer powerful affordances for enhancing learning. Innovative instructional resources tend to build upon students' visual acuity and attempt to leverage this preference for deeper learning. The school librarian can use digital library resources in the school media program to not only expose students to a richer variety of educational media, but also use the interaction with these media to build understandings and heuristics that culminate in media literacy. Kymes (2005) contrasts open, self-directed learning in the school library with structured, bench-marked approaches in the classroom. When the classroom curriculum is complemented by the use of multiple media in the school library and when the teacher and the school librarian coordinate their efforts, Kymes imper-atively states that:

> Modern school library media centers are being transformed into spaces where students can learn, use, and create media with the support of educators who value such abilities. Students who are given a vocabulary through which to critique media, skills, and tools needed for analysis, and outlets through which their voices can be heard will be able to make a difference in the society in which they live. It is the responsibility of educators – library media specialists and classroom teachers alike – to provide these skills, tools, and outlets for students (p. 277).

Media literacy is most crucially needed to foster the principles of science education, a dimension which the NSDL project staff can use to justify the need for digital libraries and to engage powerful advocates in the school library media center. When media literacy is seen through the lens of science learning, indeed, the centrality of digital library resources like those in the NSDL becomes clear. Thier (2005) indicates that when media literacy skills are approached in the realm of science, true, deep learning occurs. "[I]n the science classroom, being 'media literate' means that students...are able to compare information from different media forms and presentations...[and] to use media judiciously" (p. 266).

Further, it is through media-rich guided scientific inquiry that students can use their critical assessment of resources and newly created knowledge to spur awareness, sensitivity, and social action. Comparison and investi-gation of multiple media types to examine the same topic can help to un-cover the power relationships that may be generated and maintained by dominant groups, expose students to diverse ways of expressing and reading the world, and encourage students to recognize and value a diversity of perspectives through critiquing and learning about dominant viewpoints. Without exposure to diverse resources coupled with the skills to interpret and use them, students have little chance of transforming knowledge in responsive social action (Janks, 2000). Pairing digital libraries with school library media programs and science education has the potential to have a profound effect on the ways students learn to use information as well as how crucial the NSDL is deemed in K-12 education.

THE DIGITAL LIBRARY "CARROT"

The growth and spread of NSDL furthers the support for innovation and reform in STEM learning and teaching envisioned by the early designers in the 1990s. While early forecasts of possibilities were often defined as much by the limitations of the visionaries and shaped by their backgrounds (Kling & Lamb, 1996), many of the promises are slowly being realized and the "carrot" of high quality digital libraries is spurring reform and showing potential on many fronts. School library media specialists dream of larger collections readily available locally that would provide rapid access to rich content to support student-learning without straining school budgets (Bennett, 2003; O'Connell, 2002). Moreover, the role of the school library needs a compelling theme for revitalization and redefinition in a digital age (Simpson, 1996). Digital library developers and educational technologists envision infrastructure that will support fast searching and retrieval of large quantities of relevant information, multimedia formats that were accessible to desktop systems, and distributed storage and integrated systems for information that would make the other side of the globe as accessible as the classroom (Brown, 2000). Educators see digital libraries as increasing the possibilities for personalized delivery to meet the needs of each child and the support systems that would promote new and more powerful teaching and learning strategies (Bennett, 2003; Wallace, Krajcik, & Soloway, 1996). Policy makers are particularly supportive of digital libraries as a means to increase accountability and produce a generation of children who are technically and information literate to power the future economy (US Department of Education, 2000).

At the same time, these future visions remain less than fully realized so that the emergence of digital library technologies has yet to be fully implemented and understood, particularly in terms impacts on school media centers directly and teaching and learning more broadly. Teaching has not changed substantially, users still have great difficulty in locating and retrieving quality information effectively, wonderful collections disappear for lack of social and economic models to support them, huge questions remain about the impact of educational technologies to significantly impact student learning, and children are increasingly finding that the richest sources of knowledge are outside the school building.

Currently shifting policy priorities can serve as a "stick" instead of a carrot by hindering true transformation in the teaching of STEM topics. The success or long-term institutionalization of reform efforts sponsored by federal agencies such as NSF are routinely uncertain, both because of the lack of continuing support and because of the voluntary nature of adoption. Changing officials and political attitudes can rapidly reshape direction or scuttle emerging practices before these have been fully tested. As Belanger (1998) notes,

> Because political entities – Congress and the executive branch through the Office of Management and Budget – hold the purse strings, federal funding introduces the role of national politics – sometimes partisan, always reflecting politicians' desire to respond to the pressures they themselves encounter, especially from constituents. A federal agency like NSF, remarkably independent until its budget grew large enough for politicians to notice, has only limited choices in its policies and actions (p. 22).

Earlier technological endeavors from NSF like NSFNet connectivity initiative (the foundation for today's Internet) and Google have had massive success although impacts on education are still to be determined. Digital libraries are an extension of this initial networking reform and the hope remains that this too will have long-term and widespread positive impacts. Despite successful prototypes and small-scale efforts within NSDL, the overall concept and vision of digital libraries is unrealized and in particular, it is still unclear in how or how much these will influence schools. The "Net generation" is showing a marked change in their preferred learning (Beck & Wade, 2004; NetDay, 2004; Tapscott, 1998), but schools have yet to respond and the structures continue to inhibit the adoption of technologies already widespread outside the schoolroom door (Cuban, 2001; Schofield & Davidson, 2002). As an emerging technology, digital libraries may actually be precursor to something that is still hard to imagine.

Yet, the carrot of this innovative resource incorporated into educational settings in transformative and sustainable ways is important as it represents new policy areas where the innovation may be too immature and stable to mandate adoption. We must have mechanisms that allow testing, experimentation, and that will not be destructive if they fail or head in very unanticipated directions. Digital libraries and their potential to revolutionize the way information is located and used in school settings are a good beginning but not yet close to the envisioned thing.

REFERENCES

Beck, J. C., & Wade, M. (2004). *Got game: How the game generation is reshaping business forever.* Boston, MA: Harvard Business School Press.
Belanger, D. O. (1998). *Enabling American innovation: Engineering and the National Science Foundation.* West Lafayette, IN: Purdue University Press.

BellSouth Foundation. (2003). The growing technology gap between schools and students: Findings from the BellSouth power to teach program. Retrieved February 20, 2004, from http://www.bellsouthfoundation.org/pdfs/pttreport03.pdf

Bennett, S. (2003). Redesigning libraries for learning from http://www.clir/org/pubs/abstracts/pub122abst.html

Bilal, D. (2002). Children's use of the Yahoologans! Web search engine. III. Cognitive and physical behaviors on fully-self generated search tasks. *Journal of the American Society for Information Science and Technology, 53*(13), 1170–1183.

Blumenthal, D. (2003). Teacher's Domain: Classroom media resources from public television's WGBH. *Knowledge Quest, 31*(3), 30–32.

Brown, J. S. (2000). Growing up digital: How the web changes work, education, and the ways people learn. *Change, 32*(2), 11–20.

Corporation for Public Broadcasting. (2003). Connected to the future: A report on children's Internet use from the Corporation for Public Broadcasting. Retrieved May 30, 2003, from http://www.cpb.org/ed/resources/connected/

Cuban, L. (2001). *Oversold and underused: Computers in the classroom.* Cambridge, MA: Harvard University Press.

Falk, H. (2003). Developing digital libraries. *The Electronic Library, 21*(3), 258–261.

Fidel, R. (1999). A visit to the information mall: Web searching behavior of high school students. *Journal of the American Society for Information Science, 50*(1), 24–37.

Friedlander, A. (2003). The Internet and Harry Potter. *Information Outlook, 7*(12), 18–25.

Janks, H. (2000). Domination, access, diversity, and design: A synthesis for critical literacy education. *Educational Review, 52*(2), 175–187.

Jukes, I., & McCain, T. (2000). *Windows on the future: Education in the age of technology.* Thousand Oaks, CA: Corwin Press.

Kling, R., & Lamb, R. (1996). Envisioning electronic publishing and digital libraries: How genres of analysis shape the characteristics of alternative visions. In: R. P. Peek & G. Newby & L. Lunin (Eds), *Scholarly publishing: The electronic frontier.* Cambridge, MA: MIT Press.

Kymes, A. (2005). The library media center: At the center of media literacy education. In: G. Schwarz. & P. U. Brown (Eds), *Media literacy: Transforming curriculum and teaching. 104th yearbook of the National Society for the Study of Education* (pp. 275–278). Malden, MA: Blackwell Publishing.

Lance, K.C. (2001). Proof of the power: *Recent research on the impact of school library media programs on the academic achievement of U.S. public school students* (Digest No. EDO-IR-2001-05). Syracuse, NY: ERIC Clearinghouse on Information & Technology.

Levin, D., & Arafeh, S. (2002). The digital disconnect: The widening gap between Internet-savvy students and their schools. Retrieved September 23, 2002, from http://www.pewinternet.org/reports/

Manduca, C. A., McMartin, F. P., & Mogk, D. W. (2001). *Pathways to progress: Visions and plans for developing NSDL.* Retrieved June 18, 2005, from http://nsdl.comm.nsdl.org/meeting/archives/smete/meetings/grantees0901/whitepaper.pdf

Mardis, M. (2003). If we build it, will they come? An overview of the issues in K-12 digital libraries. In: M. Mardis (Ed.), *Developing digital libraries for K-12 education.* Syracuse, NY: ERIC Information Technology Clearinghouse.

Miller, M. L., & Shontz, M. L. (2003). The SLJ spending survey. *School Library Journal* (October 1). Retrieved May 10, 2004, from www.schoollibraryjournal.com/article/CA326338

National Research Council. (1999). *Serving the needs of pre-college science and mathematics education: Impact of a digital national library on teacher education and practice. Proceedings from a National Research Council workshop.* Washington, DC: National Academy Press.

National Science Foundation. (1998). Report of the SMETE Library Workshop. *D-Lib Magazine* (October 29). Retrieved April 10, 2000, from www.dlib.org/smete/public/report.html

National Science Foundation. (2000). *America's investment in the future: NSF celebrating 50 years* (No. NSF 00–50). Arlington, VA: National Science Foundation.

National Science Foundation. (2005). *NSF 2004 Performance Highlights* (No. NSF 05-02). Arlington, VA: National Science Foundation.

NetDay. (2004). Voices and views of today's tech-savvy students: National report on NetDay speak up for Students 2003. Retrieved Apr. 15, 2004, from www.netday.org/speakup-day2003_report.htm

O'Connell, J. (2002). Extending the reach of the school library. *School Libraries Worldwide, 8*(2), 21–26.

Recker, M. M., Dorward, J., & Reinke, D. (2003). The instructional architect: Theory and practice in the development and evaluation of digital library services. In: M. Mardis (Ed.), *Developing digital libraries for K-12 education* (pp. 107–117). Syracuse, NY: ERIC Information & Technology Clearinghouse.

Schofield, J. W., & Davidson, A. L. (2002). *Bringing the Internet to school: Lessons from an urban district.* San Francisco, CA: Jossey-Bass.

Sharma, R. K., & Vishwanathan, K. R. (2001). Digital libraries: Development and challenges. *Library Review, 50*(1), 10–15.

Silverstein, J. (2003). Next-generation children's digital reference services: A research agenda. In: M. Mardis (Ed.), *Developing digital libraries in K-12 education* (pp. 141–158). Syracuse, NY: ERIC Information & Technology Clearinghouse.

Simpson, C. (1996). *The school librarian's role in the electronic age.* ERIC Digest No. ED402928. U.S. Department of Education.

Tapscott, D. (1998). *Growing up digital: The rise of the Net generation.* New York: McGraw-Hill.

Thier, M. (2005). Merging media and science: Learning to weigh sources, not just evidence. In: G. Schwarz. & P. U. Brown (Eds), *Media literacy: Transforming curriculum and teaching. 104th yearbook of the National Society for the Study of Education* (pp. 260–268). Malden, MA: Blackwell Publishing.

Tomei, L. A. (2002). *The technology facade: Overcoming barriers to effective instructional technology.* Boston, MA: Allyn and Bacon.

U.S. Department of Education. (2000). *The power of the Internet for learning: Moving from promise to practice.* Report of the Web Based Education Commission to the President and the Congress of the United States. Washington, DC, from http://www.ed.gove/offices/AC/WEBC/FinalReport/WBECReport.pdf

Vedung, E. (1998). Policy instruments: Typologies and theories. In: M. Bemelmans-Vedic., R. C. Rist. & E. Vedung (Eds), *Carrots, sticks & sermons: Policy instruments and their evaluation.* New Brunswick, NJ: Transaction Publishers.

Vinovskis, M. (1999). *History and educational policymaking.* New Haven, CT: Yale University Press.

Wallace, R., Krajcik, J., & Soloway, E. (1996). Digital libraries in the science classroom. *D-Lib Magazine.*

Witten, I. H., Loots, M., Trujillo, M., & Bainbridge, D. (2002). The promise of digital libraries in developing countries. *The Electronic Library, 20*(1), 7–13.

Zia, L. L. (2005). The NSF National Science, Technology, Engineering and Mathematics Education Digital Library Program: New project from fiscal year 2004. *D-Lib Magazine* (June 18). Retrieved July 25, from www.dlib.org/dlib/march05/zia/03zia.html

INTEGRATING SQUEAK INTO A COMMUNITY: A COLLABORATIVE EFFORT

Barbara Hug and George Reese

ABSTRACT

Helping teachers to change practices by adopting new tools and peda-gogical approaches is of interest to a wide range of educational research-ers and practitioners. We describe a project that has addressed issues surrounding the adoption of a technology tool into a local community. We examine the impact Squeak, an object-orientated programming environ-ment, had on project participants. We observed that both teachers and students developed reasoning and problem-solving skills while using this tool. In order to be successfully integrated, an innovative educational technology requires a collaborative effort between multiple partners. We discuss implications in the context of usability, scalability and sustain-ability.

INTRODUCTION

Recent reform movements within the United States call for increased math-ematics understanding (National Council of Teachers of Mathematics

Technology and Education: Issues in Administration, Policy, and Applications in K12 Schools
Advances in Educational Administration, Volume 8, 181–199
ISSN: 1479-3660/doi:10.1016/S1479-3660(05)08013-3

(NCTM), 2000) and "science for all" (American Association for the Advancement of Science (AAAS), 1989) as well as an increased awareness of quantitative and scientific literacy (National Research Council (NRC), 1996; Steen, 2001). In order to help facilitate this objective, national organizations have established standards, Principles and Standards for School Mathematics (NCTM, 2000), *Benchmarks for Scientific Literacy*, (AAAS, 1993) and the *National Science Education Standards* (NSES; NRC, 1996) that identify key learning goals and processes that students should understand for basic quantitative and scientific literacy. The NSES emphasize the teaching of science through inquiry and situated within the context of the real world while the documents from Project 2061 stress that students should take part in a range of scientific practices. In these documents as well as the state and local documents, teachers are called on to modify their teaching practices and to engage in more student-centered instruction using a range of strategies, one of which has been the use of a variety of computer-based tools. The critical issue is how to address these frameworks and changes in teaching practices in order to help bring about change at the local and district level to improve the teaching and learning of all students. Research has shown that several issues impede progress; these issues include a crucial lack of alignment between professional development, policy issues, resources, teaching practices and large-scale assessments and the types of teaching and learning called for in the national documents (Anderson & Helms, 2001; Keys & Bryan, 2001; Lynch, 2000).

LITERATURE REVIEW

The focus of this chapter is on documenting how one collaborative partnership developed between a research I university and a local school district to meaningfully integrate a computer programming application into the district's curriculum in order to help address issues of technology education. It is important to study such cases because school districts often struggle with meaningful technology integration but in districts where technology has been integrated in meaningful ways, increased student learning and engagement has been documented (Honey, McMillan, & Carrig, 1999). We describe how we introduced to a local community Squeak, an object-orientated programming environment. Squeak enables dynamic opportunities for simulation and visualization. The authoring tool masks the sophisticated underlying program, which allow "entry" for students to engage in productive design of visualizations. Students come away with an understanding of object-orientated approaches to programming and can develop powerful thinking and problem-solving skills. We are interested in documenting how different parts of this community take up and use this tool in a range of educational settings.

Our main question is the following:

- How is a new technology successfully adopted and used within a school district?

In presenting our findings, we document how a maverick teacher has used Squeak and learn from her story how a district wide implementation of Squeak might be possible on a larger scale.

ISSUES SURROUNDING THE USE OF TECHNOLOGY IN SCHOOLS

There has been considerable skepticism with regard to technology efficacy in schools (Cuban, 1986, 1993, 2001; Noble, 1998; Oppenheimer, 1997). Particularly problematic are computers that are used for drill and practice (Manoucherhri, 1999; Mathews, 1998). Nonetheless, advocates for the use of technology in the classroom have long believed there are effective ways to use digital technologies in the classroom (Papert, 1980, 1993, 2002; Tapscott, 1998).

One report, "Does It Compute?" (Weglinsky, 1998) can serve as an illustration of how crucial the role teacher professional development is on the use of new technologies and new teaching strategies. This study highlights that in order to show positive gains in academic achievement, it is not only the professional development that is important but also the way computers are used. Both issues impact how students learn and the level of understanding they achieve. If computers are used in ways that allow students to develop higher-order thinking skills, higher gains in academic achievement were noted. Additional studies have looked at the importance of professional development offered to the teachers and have identified a series of requirements for effective professional development in regard to the use of technology. These requirements focus around developing teachers' knowledge in the use of technology in appropriate ways and to make clear the connections between the technology and the content being taught.

Computers can be used to teach explicit skills and knowledge to students or can be used to encourage students to explore options and pursue individual learning goals in ways that would not be possible without the use of technology (Bereiter & Scardamalia, 1992). These two ways can be viewed as two points on a continuum with a wide range of options between them. These different ways of thinking about computers can be used in reform-oriented ways of teaching that is more student-centered. The Department of Education (2001) released a report looking at different uses of computers in schools. In this report, they labeled as "traditional" classroom practices use of computers in drills, remediation and instruction in computer applications. The "authentic" use of technology includes the use of computers in "real-life" problems. In addition, this type of use of technology allows students and teachers to engage in learning in ways that they would not have been able to do in the absence of technology (Krajcik, Blumenfeld, Marx, & Soloway, 2000; Reese et al., 2005). It is important that students progress beyond the basic level of computer skill and knowledge and begin to understand how technology can be used in today's society.

In particular, inquiry-based approaches to using technology have been shown to produce significant gains in student understanding (Linn, 1998; Edelson, Gordin, & Pea, 1999; White & Frederiksen, 2000; Songer, Lee, & Kam, 2002; Rivet & Krajcik, 2004). It is important to note that these projects have had extensive professional development efforts aligned with the development and use of these inquiry-based curriculum materials (Blumenfeld, Fishman, Krajcik, Marx, & Soloway, 2000). Recent studies have linked the use of technology-rich, project-based science curricula with increased scores on state mandated test, at significantly higher scores than students who had not participated in the units (Marx et al., 2004).

Change in the classroom can happen with leadership and "identified and activated resources" (Spillane, Diamond, Walker, Halverson, & Jita, 2001). That is, the resources must not merely be present, but must be recognized and used in the classroom and their use supported by the immediate educational community. Given that responsibility for change in classroom practice resides primarily with the classroom teacher, it requires support from administrators (Spillane & Zeuli, 1999; Spillane et al., 2001). Currently, administrators are being pushed to justify the technology costs that they incur. With the right teacher, the right tool and the right context (Zhao et al., 2002; Zhao & Frank, 2003), effective and appropriate use of technology can happen.

In the recent literature, there has been increased documentation of alignment of professional development to the teachers' actual needs and context (Loucks-Horsley, Love, Stiles, Mundry, & Hewson, 2003; Crockett, 2002; Fishman, Marx, Best, & Tal, 2003; Borko, 2004). This has come with the recognition that professional development is crucial for the success of standards-based reform as called for in the national documents (AASS, 1993; NRC, 1996; NCTM, 2000) as well as in the recently passed the No Child Left Behind legislation. We are interested in understanding the use of technology in schools, since this is often seen as a cross-cutting area for professional development. In order for cognitively based technology tools to be taken up by a range of school districts, tool developers and educators should be concerned with issues surrounding usability, scalability and sustainability of the reform efforts (Fishman, Marx, Blumenfeld, Krajcik, & Soloway, 2004). These points have thus far not been widely studied. We are currently documenting how one piece of technology was used in a wide range of settings and the successes and challenges that we faced in the use of the tool. Here we examine our project in light of these three issues. We believe that we make a contribution to the literature as well as to the teacher and administrator communities with this study.

METHODS

This chapter is a descriptive study of a collaboration between a research university and a local school district aimed at expanding the use of an educational software, Squeak in the greater community. This project is an ongoing research effort in which we use what we do to inform our next steps, we constantly engage in self-evaluation, reflection and revision of our project. In doing so, we are participating in an ongoing iterative design of the curriculum and professional development as a design experiment (Brown, 1992; Edelson, 2002). In reporting our findings, we hope to be able to inform a wide range of audience members and impact the use of technology in the K-12 school arena.

Participants

Participants in the study included two maverick teachers (one an elementary enrichment teacher and the other a secondary mathematics teacher), and two university faculty members (one a science education faculty member and the other the director of the Office for Mathematics, Science and Technology Education). We have engaged with approximately 1,000 individuals throughout our project. Approximately 700 students participated in the project throughout the year; students were predominantly local elementary and middle grade students. Students came from a mix of socioeconomic backgrounds. They were exposed to Squeak in a variety of venues: elementary enrichment program, boys and girls club, after-school programs sponsored by the school, city community programs as well as Saturday programs. Community members included parents and guardians of participating students, interested community members, local teachers as well as school and district administrators.

Context

We are located in a Mid-Western university town and have used Squeak in a range of local settings. Our project is currently ongoing in 18 local institutions, schools, public libraries, community college libraries, University courses and out-reach programs as well as the local boys and girls club.

Squeak Application

As described at Squeakland.org, Squeak is a platform independent "media rich authoring tool" that allows an easy entrance into the interesting world of programming. The multiple platform compatibility was key to the project since a project created on one system can be opened and run on another platform. A project started at home can be continued at school. In addition, students can use Squeak throughout their K-12 years – as they develop their Squeak programming skills, they can program more and more complex models appropriate to their curriculum.

As Squeak assembles scripts from click-and-drag tiles, it allows beginners to focus on the logic of their ideas rather than syntax. In typed programming languages, an incorrectly placed space or punctuation mark causes the script to fail. Click-and-drag tiles eliminate that kind of problem for the beginner. They can test ideas rather than typing skills. Squeak scripts can be changed while they are running by adding or removing script tiles or by changing a number value in a script. Effects are immediate. Squeak projects were posted to the SqueakCMI superswiki (available through the Squeak-CMI.org website).

Data Sources

The genesis of the data that served as the basis for this chapter occurred as a result of searching for appropriate modeling and visualization tools to be used in elementary classrooms that would help address key science and mathematics standards as articulated by the national, state and local documents. At an initial professional development conference on modeling and visualization tools held during the 2003 SuperComputing Conference, project members were exposed to a variety of proprietary tools for integrating visualization technologies into the classroom. Most of these tools, such as Mathematica, Fathom, Agent Sheets and Interactive Physics, are appropriate for integration into the curriculum for secondary-level students or higher. One project member, an elementary school teacher, was interested in tools that could be used by elementary school teachers and students. One day in February 2004, as project members struggled to find ways to put the tools they knew into use and retool them for elementary school, the elementary teacher team member sent the group a note.

> I learned Squeak today. I downloaded the software, it is free, it has good tutorials and it is fun. Could I hear some opinions on whether or not it would be a good place for the [school name removed] kids to start playing around. There are rules, there are xy coordinates, and there is creativity. The software will string together commands about objects in the world created on the screen and has them move like a cartoon.

This was the first of 657 messages over the next 500 days that came from this teacher that included a discussion of Squeak. Over the next 18 months, she arranged and led 92 presentations and workshops using Squeak, and has had the program installed on the computers at 18 local institutions, schools, public libraries, community college libraries and boys and girls club computers, and university computers. Through this teacher, our group was connected to the network of Squeak users and developers, and hundreds of students and teachers in the area have learned and are using the tool. Our records of the largely electronic exchanges and the developments that this team member led are one of our most important data sources.

Additional data sources include the following: pictures and video tapes of the workshops with students, parents and community members, survey information from workshop participants, notes taken during the workshops and workshop leader reflections. Workshops were conducted during the 2004–2005 calendar year. Two extended-week long workshops were offered for students during the summer of 2004 and 2005. Additional Saturday workshops were offered for parents and children. A series of after-school enrichment courses were offered as well during the 2004–2005 school year. During these workshops, students and parents were taught how to use Squeak and encouraged to develop beginning or advanced programs as appropriate. These programs were collected and used in the data analysis for evidence of students developing skills and knowledge about computer programming. Additional data sources include detailed classroom observations of students using Squeak during the normal classroom day and student artifacts that resulted from the use of the educational tool.

Data Analysis

Data was analyzed for themes connected to usability, scalability and sustainability of Squeak as applied to our project (Blumenfeld et al., 2000; Fishman, 2004). Usability focused on the ability of teachers and students to use the tool in meaningful and appropriate ways. Scalability focused on issues past the maverick teacher by bringing up district wide implementation concerns. Sustainability focused on issues independent use by teachers following the initial professional development and the adoption of the tool by teachers and student not directly involved in our workshops. Themes were arrived at by participating in iterative cycles of data examination, discussion and consensus of key factors.

RESULTS

In our exploratory study documenting how a community adopts and uses a new software tool, we identified a number of key issues around the ideas of usability, scalability and sustainability of Squeak in the school districts and surrounding community.

Issues of Usability

In order to understand what is meant by usability, it is important to understand the whole design experiment process that is often the mechanism by which developers examine particular learning technology tools and modify them based on the needs of a few maverick teachers and their students. While a crucial process and one that has a strong research background, it is important that this approach be broadened to examine the use of the tool in a wider arena, multiple classrooms, schools and even districts. Within our own small study, we identified a series of issues that need further study related to usability of Squeak.

Student and Teacher Engagement

Unlike Fishman et al. (2004) who did not consider the use of cognitively oriented technology tools in after-school programs as part of the whole school reform process, we situated our study in the larger context of the school and surrounding community as we were interested in trying to expose as many students to the use of the application as possible and to use this as an entry into the school classroom. In doing so, we were able to see high student engagement of the tool in a wide range of settings, including the traditional classroom. We feel that it is important to consider alternative arenas of learning as well as the traditional classroom, as this might be one way of gaining access to students who are at the greatest risk of being left behind in the move toward increased technology education.

In addition to student engagement, we saw highly motivated teachers using Squeak and participating in the design research that was ongoing in the classrooms. This adoption is one illustration of what is meant by usability of a particular cognitive learning technology tool. However, it is important to identify ways in which to scale past these initial crucial teachers during the scaling of the tool.

Interacting with a More Knowledgeable Community

In selecting Squeak as an application to explore and integrate into the district curriculum, we had not anticipated interacting with a larger more knowledgeable community concerned with Squeak. However as we expanded our project, we had to modify our approach. We found that it was necessary to create a local repository for Squeak projects on a locally hosted web-server. This local computer access was supplied by the University portion of the collaboration and proved to be a key issue in solving usability issues. For example, we needed to be able to upload and store more than 1,000 Squeak projects.

A second interaction that became important as we expanded our project was the e-mail communications we had with Squeak developers and other programmers. We realized this is a strength of the application and believe that this community will be crucial for adoption by others as no curriculum is currently available for integration of Squeak into current classroom practice. We found, for example, that undergraduate and graduate students in computer science could quickly create applications in Squeak for ad hoc concepts (e.g., sine waves) that one teacher might find immediately useful but would not have the time to create on her own. This teacher would benefit greatly from communicating with the college level programmers.

Availability of Educative Curriculum Materials

The lack of both user guides and curriculum materials proved to be an issue in terms of usability and needs to be addressed in order for Squeak to scale and be sustained at the whole district level. We were fortunate to have several maverick teachers who were willing and able to make additional contacts in order to develop their own understanding about Squeak and explore how to use it in the classroom in engaging ways. The issue of materials that teachers can use and learn from is of interest to a wide range of educational researchers as well as school administrators, as teachers are being required to change their teaching practices to align with the national reform documents (Davis & Krajcik, 2005; Schneider, Krajcik, & Blumenfeld, 2005).

Limitations of Squeak

As the teachers integrated Squeak into their curriculum, it became clear that Squeak presented several limitations and could not be used to address several key ideas in mathematics (e.g., trigonometry functions), and computer science (e.g., a simple repeat loop) as it is currently available. However, one advantage of Squeak is that Squeak can be modified by a knowledgeable end user to address new areas that it previously could not. We are currently working with a University faculty member in the Computer Sciences Department to address some of these issues.

One use of Squeak we saw in a number of classrooms was as a performance portfolio tool used for assessment. An example were the projects that early elementary school students did with Squeak in modeling the solar system. Two examples are shown in Figs. 1 and 2. In both of these examples, one can see students illustrating their understanding about the solar system. In the second example, a higher level of understanding is shown by the addition of the script that allows the sun to rotate. This addition of movement illustrates the deeper understanding that the student who created this applet had about the solar system – it no longer was a static image but contained movement. The script that the first grader created to carry this out is shown on the right of the image.

By using computer programming skills, students were able to go past the simple recall facts illustrated in Fig. 1 to adding in information about how the sun moved in relation to the planets (Fig. 2). In doing so, students were able to make images of planets move around a sun and moons around planets. However, this quickly illustrated the limitations of the tool. If students at the high school level wanted to refine their model of the solar

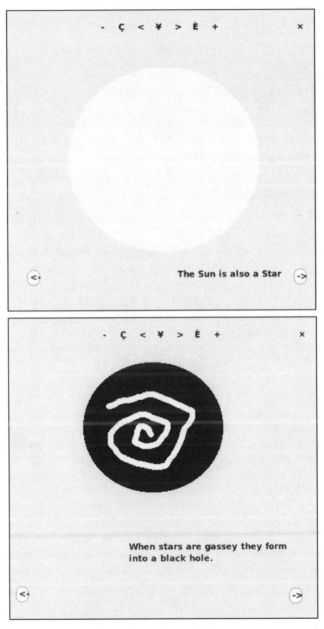

Fig. 1. First Grade Student Work.

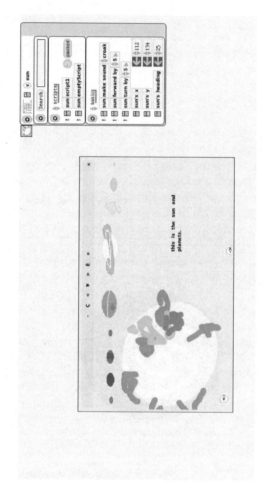

Fig. 2. First Grade Student's Model of the Solar System.

system to include elliptical orbits, even entering the equation for an ellipse, the mechanisms for doing so in Squeak are not clear.

Issues of Scalability

In thinking about issues surrounding scalability, one needs to address issues facing teachers and administrators at multiple levels. In examining how Squeak was used in the local school district and the surrounding community we situated our work in, we identified several issues that need to be addressed in order for Squeak to be taken up by additional teachers.

Financial and Time Constraints

A key issue in the selection of a tool is the initial and continuing cost of the tool to the district and the individual. Squeak is free and open source. With free, open source software, one can focus on how the software can be used in a range of different settings. In addition to being a free application, Squeak is an application that can run on multiple platforms. In using Squeak, students can elect to save their projects to a server that can be accessed through the Internet. Because of this feature, students can work on a project at home and access it at school. These factors all contributed to the selection of Squeak as a tool that could work in a range of environments and as such be scalable.

An additional issue we identified was the extended amount of time required to learn how to use Squeak. There appears to be a more challenging learning curve for teachers than for students. This raises the issue of necessary time investment for teachers before they are comfortable with using Squeak in the classroom. This paradox might not be surprising to many since students tend to be willing to explore without detailed manuals, while teachers are more hesitant. The adults in our workshops were less inclined to explore and more likely to request detailed instructions on procedures. This experience with adult learners as well as our own experience in developing models for use in the classroom as well as necessary professional development materials, we realized that Squeak was an application that one could learn the basics of quite quickly, but it would require an extensive exploration and time to master. Due to the issues raised here, we have begun to question if our initial vision of students programming through Squeak might not be possible due to pressures on and within schools today.

In addition, as we developed curriculum that included Squeak projects, we realized that it would be difficult to develop accurate models that students could use to learn specific science and math concepts. This development process has required large amounts of time, and time is a commodity that teachers do not have in surplus. This time requirement has reemphasized the need for educative curriculum materials to achieve widespread use of the tool. When the use of Squeak was examined with regard to scalability issues, it became clear that these materials would need to address the curriculum in different states and support a range of teaching environments and abilities.

Issues of Sustainability

In thinking about sustainability of a particular tool, one hopes that the use of a particular tool will continue past the time that the developers are in the classroom or community. This extended use is the key point to sustainability (Fishman et al., 2004). For our study, the issue of sustainability cannot yet be addressed. When the necessary curriculum materials and support to make Squeak scalable exists, then we expect issues of sustainability to emerge. We hope that the use of Squeak will become part of the standard tools that teachers use when teaching visualization or modeling. We believe that the pedagogical practice will be one that aligns with the national documents and encourages the use of higher-order thinking skills. However, until Squeak has succeeded at being scaled, we cannot begin to investigate these issues. Nonetheless, we do believe that they will become important.

CONCLUSIONS: LESSONS LEARNED

The power of Squeak is that it is free and that, as an authoring tool, it is open-ended and empowers inquiry. We know that using computers for demonstrating/illustrating an understanding of new topics and for simulations and modeling is associated with higher mathematics scores than other uses such as drill and practice (U.S. Department of Education, Office of Educational Research and Improvement, & National Center for Educational Statistics, 2001). Similar trends are seen for science learning especially when embedded within extended project-based learning environments (Marx et al., 2004; Schneider, Krajcik, Marx, & Soloway, 2002).

Developing the Appropriate Models

Using and constructing models is a key aspect of the nature of mathematics and science. In addition, modeling is one way to investigate phenomena since it enables the student to organize, visualize and test predictions about the phenomena. Squeak is one way that students can develop models about the concepts that they are learning about in their school curriculum or about ideas that interest them. As is shown in the examples in the previous section, we have had success with the use of Squeak in the study of astronomy and in other disciplines not shown. With an hour's worth of Squeak lessons, children can draw a sun, the planets and set them in orbits around the sun. The more factual knowledge the student has, the more accurate the model becomes. In fact, the effort of building the simulation can cause a child to verify information she was uncertain of, or seek new facts to make her model more accurate. The relative sizes of the planets, their apparent color, their relative distances from the sun are details that all become more and more important to the students as they work. It has been obvious to us as we ask children to create a model of a solar system that they know many facts but that doing the simulation gives them a chance to put what they know into action together in a whole view. There is a moment when the scripts are first started and the planets move that is very powerful. It is also a moment of concern to the programmer when the planets do not move in ways that she expected to see them move. Even nine-year-old programmers expect good orbits and seek more information either about Squeak or about astronomy if their model does not match their expectations.

We have seen some mathematic applications for Squeak with young children. One of the first projects students make is to draw an object and write a script that includes the phrase 'forward by 5.' The default forward is a positive direction on the 'y'-axis. Children are surprised that forward goes up. They are not surprised when they find out if they click on an arrow and change the number from 5 to 4 and then to 3, 2 and 1 that the object moves slower and slower. If there is time when they are clicking to ask "What will the object do when you reach zero?" they will say, "It will stop," or "do nothing". They will also willingly check to see if there is another number below zero. When they try a number below zero and their object moves down on the screen they see negative 1 is useful and are on the road to understanding positive and negative integers. In their explorations, students learn about "if-then" statements, probability and variables (see Fig. 3). In the example shown here, the student has created a script that illustrates an "if-then" statement. The student set up a situation so that if a particular color present in the drawing of the fish sees a particular color present in the drawing of the jelly fish, the "alive" fish hides and the skeleton of the fish rises above the jelly fish (bottom panel).

Squeak-based materials could be sustainable even given the constraints that are currently present around the usability and scalability. However,

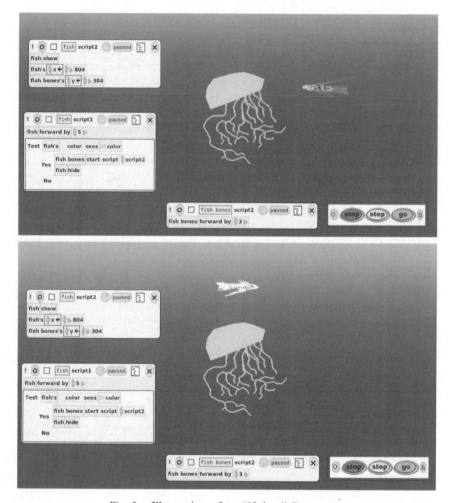

Fig. 3.   Illustration of an "if-then" Statement.

teachers are concerned with meeting standards and the external expectations of the school communities (parents, legislatures, etc.) and it remains to be seen whether tools that have clear educational benefit within themselves, as seen from the cases of our workshops and classroom activities, are recognized as beneficial for meeting external education standards. If teaching students how to reason, program and problem solve improves content learning and understanding, then using this tool is justified.

REFERENCES

American Association for the Advancement of Science (AAAS). (1989). *Science for all Americans.* New York: Oxford University Press.

American Association for the Advancement of Science (AAAS). (1993). *Benchmarks for science literacy.* New York: Oxford University Press.

Anderson, R. D., & Helms, J. V. (2001). The ideal of standards and the reality of schools: Needed research. *Journal of Research in Science Teaching, 38*(1), 3–16.

Bereiter, C., & Scardamalia, M. (1992). Cognition and curriculum. In: P. Jackson (Ed.), *Handbook of research on curriculum* (pp. 517–542). New York: MacMillan.

Blumenfeld, P., Fishman, B., Krajcik, J., Marx, R., & Soloway, E. (2000). Creating usable innovations in systemic reform: Scaling up technology-embedded project-based science in urban schools. *Educational Psychologist, 35*(3), 149–164.

Borko, H. (2004). Professional development and teacher learning: Mapping the terrain. *Educational Researcher, 33*(8), 3–15.

Brown, A. (1992). Design experiments: Theoretical and methodological challenges in creating complex interventions in classroom settings. *Journal of the Learning Sciences, 2*(2), 141–178.

Crockett, M. (2002). Inquiry as professional development: Creating dilemmas through teachers' work. *Teaching and Teacher Education, 18,* 609–624.

Cuban, L. (1986). *Teachers and machines: The classroom use of technology since 1920.* New York, NY: Teachers College Press.

Cuban, L. (1993). Computers meet classroom: Classroom wins. *Teachers College Record, 95*(2), 185–210.

Cuban, L. (2001). *Oversold and underused computers in the classroom.* Cambridge: Harvard University Press.

Davis, E. A., & Krajcik, J. (2005). Designing educative curriculum materials to promote teacher learning. *Educational Researcher, 34*(3), 3–14.

Department of Education. (2001). *Overview of Technology and Education Reform.* Report available on-line at http://www.ed.gov/pubs/EdReformStudies/EdTech/overview.html

Edelson, D. C. (2002). Design research: What we learn when we engage in design. *The Journal of the Learning Sciences, 11*(1), 105–121.

Edelson, D. C., Gordin, D. N., & Pea, R. D. (1999). Addressing the challenges of inquiry-based learning through technology and curriculum design. *The Journal of the Learning Sciences, 8,* 391–450.

Fishman, B., Marx, R., Best, S., & Tal, R. (2003). Linking teacher and student learning to improve professional development in systemic reform. *Teaching and Teacher Education, 19*(6), 643–658.

Fishman, B., Marx, R., Blumenfeld, P., Krajcik, J. S., & Soloway, E. (2004). Creating a framework for research on systemic technology innovations. *Journal of the Learning Sciences, 13*(1), 43–76.

Honey, M., McMillan, K., & Carrig, F. (1999). Perspectives on technology and education research: Lessons from the past and present. Paper presented at the The Secretary's Conference on Educational Technology – 1999.

Keys, C. W., & Bryan, L. A. (2001). Co-constructing inquiry-based science with teachers: Essential research for lasting reform. *Journal of Research in Science Teaching, 38*(6), 631–645.

Krajcik, J., Blumenfeld, P., Marx, R., & Soloway, E. (2000). Instructional, curricular, and technological supports for inquiry in science classrooms. In: J. Minstrell & E. v. Zee (Eds), *Inquiring into inquiry learning and teaching in science* (pp. 283–315). Washington, DC: AAAS.

Linn, M. C. (1998). The impact of technology on science instruction: Historical trends and current opportunities. In: B. J. Fraser & K. G. Tobin (Eds), *International handbook of science education* (pp. 265–294). Dordrecht, The Netherlands: Kluwer.

Loucks-Horsley, S., Love, N., Stiles, K. E., Mundry, S., & Hewson, P. W. (2003). *Designing professional development for teachers of science and mathematics* (2nd ed.). Thousand Oaks, CA: Corwin Press.

Lynch, S. (2000). *Equity and science education reform*. Mahwah, NJ: Lawrence Erlbaum Associates, Inc.

Manoucherhri, A. (1999). Computers and school mathematics reform: Implications for mathematics teacher education. *Journal of Computers in Mathematics & Science Teaching, 18*(1), 31–48.

Marx, R. W., Blumenfeld, P. C., Krajcik, J. S., Fishman, B., Soloway, E., Geier, R., & Tal, R. T. (2004). Inquiry-based science in the middle grades: Assessment of learning in urban systemic reform. *Journal of Research in Science Teaching, 41*(10), 1063–1080.

Mathews, J. (1998). Study links lower grades to computer use. *Washington Post*, September 30, p. A3.

National Council of Teachers of Mathematics (NCTM). (2000). *Principles and standards for school mathematics*. Reston, VA: National Council of Teachers of Mathematics.

National Research Council (NRC). (1996). *National science education standards*. Washington, DC: National Academy Press.

Noble, D. D. (1998). The regime of technology in education. In: L. E. Beye & M. W. Apple (Eds), *The curriculum: Problems, politics, and possibilities* (pp. 267–283). Albany, NY: State University of New York Press.

Oppenheimer, T. (1997). The computer delusion. *The Atlantic Monthly*, July, pp. 45–61.

Papert, S. (1980). *Mindstorms*. New York, NY: Basic Books.

Papert, S. (1993). *Obselete skill set: The 3 Rs. Literacy and letteracy in the media ages. Wired, 1*. Available at http://www.papert.org/articles/ObsoleteSkillSet.html

Papert, S. (2002). Squeakers – Chapter 16. In: J. Shasky & B. MacBird (Eds), *Squeakers (DVD)*. Muncie, IN: Ball State University.

Reese, G. C., Dick, J., Dildine, J. P., Smith, K., Storaasli, M., Travers, K. J., Wotal, S., & Zygas, D. (2005). Engaging students in authentic mathematics activities through calculators and small robots. *Technology-supported mathematics learning environments: Sixty-seventh yearbook* (pp. 319–328). Reston, VA: National Council of Teachers of Mathematics.

Rivet, A. E., & Krajcik, J. S. (2004). Achieving standards in urban systemic reform: An example of a sixth grade project-based science curriculum. *Journal of Research in Science Teaching, 41*(7), 669–692.

Schneider, R. M., Krajci, J. S., & Blumenfeld, P. (2005). Enacting reform-based science materials: The range of teacher enactments in reform classrooms. *Journal of Research in Science Teaching, 42*(3), 283–312.

Schneider, R. M., Krajcik, J., Marx, R. W., & Soloway, E. (2002). Performance of students in project-based science classrooms on a national measure of science achievement. *Journal of Research in Science Teaching, 39*, 410–422.

Songer, N. B., Lee, H.-S., & Kam, R. (2002). Technology-rich inquiry science in urban class-rooms: What are the barriers to inquiry pedagogy. *Journal of Research in Science Teaching, 39*(2), 128–150.

Spillane, J. P., Diamond, J. B., Walker, L. J., Halverson, R., & Jita, L. (2001). Urban school leadership for elementary science instruction: Identifying and activating resources in an undervalued school subject. *Journal of Research in Science Teaching, 38*(8), 918–940.

Spillane, J. P., & Zeuli, J. S. (1999). Reform and teaching: Exploring patterns of practice in the context of national an state mathematics reforms. *Educational Evaluation & Policy Analysis, 21*(1), 1–27.

Steen, L. A. (2001). Quantitative Literacy. *Education Week on the Web, 21*(1), 58.

Tapscott, D. (1998). *Growing up digital: The rise of the net generation.* New York, NY: McGraw-Hill.

U.S. Department of Education, Office of Educational Research and Improvement, & National Center for Educational Statistics. (2001). *The nation's report card: Mathematics 2000* (NCES 2001-517 by J.S. Braswell, A.D. Lutkus, W.S. Grigg, S.L. Santapau, B. Tay-Lim, and M. Johnson). Washington, DC

Weglinsky, H. (1998). *Does it compute? The relationship between educational technology and student achievement in mathematics.* Princeton, NJ: Educational Testing Services. Available at http://www.ets.org/research/researcher/pictechnolog.htm

White, B., & Frederiksen, J. R. (2000). Metacognitive facilitation: An approach to making scientific inquiry accessible to all. In: J. Minstrill & E. H. van Zee (Eds), *Inquiring into inquiry learning and teaching in science* (pp. 331–370). Washington, DC: AAAS.

Zhao, Y., Pugh, K., Sheldon, S., & Byers, J. L. (2002). Conditions for classroom technology innovations. *Teachers College Record, 104*(3), 482–515.

Zhao, Y., & Frank, K. A. (2003). Factors affecting technology uses in schools: An ecological perspective. *American Educational Research Journal, 40*(4), 807–840.

COLLABORATIVE LEARNING ENVIRONMENTS: DEVELOPING SMART CLASSROOMS IN THEORY AND IN PRACTICE

Bryan Carter and Tim Linder

ABSTRACT

This chapter will outline the theory behind collaborative learning environments and describe several projects that best exemplify these theories and how best to incorporate them into the learning styles of the Net Generation's way of learning. Through partnerships with the St. Louis science center and the Children's Museum of Manhattan, visuality and interactivity have been incorporated into displays that demonstrate how these sorts of projects encourage students to collaborate in different ways as well as how teachers can introduce material in a variety of multidisciplinary formats.

This chapter will outline both the learning theory behind collaborative learning environments as well as describe several projects that have been done with the St. Louis science center and the Children's Museum of Manhattan, which demonstrate how these sorts of projects encourage students to collaborate in different ways as well as how teachers can introduce material in a variety of innovative formats.

Technology and Education: Issues in Administration, Policy, and Applications in K12 Schools
Advances in Educational Administration, Volume 8, 201–211
Copyright © 2006 by Elsevier Ltd.
ISSN: 1479-3660/doi:10.1016/S1479-3660(05)08014-5

Its not uncommon for students who are a part of the "Net Generation" to multitask on a regular basis and actually do it quite effectively. As the Millennials move through elementary and secondary school and on into their post-secondary tenure, more educators are beginning to realize that the new crop of students are often prepared quite differently than previous generations. Although many have defined the "Millennials," few have provided the practicalities or the impact this generation will have on today's educational process. As students become teachers and as teachers become students it is important to find a way to communicate through ways in which the Net Generation is familiar. By relating to the Net Generation's skills and learning strategies, a new form of teaching has emerged. This methodology is best exemplified in a collaborative learning environment, and through this form of teaching and learning, students often discover, explore, learn, and evaluate ways in which they are both familiar and proficient.

However, before one jumps into teaching within a collaborative learning environment it is necessary to first understand how the Net Generation has previously gained success in experiential learning. In an experiential learning environment, students are responsible for the knowledge they obtain during their experiences working with projects and assignments. Each student adapts to each project by working through the process together. This group environment, no matter the size, is a powerful brainstorming tool that helps each student become more flexible with ideas by opening their minds to other options before applying a collaboratively produced solution to a problem (Scardamalia & Bereiter, 1991, pp. 37–40). Furthermore, as students apply these skills and experiences to the outside world, they are often provided an increased opportunity to succeed. Being presented with multiple solutions to a problem, which they may not have considered outside of the group learning environment, often increases their critical thinking skills. This is a very different way of thinking and learning than previous generations.

It is important to illustrate one difference that distinguishes the Net Generation from other generations. The Net Generation, whose research methods are often shallow and impatient, tends to utilize the research tools of technology, especially the Internet, in a regurgitating manner. This generation tends to avoid exploring any project in-depth because the information is always readily available. As they progress toward higher education they often face many challenges presented by college and university professors who are either not aware of or sympathetic to the diverse learning styles of their generation (Oblinger & Oblinger, 2005 pp. 1–4). Generational trends have shown that the Net Generation differs from previous generations because they learn from an experiential learning cycle that is typically defined as "learning by doing." Furthermore, the technologies of today, especially computerized visualization, have inspired new modes of thinking and learning. Learning by designing computer models of the subject matter being studied, a common form of "visual thinking," is an increasingly wide-spread practice (Winn, 1993, p. 4). Because of the role images play in visual thinking and because visualization frequently depends upon story telling (or "story boards"), these new modes of learning often present opportunities for previously unimaginable collaboration between the arts and sciences. Advances in learning often require the unlearning of familiar but outdated ideas. Having been schooled in a variety of exacting disciplines, usually divided into sciences and arts, scholars may be unaware of the ways in which these segregated disciplines present barriers for advances in learning.

With this in mind, the Net Generation's educational process needs to evolve to incorporate technologically based collaborative learning environments to be successful. This is where instructors need to find a way to effectively communicate with students. While the experiential learning cycle is beneficial for learning utilization skills; however, it should be noted that the experiential learning cycle may not be beneficial for cognitive skills.

Digital communication in the classroom, to some, may seem like a distraction or a needless methodology that caters to the whims of students who are familiar with forms of communication that are more commercial than academic. When designing a computer-mediated communication environment, whether it be a more visually "heavy" one or one which focuses more so on textual communication, there are several factors to consider. For instance, the visual, tactile, and auditory nature inherent within true virtual reality environments makes them extremely attractive to faculty who wish to expose their students to the context in which their disciplinary content was originated. These environments, however, are not always practical because of cost, resources, or lack of exposure to the potential impact they may have on students by faculty who are remotely interested. Thus, some of those interested in computer-mediated communication lean toward text-based environments like Blogs, chat rooms, or discussion forums. All are interesting and have positive and negative features. The reflexive nature of all computer-mediated communication designs runs similar to that which we experience in face-to-face communication. As the technology that supports such communication continues to progress, so will the nature and speed in which the reflexivity occurs.

From the instructor's standpoint, motivating students who have admittedly become lazy due to the influx of technology has become an issue. The majority of students in today's universities and colleges have confessed to plagiarizing information from the Internet believing that they "won't get caught." Furthermore, students today are able to freely access programs that are copyrighted without fear of prosecution. The Internet, as it stands today, does not have a way to defend copyright protected materials that have been uploaded for free downloading. Net Generation members trust the Internet, the materials they obtain, and the information they see without question.

There are two different types of environments that should be explored by institutions in order to most effectively reach those of the Net Generation. The Millennials are comfortable functioning within a collaborative environment, this is the norm. However, the control that the major universities exert over their servers often limits access, monitors actions, and tend to prevent collaborative networking in a manner most familiar to students using it. This is counter productive; however, as instructors adapt to meet the needs of their students there has emerged an increased use of remote, web-based collaborative programs that are shared within a classroom or a course in order to open up discussion and allow for the free flow of information. This relaxed environment encourages students to talk more among their peers and with their instructor in a manner they might not have done originally.

As instructors, born on the cusp of Generation X and the Net Generation, there have been several opportunities for us to experience and observe the digital divide that occurs in the student and teacher relationship. This relationship must be adaptive for progress to occur. Case in point, when a teacher becomes a student to open more avenues of communication and learn extra tips, "cheats," to updated software that have been mastered by the "student" in its original form. This is part of the definition of a collaborative learning environment that has been the norm for the Net Generation, even if it is not consciously realized. Collaborative learning helps those of us who are teachers to evolve along with the progresses that technology has made and will continue to make. However, collaborative learning is not limited to the utilization of programs and skills. It encourages students to interact more readily and easily with peers and instructors. Furthermore, it allows instructors to introduce material in a variety of formats to help bridge the "generational" digital divide.

The generational digital divide is the result of multiple external factors that include, but are not limited to:

Age – it has been proven that the earlier one starts with programs the more adaptive they are to become with other programs and skills.

Finance – many instructors are at the mercy of their departments and of their universities. Thus, instructors tend not to have the most reliable technology and information to communicate with students.
Access – students are faced with the dilemma of not having the resources or access to compete with the ever-evolving technology industry.
Training – educators are having trouble finding access to training to utilize technology in the classroom.

With the Net Generation being dependent on technology it is imperative to relate with them in as many ways possible, using the most innovative techniques available, and as a student put it "technology should be used in the classroom because it is a part of our culture. We will be forced to use it in our jobs and in the future, so we might as well incorporate and learn it now" (B. Carter, personal communication, April 3, 2005). With this realization staring everyone in the face, incorporating technology into education is a necessary task that should engage the instructor as well as the student. We are all products of our environment, and technology has become our world. This notion is easily exemplified through a questionnaire given to students in the Spring of 2005.

The survey queried 70 students in an American literature class at Central Missouri State University to assess the relationship between technology, students, and instructors. Their responses suggest that they are not only very comfortable with technology but expect their teachers to use it.

85.7% students find themselves fascinated with new technologies.
90.5% students feel that they learn best by doing.
90.5% of students prefer experiencing to reflecting.
95.2% of the students are more comfortable composing documents online rather than longhand.
100% of the students disagree with the following statement "Technology use in the classroom is a barrier to my learning."

The larger question really is: what is the nature of academic communication and in what environment must that communication take place in order to be "acceptable" in the eyes of more traditional scholars. There is no question that there is an ongoing educational revolution between traditionalists and those on the bleeding edge as instructional technology becomes increasingly sophisticated. For example, how subjects are being studied is researched in multidisciplinary ways (combining researchers from many disciplines on projects that create special vocabularies and techniques specific to the project and accessed in smart spaces and networks). This is increasingly becoming a collaborative endeavor between students and faculty modeled or performed to incorporate a variety of sensory input and addressing a multitude of learning styles.

Smart classrooms are one of the more interesting recent developments. This includes networking educational facilities with other similar classrooms as well as scientific organizations and museums. When curricula is incorporated that can either be modified or that can modify itself based on pre-programmed sets of information the end result is having smart curricula that can be distributed in a number of ways:

Wireless access to a course management system
Videoconferences on a variety of channels
Virtual 3D experiences of the subject matter being modeled
PDAs supplementing the virtual experiences or E-tablets
Holography in the virtual experiences
Data mining
Shared virtual spaces.

There are a plethora of projects currently in development that address many of the ideas above. The Virtual Harlem Project is one that not only is very advanced, but also well ahead of its time when first developed in 1997.

The Virtual Harlem Project allows students not only to visualize a historical context of the Harlem Renaissance, which is the setting of several fictional texts, but it also enables them to navigate through streets, to interact with historical characters (through questions and audio cues), and to participate in its design. When students "build" the setting for their readings, their enthusiasm for research tends to increase.

To date, approximately ten square blocks of Harlem, NY have been reconstructed in a virtual reality-learning environment. This environment gives students an unprecedented view of the cultural wealth and history of one of the most productive periods in African-American culture – the Harlem Renaissance, circa 1921–1930. Currently, research materials contributed by students help to refine and expand upon this base. Students not only do interdisciplinary research on the time period but also see its results in Virtual Harlem, providing new dimensions to their understanding of the Harlem Renaissance. Learning of this sort is only possible in a virtual environment because the goal of Virtual Harlem is to simulate the real-world situations and settings that no longer exist in the forms they had during the 1920s and 1930s. Historic figures are no longer living, buildings have been torn down, moved, or have decayed to the extent that they are no longer recognizable, and the style of dress and use of language has changed over the years. It is anticipated that by placing users in the context in which a work of art or literature was created that their research will be more comprehensive. The Virtual Harlem environment is not, at this point, an exact replica of the Harlem landscape. There are several representations of cultural landmarks like the Savoy Ballroom, the Apollo Theater, The Theresa Hotel and others that have been recreated based on black and white photographs. The immediate area surrounding these landmarks is accurate. There are plans underway to revise the current environment to reflect a more historically accurate rendition of Harlem of the 1920s and 1930s. This redevelopment will include higher resolution images and textures, more realistic figures, higher quality audio, and the incorporation of video and animated figures.

There are many similarities in developing engaging and educational digital media applications for the classroom as compared to interactive museum galleries. Often the same techniques, imagery, and content can be used. However, there are several differences which can make the development of an interactive museum even more challenging. An interactive kiosk called Harlem Renaissance 2001 (HR2K1) was developed as an offshoot Virtual Harlem. This kiosk was created for the Children's Museum of Manhattan in New York, NY (http://www.cmom.org/). Users experience a similar version of Virtual Harlem except with a few distinct differences; HR2K1 was developed for children ages 12 and under. Users navigate a limited version of the experience given in Virtual Harlem by traveling back in time where the visitor meets young children from 1930s who are guides that help the visitor explore the space. The goal of those playing is to navigate the streets of Harlem until their character reaches the Apollo Theater. Once at the Apollo, the user interacts with members of a band that is performing on the stage and can create jazz style music with them, reminiscent of that which was popular during the early 1930s.

While much of the same content was transferred from Virtual Harlem to HR2K1, several changes were needed because of the differences between classroom and museum. One of the hardest challenges to overcome is being able to deliver content that is engaging and educational to a broad range of ages and backgrounds. The Children's Museum of Manhattan is geared toward children from ages 1 to 12, which is an even more focused age range than most other educational museums. The first step in developing an interactive is to choose an age range so the experience can be geared toward the user's level of understanding. Language barriers can also be overcome in the same manner. This can be done with Radio Frequency ID cards, which are an advanced way of gearing exhibits to individual users where each person that enters the museum, specially designed speakers were installed which directed sound to an area only around the user.

A third obstacle is limited time for user experience. Typical length of experience for an interactive kiosk in a museum is usually no longer than five minutes. Interactives need to be very efficient in the way they educate the users, and its interface needs to be very intuitive so it is not a hindrance. Interactives also need to be short so waiting does not occur if the exhibit becomes very popular. Flow is an important aspect of interactive museums.

The last challenge is making sure the application is easily used and understood without the aide of direction or instruction from a teacher or parent. Not only do these interactives need to be easily used, effective educationally, and entertaining to the target group of children, but they should also reach other users outside the target. Parents, teens, and seniors also enter these museums to aide children with exploration of exhibits, but at the same time observe the interactive. With careful planning, the interactive will provide entertainment and education to them as well. This challenge is often overcome by utilizing the dynamic nature of digital media. The exhibit has been modified so that the user can control the experience. For instance, in HR2K1 instructions were imbedded as part of the interactive to prevent confusion and frustration for the child but presented in a way that any adult can also easily grasp.

Often there is a "disconnect" between the way students use their computer at home or in a public setting and the way it is utilized in classroom education. Prensky calls the cultural division between those who grew up with technology as "digital natives" and those who did not as "digital immigrants" (Prensky, 2001, p. 1). One way to bridge this gap is to merge video games and educational content through digital media. This type of "edutainment" pulls similar principles from video game design and mixes it with educational content. A hybrid teaching tool like this can easily be created in response to the growing need for an environment suitable for adapting the growing use of technology within a dynamic, multidisciplinary society. A good example of this idea is the Virtual Reality Biology Lab for high school biology students, which was created to merge technology and instruction together.

The VR Bio Lab offers an interactive simulation of real laboratory processes to help instruct students in the process of photosynthesis in plants. The application is graphically designed to resemble a space station and shares a similar look and feel to modern video games. It begins with a movie that shows the inner structure of a plant leaf to view a model of the molecular structure of a plant's photosynthesis mechanism. After the movie the user makes his way to the lab and conducts an experiment. After preparing a sample of leaf spinach by washing it and chopping it in a blender, the students centrifuge the sample to separate the liquid from the solid matter. The tests can then be performed in a dark room to find the CO_2 content by observing the sample under different colors and intensities of light. Students gain a better understanding of the working of photosynthesis through this entertaining and dynamic application in a game-type setting that provides numerous rewards for students as they learn.

Video games offer a challenge and reward in much different ways than movies or books, which appeals to students who experience the VR Bio Lab. When playing a video game a person expects to "do," not to "watch." They expect a fair chance at completing a task in the game, but they also understand the realities that it will take trial and error to progress through the environment. Most users do not want to repeat processes too many times, but this failure and repetition until completion can give a sense of achievement.

Video games are similar to education in that lessons can often be taught through defeat. They often give players the ability to fantasize, become someone else, and be taken to another place and time. The VR Bio Lab was created to look like a space station for this reason. As a student completes the challenges and tasks within the lab they forget about the process and have fun learning the material. These techniques are used to create an emotional experience for the user similar to many other forms of entertainment, such as movies that strive to engage the user to the point of his or her feeling part of the experience. Video gamers want to feel something when they interact with the game. They want to be immersed in the experience. Therefore, the interface needs to be as transparent as possible and should not shatter the user's suspension of disbelief.

Applications such as the VR Bio Lab can enrich education and maintain commitment to learning. Often the learning experience will continue long after completing the interactive through discussions and comparing strategies with classmates. Another benefit to edutainment is that every student is usually assured participation. It can often be used in a home setting where a student may feel more comfortable and less likely embarrassed by making mistakes. While playing/learning in a personal setting the gap between using technology for education and entertainment can be reduced even more. Furthermore, applications can be updated as technology and science progress together.

Interactives can also be designed to reinforce the usefulness of collaboration through computers for educational purposes and not just as a conversation tool. One example is Cyberville. In this exhibit, located in the

St. Louis Science Center, players are invited to build a structure in Cyberville, a virtual community situated within the museum. Players work together by assuming the roles of an architect, shipper, and builder. They communicate with each other through computer stations themed for each job. Each role has specific tasks that are given as entertaining interactives, scenarios, and puzzles. A large screen surrounded by the three stations shows the complete cyberworld and displays the e-message network between the players. After everyone offers their input, they see the structure come to life on the big screen, vividly demonstrating the importance of communication using computer networks and dependence on others to accomplish a common goal.

There are several assumptions behind the incorporation of game engine and interactive technology into education. One is that some learners will come to the classroom already familiar with game play and navigation (cognitive mapping skills) and therefore be less intimidated by the interface. By lowering the level of initial intimidation of navigation alone, we anticipate that learners will concentrate more on content retrieval and interaction than lumbering through an environment with little or no control (Alexander, Kulikowich, & Jetton, 1994, pp. 235–238). Second, we recognize that Net Generation learners see the use of technology as a means to an end and although they may not be as familiar with the inner workings of the technology they use, they have mastered "how" to use it to get what they want. Third, context is everything to this generation of learners. They tend to assign importance to meaning and relevance. If it means nothing to them and see it as not relevant to their lives and what they want, then the learning sometimes has little relevance (Bransford, & Johnson, 1973, p. 390). Here is where context plays an important role. Through contextualization, students are thrust into a setting where the character they assume must pay attention to details in the "lesson" in order to survive. The character must also communicate and collaborate with other users within the environment and with the environment itself in order to be successful. Through this willful suspension of disbelief, the simulation takes on an entirely new "meaning" to the learner.

Educators who embark down this path are forging a new path for instructional delivery, one which may change the face of teaching as we know it. Technology is here to stay and although there will always be those who gravitate toward more "traditional" modes of instruction, the real question is, "are they teaching that way for themselves or for the sake of the students?" Teaching has always been a profession that requires us to modify our methodologies based on the changing times and the ever-changing nature of our students. How far individuals are "willing" to change cannot be directed, but how far we must change collectively is something that we cannot escape. Through the use of new modes of instruction, interactive media, and by harnessing the imagination of Net Generation learners, educators today have one of the most provocative opportunities in history to radically change the way teaching and learning occur in both the traditional classroom and from within virtual environments.

REFERENCES

Alexander, P. A., Kulikowich, J. M., & Jetton, T. L. (1994). The role of subject-matter knowledge and interest in the processing of linear and non-linear texts. *Review of Educational Research, 64*, 210–252.

Bransford, J. D., & Johnson, M. K. (1973). Consideration of some problems of comprehension. In: W. Chase (Ed.), *Visual information processing* (pp. 383–438). New York: Academic Press.

Oblinger, D., & Oblinger, J. (Eds). (2005). Educating the net generation. Educause.

Prensky, M. (2001, October). Digital natives, digital immigrants. Retrieved June 1, 2005, from http://www.marcprensky.com/writing/Prensky%20-%20Digital%20Natives,%20Digital%20Immigrants%20-%20Part1.pdf

Scardamalia, M., & Bereiter, C. (1991). Higher levels of agency for children in knowledge building: A challenge for the design of new knowledge media. *The Journal of the Learning Sciences, 1*, 37–68.

Winn, W. (1993, August). A conceptual basis for educational application of virtual reality. Human. Retrieved June 1, 2005, from http://www.hitl.washington.edu/publications/r-93-9/

CAN WE TALK? COMMUNICATION TECHNOLOGIES, SOCIAL INFORMATICS, AND SYSTEMIC CHANGE

Barbara Monroe

ABSTRACT

Asynchronous communication technologies (ACT), such as email, list-servs, and online discussions, have been slow to catch on in K-12 classrooms. Not coincidentally, these are potentially the most transformative of all technologies and the ones most difficult to integrate into a traditional classroom. Teacher training, technical support, and access do not really explain this glaring exclusion. The theoretical standpoint of social informatics– or the ecology of technology and social systems– gives us a productive way of understanding technology's impact– or lack thereof – in school settings. More specifically, the individual/organizational, institutional, national, and societal contexts impede or propel technological integration in any given setting. In light of these contexts, one teacher's successful integration practices are examined. While teachers can effect change in their own classrooms, only administrators can truly effect systemic change, ironically working from the grass-roots up, as one district success story illustrates.

Technology and Education: Issues in Administration, Policy, and Applications in K12 Schools
Advances in Educational Administration, Volume 8, 213–229
ISSN: 1479-3660/doi:10.1016/S1479-3660(05)08015-7

In 1995, one in seven Americans was online; in 2005, two of every three Americans were online (Almasy, 2005). Clearly, the Internet has transformed the way we live, work, play, date, bank, auction, shop, file, and communicate. It has also transformed the way we learn, as distance learning opportunities increase to include everything from job training to college degrees.

Why then has not technology substantively changed the way we teach in physical K-12 schools? In his introduction to the Visions 2020 Report, Secretary of Education Dr. Rod Paige noted,

> Indeed, education is the only business still debating the usefulness of technology. Schools remain unchanged for the most part despite numerous reforms and increased investments in computers and networks. The way we organize schools and provide instruction is essentially the same as it was when our Founding Fathers went to school. Put another way, we still educate our students based on an agricultural timetable, in an industrial setting, but tell students they live in a digital age.
>
> (U.S. Department of Education (DOE), 2005b, The Plan section, para. 3)

Even though all schools, at least theoretically, have access to the Internet, "it is business as usual" (DOE, 2005c, Tear Down Those Walls subsection, para. 2) inside classrooms. The technologies that have found a home there – word-processing, web-publishing and – researching, and presentational applications (such as PowerPoint and video) – have been embraced precisely because they support traditional practices.

Meanwhile, the potentially most transformative technologies – namely, asynchronous communication technologies (ACT), including email, listservs, and online discussions– go underutilized (Becker, Ravitz, & Wong, 1999; Becker & Riel, 2000; Cuban, 2001). Synchronous communication technologies, such as chat and videoconferencing, are difficult to schedule and therefore hard to incorporate in daily plans. ACT are not. Why then do so few teachers use ACT in an integral way? And how do so many K-12 administrators, perhaps unwittingly, perpetuate this status quo?

Usually named and blamed are inadequate teacher training, access, technical infrastructure. But even as teacher preparation programs are requiring education technology courses and even as most districts are focusing more on improving the technical infrastructure, teachers are still disinclined to integrate ACT into their classroom practices. In order to address the complexity of ACT use specifically, as well as the issue of technology integration in K-12 education more generally, I will first examine one teacher's pedagogy that effectively integrates ACT and then apply that example to an ecological view of technology innovation and implementation. My analysis aims to advocate, ultimately, for the role of individual agency – teachers as well as administrators – in effecting systemic change.

ACT IN THE CLASSROOM

Ryan Bretag,[1] an English teacher at Hinckley-Big Rock High School in Illinois, a rural community outside Chicago, routinely conducts online discussions with his two American literature classes and two Women's Studies classes for the four years that he has been teaching. He also invites other schools, parents, and family members to participate. The discussions are integral to a larger assignment as well as integrated into offline class discussion. For example, for a unit on modernist short stories – an assignment actually designed by teacher Paul Turtola at Foran High School in Connecticut, whose students joined Bretag's online – students from the two schools were to read six short stories from a provided list, discuss them online in self-started topics, consult secondary sources, and then write essays on modernist elements in hypertext. Because almost of his students are white and middle-class, Bretag has sought out diverse partners with different views, hosting wired discussions on Shakespeare with overseas schools and on *The Adventures of Huckleberry Finn* with two other schools, one a racially diverse school in Boston.

Bretag uses a free, open-source online discussion board, hosted by his own Internet Service Provider (ISP) on his own website. The e-board has a full range of capabilities: instant messenger, private message, polling (i.e., an automatic tallying system that allows users to vote on questions like "How many of you thought *Catcher in the Rye* was funny?"), and personal email notification when replies are posted in a thread. Students post both in class, at study hall, and at home. Online discussion is used to complement other discussion formats: Socratic seminars, small-groups, whole-class. Typically, students will post in-class for, say, 30 minutes, and then break into small groups and discuss in person for the remainder of the period, the table discussions based on the most popular threads that emerged online. Students are free to move from table to table as they wish. These online discussions also spill over beyond the class period, as students post from home, not just during the school year, but also during the upcoming summer, as wired discussions will be used for the first time to support the summer reading program (R. Bretag, personal communication, June 21, 2005).

BENEFITS OF ACT

This built-in connection between online and oral discussion, according to Bretag, is key to maximizing the benefits of the wired format. Historically teachers have been slow to adopt new technologies when a cost/benefit analysis does not show clear value-added – that is, when the cost in time and effort, not just money, is simply not worth the benefit (Cuban, 1993). What then are the benefits of ACT?

Again, according to Bretag, online discussions provide invaluable re-hearsal time, especially for shy students or students simply less adept at oral communication. They find their voices and built their confidence. Unlike oral discussions, no one student or group can dominate online, allowing all students floor-time. More important, they learn to engage in dialogic, dy-namic inquiry, asking questions, venturing other viewpoints, offering clar-ification and supporting evidence, with the goal of deepening understanding rather than looking for the right answer. Their writing, oral communication, and critical thinking skills all improve (R. Bretag, personal communication, June 21, 2005). Paul Turtola, whose students joined Bretag's online for the Modernist Short Stories unit, found that talking online helped his students see multiple perspectives that an oral discussion could never have produced in such detail and gave them a chance to venture risky positions and brave negative and positive feedback. His students were "motivated to sound 'smart' in front of their peers, and they have even admitted ... that they [had] fun" (personal communication, June 21, 2005).

Simply put, Turtola's and Bretag's students are more engaged using ACT than they are without it. Engagement is no small matter when 40–60% of students are chronically disengaged in high school (McLaughlin, & Blank, 2004). On one level, students might be more engaged with ACT because these, along with instant- and text-messaging, are their own communication tools. As such, ACT provides a bridge between their in-school and out-of-school literacies. Using ACT also links the world of school with the world of work. It may be argued that when the novelty of using ACT wears off, students will be less engaged, even bored, once again. Even so, ACT will remain more relevant, and more prevalent, than paper-and-pen communi-cation in their futures – a point that even the most alienated student can not fail to see.

One step beyond engagement is critical engagement that is, connecting students from different walks of life – be they different tracks within the same school or different schools serving different demographics. This was Bretag's most immediate goal in seeking out online partners for his students, which he accomplished when two other schools joined his classes' Huck Finn discussion, one from a racially diverse Boston school. The results Bretag summed up in one word: "WOW" (personal communication, June 22, 2005). In an age when the level of public discourse has devolved into malicious, mud-slinging sound-bites and Presidential debates are limited to two-minute statements, ACT gives students a way to practice engaging in dialogue with others with dissimilar views, born of different subject positions in the world. Whether or not they arrive at consensus, they nonetheless can achieve a more nuanced understanding of the complexity of any issue – even when that issue is something as seemingly innocuous as, for example, whether or not *Catcher in the Rye* is funny, when diverse readers' responses might nonetheless expose gender, class, and age differences in humor preferences. Unlike oral discussions, all students have equal opportunity to "talk" online and therefore a chance to practice critical, civil, and civic engagement in a more thoughtful, deliberate manner, their words a matter of public record (Monroe, 2003).

In short, ACT holds the potential of transforming education by connecting students to others outside the classroom walls and collapsing the time frame of the class period, among other changes that ripple through the system and back again, as I will discuss in greater detail later in this chapter. These spatial and temporal extensions, enabled by individual and group asynchronous communication, were simply not possible in a sustained way before the Internet revolution.

SOCIAL INFORMATICS AND ACT

Given these benefits, why has ACT not caught on in most schools? To adequately answer that question, we need a better understanding of the interdependent roles – or what might be called the ecology– of technology and social systems. Simply put, technological and social contexts cannot be separated when analyzing a technology's impactthe premise that undergirds a relatively new field of Internet sociology called *social informatics.*

Rather than just looking at computers as tools and focusing on how they are used, social informatics also takes into account the organizational context that sustain computer services as well as the belief systems that animate that context, at all levels: individual/organizational, institutional, national, and societal. In other words, social informatics investigates how "technology-in-use and social worlds co-constitute themselves in highly intertwined fashion" (Warschauer, 2003, p. 206). For example, one study that evaluated the impact of computers on local governments in 500 cities found that hardware and facilities played only a minor role. Far more important were the organizational systems governing computer use, the overarching vision, funding sources and processes, and other struggles among an array of stakeholders, including vendors, employees, and citizens (Warschauer, 2003).

Social informatics stands in stark contrast to other theories of technology, most notably determinism and instrumentalism. Technological determinism maintains that technology holds an independent impact on social systems. Typical determinist projects might be to measure the impact of television on children or the impact of computers on learning. Whereas the determinism holds that technological impact is inherent and inevitable, instrumentalism sees it as largely indifferent – neither good nor bad, just neutral. Both approaches fail to capture the ecology of technology and social systems (Warschauer, 2003).

The case of the printing press neatly highlights how social informatics departs from other theories of technological impact. Because of the printing press, printed texts became affordable and widely available, laying the foundation for modern scholarship and private, unmediated learning. The publication boom of the 15th–17th centuries fueled the Protestant Reformation, challenging the authority of the Catholic Church. Moveable type also transformed the way information was presented, i.e., charts, footnotes, indexes. But moveable type in and of itself did not cause these changes; for it did not trigger a similar chain reactions of change in China, where it was first introduced 400 years earlier. Why then did it take hold in Europe? Other changes were afoot in early modern Europe, including the rise of capitalism, colonialism, humanism, and nationalism. Thus, the printing press did not come from outside and impact social systems. It "emerged from the inside and interacted with other elements of society in an ecological fashion" (Warschauer, 2003, p. 205). Put another way, social informatics might be seen as a kind of "soft" determinism. Whereas hard determinism holds that technology automatically causes change, soft determinism maintains that technology enables social change – sometimes, given the right time and place, under the right conditions (Warschauer, 2003).

Those conditions include the human factors, not only at the individual/ organizational level, but also at the institutional, national, and societal levels. Both individual agency and social structure are mediated by institutional life, which define and structure how people act and relate to one another. Further, individuals and institutions all exist within a society that supports unequal power relationships (Feenberg, 1991). In the educational context, clearly certain structures and relations need to change, if ACT is ever going to take hold. It is a commonplace in the field education that, for maximum effectiveness, technology has to be fully integrated, not just an "add-on." But given the current configuration of most classrooms and institutions, ACT cannot help but be an add-on.

SOCIAL INFORMATICS IN ACTION

If we look back at the example of Ryan Bretag's class discussed earlier, we can see that certain factors at all levels – individual/organizational, institutional, national, and societal – work together to enable successful integration of ACT. And even though certain factors also work against him, Bretag has managed to overcome these obstacles. That he is able to do so is testimony to individual agency to effect change in one's own classroom.

Individual/Organizational Level

Four features of Bretag's pedagogy stand out as significant to fully integrating ACT: non-traditional classroom management style; constructivist pedagogy; project-based curriculum design; and democratized power relations. A more in-depth look at of each of these features follows.

Non-Traditional Classroom Management
The first significant feature of Bretag's methods is his classroom management style. Traditional classroom management needs to change if ACT is to be successfully integrated and have maximal impact. When most of the class time is used in oral whole-class discussion moderated by the teacher or when teachers believe that students need to be doing the same thing at the same time, ACT will not fit. Notice that Bretag uses a kind of hybrid-studio model to organize the class period. Students have their assignment – i.e., to read, discuss, and write about six modernist short stories from the list by a certain date – and they are allowed to proceed at their own pace and make their own choices in fulfilling that assignment. Departing somewhat from a pure studio model, however, Bretag does structure students' time to a certain degree, typically having them on computers for a portion of the period and then moving them to oral communication in small groups sitting at tables or stations, discussing key topics from the online discussion, with students free to circulate from table to table. Early studies of technology integration have found that elementary school classrooms are generally more successful than are high school classrooms, in large part because

elementary classrooms are more commonly organized around stations that
students can move to or from, as they work through their day (Becker &
Riel, 2000; Cuban, 2001).

Constructivist Pedagogy

A second significant feature that enables Bretag to integrate ACT effectively
is his constructivist pedagogy. Teachers generally tend to choose the technologies that support their pedagogy. And insofar as most teachers practice
traditional pedagogies, they are most likely to use word-processing, web
publication and research, or presentational technologies themselves and ask
students to use these too. All of these uses of technology support existing
educational practices of writing papers and presenting ideas. All that has
changed really is the medium, and in some cases, the audience: whereas
students typically write for their teacher, publishing their work on the web
potentially reaches readers beyond the classroom walls. Whereas these uses
may or may not be enlisted to support either teacher-centered or student-
centered pedagogies, ACT clearly supports constructivist pedagogies – and
only constructivist pedagogies.

   As we see from Bretag's classroom, he clearly works from the premise that
students are in charge of their own learning and their own knowledge making, working collectively. In a classroom where the teacher gives multiple
choice tests and where there are right and wrong answers, ACT simply does
not work. Anecdotal evidence provides a vivid counterexample taken from
another school. In that school, an English teacher always assigned students
the questions at the end of stories in their textbook. Daily, these written
answers were collected and checked or not, without oral discussion of the
stories at all. When a student asked one day if the class could post their
answers to an electronic discussion list, her teacher was totally confused. He
said students would cheat, simply copying what others had said. Insofar as
his assignment did have right and wrong answers, he was correct in assuming
that students would cheat. (In fact, cheating was rampant in this class already, students viewing the daily assignment as busy work to simply be
completed for a grade.) When an assignment, however, does not have a right
or wrong answer, only better or worse answers based on multiple perspectives, then students' diverse responses help built new knowledge.

Inquiry-/Project-Based Curriculum Design

As the above example illustrates, constructive pedagogy only works with
certain kinds of curriculum designspecifically, an inquiry-/project-based curriculum design, the third significant feature that enables ACT integration.

Bretag's modernist short stories unit is a project-based unit that asks students to arrive at their own conclusions about how modernism plays out in six stories of their choosing. The assignment is structured not only to allow but actually to require critical collaborations through the process of producing the project. Again, studies in effective technologies integration stress the importance of inquiry-based learning, where students investigate open-ended questions (Warschauer, 2003; Cuban, 2001).

Democratized Power Relations
The three features previously discussed – fluid classroom organization, constructivist pedagogy, and inquiry-/project-based curriculum – interdependently predicate and are predicated upon restructuring the traditional hierarchical relationship between teacher and students (Faigley, 1992). This is the fourth significant feature that enables successful ACT integration. In contrast, word-processing, web-publishing and -researching, and presentational technologies do not require change in the power structure of the classroom and thus are more easily integrated.

Bretag participates on the same level as his students in the online discussions– and his words apparently have no more weight than a student's or even a participating parent's. To be sure, he still holds the power of the grade, but even in that regard, students seem less motivated by grades than they are by wanting to learn, asking their own questions and offering support or refutation for others' viewpoints– a point that Bretag's students made in their online discussion on *Catcher in the Rye*. Generally speaking, horizontal networks are much more durable, flexible, and individually empowering than top-down, vertical networks. They are also almost impossible to contain and destroy (as we have sadly seen with terrorist networks). This fact is both the boon and bane of ACT: teachers are afraid of giving students this much power.

Institutional Level

Even when teachers like Bretag want to incorporate ACT in their classroom practice, they have to work within an institutional context that usually is not conducive to the individual/organizational changes discussed above. This is the second level, according to the social informatics model, that negatively or positively affects a technology's impact.

One common constraint at the institutional level is the time schedule. In schools where a class period runs under an hour, using computers is a time commitment that few teachers feel they can make. Although Bretag sees ACT valuable enough to take up half a period in online discussion, most teachers would not, especially in the age of No Child Left Behind (NCLB), a larger contextual concern adversely affecting experimental pedagogies (a point I will return to in the next section).

The issue of time is especially critical when school districts organize their computer resources in centralized labs, where teachers have to sign up to use computers on a limited number of usually nonconsecutive days. In the stated interest of fairness – insuring that everyone has access to the lab – such policies virtually insure that computers will be used on an irregular basis and for certain uses, such as Internet research. Further, valuable class time is lost when students have to leave their classrooms and walk to the lab or library. Computers may also be concentrated in libraries and media centers, where once again use is limited to searching local collections and the Internet. A school district's acceptable use policies, especially those that prohibit accessing personal email or instant messaging, can also restrict access and use in ways that can support the status quo. When computers are distributed within classrooms, however, teachers are much more likely and more much successful in integrating ACT in daily instruction, as we see in Bretag's case, with enough computers for each student in the instructional classroom. But even having 4-8 computers in the classroom can make the difference in how often and in what ways they will be used (Becker, Ravitz, & Wong, 1999; Becker & Riel, 2000; Cuban, 2001).

National Level

Besides individual/organizational and institutional levels in the social informatics model that greatly affects a technology's impact at any given time, a third level is the national level.

Of course, individual early adopter teachers can integrate ACT into their daily practice without institutional support. For example, Bretag's own personal ISP hosts the software he uses for his online discussions. Most teachers, however, do not have the time, energy, and sheer conviction that ACT is worth this extra unsupported effort, especially in light of the national context in the first decade of the 2000s. Despite evidence that successful technology integration can dramatically improve student engagement, teaching to the test is common practice in the era of NCLB legislation that mandates high-state testing. What gets tested, gets taught. Even when these tests require writing, they ask for – and evaluate in terms of – print literacy skills. For example, students might be asked to write a mock letter (rather than an email message) to the principal, requesting that specific improvements be made to the school grounds. Electronic skillsthe ones that dominate social and work worlds today and facilitate individual communication and group collaboration processes – go unrecognized. With the narrow focus on academic literacy, high-stake testing fails to take into account the multiple literacy sites in students' futures.

NCLBwith its obsession with quantifiable accountabilityworks to impede effective technology integration, even within the National Education Technology Plan (2005). The Plan's seven-step action plan calls for an improvement in teacher training, specifically stating the need to

- Improve the preparation of new teachers in the use of technology.
- Ensure that every teacher has the opportunity to take online learning courses.
- Improve the quality and consistency of teacher education through measurement, accountability and increased technology resources.
- Ensure that every teacher knows how to use data to personalize instruction. This is marked by the ability to interpret data to understand student progress and challenges, drive daily decisions and design instructional interventions to customize instruction for every student's unique needs. (DOE, 2005a, The Future is Now subsection).

Notice that the first bullet above vaguely states that new teachers need to learn how to use technology. Specific ways and whys are suggested in the other bullets, two stressing the importance of using data for accountability, including measuring effectiveness of teacher education programs themselves, and a third bullet pointing to the need for teachers to take online courses for ongoing professional development purposes. Like typical determinist projects, this approach assumes that technology impact is inevitable and measurable. What is lost is an understanding of how social systems and technology use are interdependent, changing both in the process. Without the perspective of social informatics, the plan's focus is shifted away from transforming education and shifted toward producing test scores and reports required by NCLB, thereby reproducing the status quo rather than transforming the future.

Societal Level

At the most systemic level of all, the societal level (to return to the social informatics model), NCLB also works in other subtle but insidious ways to exacerbate the educational divide in this country. In schools serving high-poverty communities, teachers are often mandated to prepare students for the test, having them "practice" sometimes for weeks on end, largely using direct-instruction methods, and focusing on information transmission rather than knowledge construction. Ironically, these are the very means and ends that increase these students' passivity and alienation at worst.

NCLB has effectively hijacked the computer revolution in low-income schools in other ways as well. Money that might otherwise go for ACT is being channeled for database technologies to meet the reporting requirements of NCLB and to identify strategies for raising test scores and meeting school improvement goals ("Electronic transfer," 2005). Further, computer resources in low-income schools in particular are increasingly reserved for stand-alone programs, such as Accelerated Reader, a computerized program of multiple-choice tests to check basic reading comprehension of select books, and Nova, a credit-retrieval program for students at risk for dropping out. In schools with limited resources, student access to computers is especially critical because home access is also limited. Notice that Bretag is able to sustain ACT as a regular feature of his pedagogy because his students have home access. For teachers in schools serving low-income communities, home access is not a viable option. Even though home access is increasing rapidly in these areas, other differences will affect students' home use – differences such as family size, childrearing practices, and location of computers in the home (i.e., in public family areas rather than private bedrooms) (Monroe, 2004). All of these factors, variously configured, ensure that it will be business as usual inside our poorest schools.

Further, teachers who do not use ACT say that they fear that students will post inappropriate messages or socialize or organize gang activity or cheat or otherwise wander off-task. These fears predominate in schools that serve low-income students or students of color (Becker, Ravitz, & Wong, 1999; Monroe, 2004; Warschauer, 1999, 2003). In classrooms where teachers see themselves as co-learners, as does Bretag, ACT does not evoke the same fears. Notably, Bretag's school serves white, middle-class students, so community as well as school attitudes toward student empowerment differ sharply from those in nonwhite, low-income schools, where obeying authority and being seen and not heard are major tenets of childrearing– and schooling (Lareau, 2003). Thus power relationships from the societal level-including cultural differences and racial and class prejudiceimpinge on and get reproduced at the individual/organizational level of the educational social system, self-stoking the status quo.

TEACHER PREPARATION REVISITED

The National Education Technology Plan states that the issue of how to use technology effectively to enhance learning is still an open question: "Teachers have more resources available through technology than ever before, but have not received sufficient training in the effective use of technology to enhance learning. Teachers need access to research, examples, and innovations as well as staff development to learn best practices" (DOE, 2005a, The Future is Now subsecton). Interestingly, of all the success stories linked to each of the seven steps in the action plan, none highlights students using ACT. In fact, the only use of ACT in any of these success stories is the so-called "e-solution" for professional development for teachers.

If "teachers need access to research, examples, and innovation," then Ryan Bretag offers one such example. How did he learn to use the kind of sophisticated online discussion board that he uses with his classes, both operationally and pedagogically? Not in his teacher preparation program, at least not directly. But he does credit that program with showing him some of the possibilities of ACT, when one of his professors required that pre-service teachers post responses in a personal blog to the reading each week. More importantly, Bretag says that his program always encouraged them to see themselves as teacher-researchers, not just teacher-followers. Together those influences propelled him to seek out ways to use ACT to enhance discussion – a personal project that he has pursued since entering the profession four years ago (personal communication, June 28, 2005).

More important than learning to simply operate specific applications, teacher preparation programs need to spend more time on the pedagogy – which is still being invented, awaiting the next generation, like Bretag, to walk point in discovering new ways to use networks in their teaching and class managing. For example, email might be used to send students feedback on work-in-progress – either individually or to small groups – and listservs might be used to post clarifications on assignments or reminders of due dates or post follow-ups to class discussions. These means do not simply replicate old methods, such as writing comments on student papers, for they are dialogic and co-lateral, rather than one-way, top-down communication, allowing and inviting students to respond or even initiate communication to the teacher or class or both. Like Bretag's own teacher preparation program, professors themselves have to model, if not specific practices, at least the gumption to experiment with their own pedagogies and class management styles. If teachers tend to teach the way themselves have been taught, then teacher educators need to show, not just tell, how to take risks and develop new pedagogies.

TEACHERS AND ADMINISTRATORS AS
CHANGE AGENTS

By his own account, Ryan Bretag is lucky, for he has unwavering support for his technology-infused classes all the way up, from his colleagues to this department, building, school, and district administration. He has led district in-services sessions on incorporating online discussions, and now several of his colleagues are implementing the practice K-12, although high school teachers, he notes, seem to have more trouble integrating technology because they tend to be more content-focused. He credits the district's leadership – specifically, the technology coordinator, the superintendent, and the Board of Education – with providing the vision and the practical support to sustain efforts to transform learning in his district (personal communication, August 14, 2005).

Although it is infinitely harder to integrate ACT without the kind of administrative support Bretag enjoys, teachers are still figuring out ways to sidestep some of the hurdles inherent in their respective individual/organizational, institutional, national, and societal contexts. They are finding free collaboration applications, getting hosting space from their personal ISPs, and paying for their own server space (as a recent query to a national listserv for English teachers revealed), rather than dealing with firewalls and limited storage space on school servers. They are seeking out online partnerships for their students, networking at professional conferences and on national listservs. Student access to Internetworked computers is still a significant hurdle, especially in rural, urban, and other low-income schools. Although a few teachers get grants for classroom equipment, a more viable and long-lasting direction is to serve on the district's technology planning team. Barring that possibility, teachers can also make use of the computers that a school does have, arguing for more open access policies that would allow student use of computers in any and all instructional areas of a building, before, during, and after school.

Yet, even though teachers can start the revolution in their own classrooms, they cannot effect systemic change alone. That job falls to K-12 administrators. The success story of Klein School District provides a vivid illustration of the role of administrative vision and policy in instituting change across a district, affecting all teachers, all classrooms, incrementally but at the same time. Rather than simply "greasing the squeaky wheel" of early adopting teachers who want and will use technology effectively, as is often the case, Klein administrators set out to address the equity issue among teachers and classrooms, but not with top-down mandates. Rather, they convened a broad-based team made up of teachers, parents, students, and principals that, in turn, developed the district tech plan with input from all stakeholders. That plan established that all classrooms across the district would have the same technology resources: four student computers; one teacher workstation that can also be used by students; one interactive white board; one LCD projector with a document camera; and one set of assessment tools (DOE, 2005d, Technology Baseline Standard Initiative subsection). Also important to this district's successful tech plan was administrators' support, district staff providing training and in-class support, and teachers collaborating on developing lessons. Interestingly, "[n]o organizational change was needed at the district or campus levels. The main change occurs in the classroom as the technology tools provide for an increase in targeted small group instruction and a decrease in large, whole-group, instruction" (DOE, 2005d, Technology Baseline Standard Initiative subsection).

Without the support of the institutional context, technology integration – and "the dramatic results in student engagement and teacher efficiency" (DOE, 2005d, Technology Baseline Standard Initiative subsection) – would not have had the same institutional impact, nor would have all teachers have adopted new practices. But it was the principals – whose leadership, support, and "expectations for changing teaching and learning strategies" – who were the most critical to both the initial and sustaining success of this plan (DOE, 2005d, Technology Baseline Standard Initiative subsection).

Klein's early success can already be anecdotally measured in terms of increased student engagement, more independent learning, "more higher order thinking with greater ease," and more "depth and complexity in learning" (DOE, 2005d, Technology Baseline Standard Initiative subsection). And it is this kind of success that may ultimately translate into the quantifiable terms – i.e., higher test scores and lower drop out rates – that even NCLB can value.

THE TIME IS RIPE

As discussed earlier, hard determinism holds that technology automatically causes change, while soft determinism maintains that technology enables social change – sometimes, given the right time and place, under the right conditions (Warschauer, 2003). Although email and listservs have been around for more than 10 years, schools were in no position to embrace these innovations back then.

But things have certainly changed since 1994, when the first web browser appeared. Then, schools were not online; now, they are. Although student access within schools is still problematic, as we have seen, home access and other access points in the community are increasing. In 1994, most Americans did not have experience accessing the Internet; now most students have grown up with computers, and children and adolescents are more likely to be tech-savvy than adults (DeBell, 2005). Even in low-income schools, home Internet use has surged: more than two-thirds of low-income households have access ("Study: 'Digital divide' shrinks,"among U.S. kinds, 2003). Classes dedicated to basic computer skills and keyboarding are now antiquated; they needlessly tie up computers and class time that could be used more productively.

In short, schools are now historically poised – whereas they were not earlier – to ride the next wave of technological innovation. That next wave is the recent surge in "social" software, i.e., blogs, wikis, drupal. These applications are social in that they allow for interactivity and collaboration between authors and readers. In the mid-1990s, schools did not have the infrastructure to provide email to students and teachers. Many still do not. But open source and free web-based resources now make it easier for individual teachers – like Ryan Bretag – to start the revolution themselves, grass-roots up. Even the U.S. Department of Education (DOE, 2005c) website proclaims, "Tear Down Those Walls. The Revolution is Underway."

NOTES

1. I would like to thank Ryan Bretag and Paul Turtola, the two teachers whose work and words I cite in this chapter, for allowing me to interview them via email and for sharing their insights with the profession. I am especially indebted to Ryan, whose classroom practice I weave throughout by way of illustrating how individuals can and do have agency to affect social change in their own corners of the world.

REFERENCES

Almasy, S. (2005). The Internet transforms modern life. *CNN.com.* (June 19). Retrieved June 20, 2005, from http://www.cnn.com/2005/TECH/internet/06/23/evolution.main/index.html

Becker, H. J., Ravitz, J. L., & Wong, Y. T. (1999). *Teacher and teacher-directed student use of computers and software.* Teaching, Learning, and Computing: 1998 national survey, report #3. Irvine, CA: Center for Research on Information Technology and Organizations (November).

Becker, H. J., & Riel, M. M. (2000). *Teacher professional engagement and constructivist-compatible computer use.* Teaching, Learning, and Computer: 1998 national survey, report #7. Irvine, CA: Center for Research on Information Technology and Organizations (December).

Cuban, L. (1993). *How teachers taught: Constancy and change in American classrooms 1890–1990* (2nd ed.). New York: Teachers College Press.

Cuban, L. (2001). *Oversold and underused: Computers in the classroom.* Cambridge, MA: Harvard University Press.

DeBell, M. (2005). Rates of computer and Internet use by children in nursery school and students in kindergarten through twelfth grade: 2003. *National Center of Education Statistics.* Retrieved June 30, 2005, from http://nces.ed.gov/pubsearch/pubsinfo.asp?pubid=2005111

Electronic transfer: Economic and policy forces are moving technology dollars in new directions. (2005). *Edweek.org.* (May 5). Retrieved June 30, 2005, from http://www.edweek.org/ew/articles/2005/05/05/35exec.h24.html

Faigley, L. (1992). *Fragments of rationality: Postmodernity and the subject of composition.* Pittsburgh, PA: University of Pennsylvania Press.

Feenberg, A. (1991). *Critical theory of technology.* New York: Oxford University Press.

Lareau, A. (2003). *Unequal childhoods: Class, race, and family life.* Berkeley, CA: University of California Press.

McLaughlin, M., & Blank, M. (2004). Creating a cutlure of attachment: A community-as-text approach to learning. *Edweek.org.* (November 10). Retrieved June 21, 2005, from http://www.edweek.org/ew/articles/2004/11/10/11mclaughlin.h24.html?querystring=culture%20attachment

Monroe, B. (2003). Let their fingers do the talking: Class discussion online. *Inland: A Journal for Teachers of English Language Arts, 25*(2), 11–12.

Monroe, B. (2004). *Crossing the digital divide: Race, writing, and technology in the classroom.* New York: Teachers College Press.

Study: Digital divide shrinks among US kinds. (2003). *CNN.com.* (March 20). Retrieved April 18, 2003, from http://www.cnn.com/2003/TECH/internet/03/20/digital.divide.reut/

U.S. Department of Education. (DOE). (2005a). A National Education Technology Plan: The Future is Now. In *The National Education Technology Plan.* Retrieved June 30, 2005, from http://www.nationaledtechplan.org/theplan/Recommendations.asp

U.S. Department of Education. (DOE). (2005b). The Plan. In *The National Education Technology Plan* (para. 3). Retrieved June 30, 2005, from http://www.nationaledtechplan.org/background.asp

U.S. Department of Education. (DOE). (2005c). Tear Down Those Walls. The Revolution is Underway. In *The National Education Technology Plan* (para. 2). Retrieved June 30, 2005, from http://www.nationaledtechplan.org/theplan/TearDownThoseWalls.asp

U.S. Department of Education. (DOE). (2005d). Technology Baseline Standards Initiative. In *The National Education Technology Plan.* Retrieved June 30, 2005, from http://www.nationaledtechplan.org/stories/spring.asp

Warschauer, M. (1999). *Electronic literacies: Language, culture, and power in online education.* Mahwah, NJ: Lawrence Erlbaum.

Warschauer, M. (2003). *Technology and social inclusion: Rethinking the digital divide.* Cambridge, MA: The MIT Press.

UBIQUITOUS COMPUTING: RETHINKING TEACHING, LEARNING, AND TECHNOLOGY INTEGRATION

Karen Swan, Dale Cook, Annette Kratcoski,
Yi Mei Lin, Jason Schenker and Mark van 't Hooft

ABSTRACT

Ubiquitous access to digital technologies is becoming an integral part of our business, home, and leisure environments, yet despite a quarter century of educational technology initiatives, ubiquitous computing remains conspicuously absent from our schools. In this chapter, we argue that simply putting more computers in schools will not solve the problem, but rather that teaching, learning, and technology integration need to be reconceptualized within a ubiquitous computing framework before the full educational possibilities inherent in digital technologies can be realized. Using examples from our laboratory classroom, we discuss how teaching needs to be reconceived more as "conducting" than "instructing"; how learning needs to become more the responsibility of the student, and located with her in an expanded space and time that extends beyond the classroom; and how technology integration needs to be understood not as an add-on, device-driven enterprise, but one motivated by teaching and

Technology and Education: Issues in Administration, Policy, and Applications in K12 Schools
Advances in Educational Administration, Volume 8, 231–252
ISSN: 1479-3660/doi:10.1016/S1479-3660(05)08016-9

learning needs and in which multiple technology choices are readily available to teachers and students both within and beyond the classroom.

Digital technologies are for education as iron and steel girders, reinforced concrete, plate glass, elevators, central heating and air conditioning were for architecture. Digital technologies set in abeyance significant, long lasting limits on educational activity.

McClintock, 1999

The most pressing strategic problem for the evolution of public education in the digital age is this: How to restructure a school computer culture that was shaped by conditions that no longer apply.

Papert, 2002

In *The Educators Manifesto* (1999), Robbie McClintock argues that the innovations in communications and digital technologies have the potential to dramatically change teaching and learning. He identifies three areas where technological innovations have already changed what is educationally possible.

The first of these is the Internet and broadband communications networks. McClintock maintains that these have the potential to change schools and classrooms from isolated places with relatively scarce access to information to ones with rich connections to the world and all its ideas. He argues that basic pedagogical approaches must accordingly change from ways of disbursing scarce knowledge to ways of enabling students "to use with purpose and effect their unlimited access to the resources of our cultures" (McClintock, p. 12).

The second area in which McClintock thinks digital innovations are changing what is educationally possible involves multimedia. Multimedia, he maintains, "make it increasingly evident that the work of thinking can take place through many forms – verbal, visual, auditory, kinetic, and blends of all and each." (McClintock, p. 13) Basic educational strategies, he argues, must accordingly be broadened to include intellectual recognition of skills in such areas, now too often relegated to the periphery of school curricula.

Thirdly, McClintock points to digital tools designed to "augment human intelligence" (Engelbart, 1963); tools ranging, for example, from digital calculators, word processors, databases, and spreadsheets to very complex modeling, statistical, and graphical software. He notes that these tools automate lower-level intellectual skills, allowing their users to concentrate on higher-level thinking, and argues that the basic curricular question "What knowledge is of most worth?" must accordingly be rethought.

McClintock maintains that his observations are not normative, but rather factual. Digital technologies change what is educationally possible. The key word here is "possible." Indeed, the digital revolution may have changed what is educationally possible, but actual teaching and learning have changed little since the last great media revolution, that of printing. In part, this is because of the way computing devices have been placed in schools and classrooms. Until access to computers is ubiquitous, until every student has access to appropriate digital technologies whenever and wherever he or she needs them, what is possible will remain mere potential. Seymour Papert, for example, asks us to consider what impact the technology of writing might have had on education if there were only three or four pencils in a classroom or students went to a "pencil room" once a week to use them (Kyle, 2000).

However, ubiquitous access to computing technologies is not enough to make what is possible a reality in schools and classrooms. In this chapter, we will argue that simply putting more computing devices in schools will not revolutionize teaching and learning, but rather that teaching and learning need to be reconceptualized within a ubiquitous computing framework for the educational possibilities inherent in digital technologies to be realized. Using examples from work in our laboratory classroom, we will discuss (1) how teaching needs to be reconceived more as "conducting" than "instructing"; (2) how learning needs to become more the responsibility of the student, and located with her in an expanded space and time that extends beyond the classroom; and (3) how technology integration needs to be understood not as an add-on, device-driven enterprise, but one motivated by teaching and learning needs and in which multiple technology choices are readily available to teachers and students both within and beyond the classroom.

BACKGROUND

The term "ubiquitous computing" was introduced by Mark Weiser of Xerox PARC who wrote, "The most profound technologies are those that disappear. They weave themselves into the fabric of everyday life until they are indistinguishable from it." Weiser envisioned ubiquitous computers as embedded in the environments we inhabit; others have seen them as devices we carry through those environments (Kay, 2005); while others still have maintained that what is most important about ubiquitous computing in schools is the provision of 1:1 computing (Papert, 1980, 2002; Silvernail & Lane, 2004).

In our work, we view ubiquitous computing as encompassing all three of these notions, as well as the importance of Internet connectivity. We view ubiquitous computing as involving learning environments in which all students have access to a variety of digital devices, including computers connected to the Internet and mobile computing devices, whenever and wherever they need them. Our concept of ubiquitous computing is centered on the notion of technologies which are always available but not themselves the focus of learning, and the idea that students and teachers can make informed choices about which technologies to use for particular tasks. We further view ubiquitous computing environments as not bound by the walls of the classroom, but rather both portable and at least partially virtual.

Nonetheless, our work at the Research Center for Educational Technology (RCET) is grounded in ongoing research taking place in a unique classroom located at Kent State University. Each year RCET brings eight local teachers and their classes to spend six weeks in Kent State's SBC Ameritech Classroom (SBCAC) working on thematic units drawn from their regular curricula and instructional schedule for the time they are visiting the SBCAC. Thus, most teachers adapt lessons and units they have been doing for several years to utilize the technological possibilities available therein.

The SBCAC is a ubiquitous computing classroom. It is currently equipped with enough desktop and wireless laptop computers to provide all students with access to up-to-date computing capacity and Internet access, enough handheld and mobile computing devices for all students to take with them beyond the classroom, distance learning capability via a variety of interactive video technologies, presentation systems, scanners, printers, digital cameras, video and audio recorders, three VCRs, video editing equipment, CD and DVD burners, digital microscopes and scientific probes, wireless Interwrite School Pads, Graphire pads, a Logo robot turtle, and a wide variety of software to support teaching and learning. The SBCAC classroom and its yearly program of extended residences for local classes thus gives teachers and students a chance to explore the educational possibilities afforded by ubiquitous access to digital computing.

The SBCAC is also a laboratory classroom. It is equipped with an observation room with one-way glass through which researchers can observe teachers and students as they study traditional curricula in an extraordinary environment. The classroom has four ceiling-mounted cameras and stationary microphones located at all desks and tables throughout the room, as well as wireless mobile microphones to capture teachers and other presenters (including student presentations). From any one of four stations in the observation room, researchers can use touch screen control panels to manipulate the cameras to record as many as four simultaneous digital videos at a time. In addition, digital cameras are available to document class activities both within and outside the classroom. All student work is collected in electronic portfolios. The SBCAC and its yearly program of extended residences thus gives RCET researchers a chance to study teaching and learning in a ubiquitous computing environment, in depth and across a variety of grade levels, subject areas, teachers, and students.

In the sections that follow, we will draw from our SBCAC experiences to discuss the issues involved in rethinking teaching and learning from a ubiquitous computing perspective. We conclude with some comments on rethinking technology integration in that light.

RETHINKING TEACHING

In *The Educators Manifesto* (1999), Robbie McClintock argues that the digital technologies available today have changed what is pedagogically possible in classrooms. To take advantage of these possibilities, teaching must be rethought; the role of the teacher must be reconceived within a ubiquitous computing context. Three related areas of rethinking seem particularly relevant. For the pedagogical possibilities inherent in ubiquitous computing to be fully realized, teaching must be reconceptualized as conducting learning; it must no longer be thought of as bound by the school building or the school day; and the content and focus of teaching must be redefined to meet the needs of the 21st century.

Rethinking Teaching from Instructing to Conducting

First, as McClintock (1999) suggests, ubiquitous computing means classrooms no longer need be isolated places with very limited resources, but rather should be reconceived as portals with access to abundant resources and rich connections to the world. Teaching, accordingly, need not be confined to walking all students through a limited set of materials, but rather can and should be reimagined as supporting each and every student's learning with materials appropriate to his or her abilities and interests. Teaching needs to be thought of less as instruction and more as the facilitation of learning. We like to think of the role of the teacher in a ubiquitous computing classroom as similar to the role of a conductor of an orchestra. The conductor's job is to bring together the disparate voices of the orchestra to bring to life a common musical theme. Similarly, the role of a teacher in a ubiquitous computing environment is not only to support individual learning, but to blend individual learning into a shared class experience.

Although this not only seems, but is, in some sense antithetical to the standards-based frame dominating American K-12 education today, standards just proscribe what students should know, not how they should learn it, and certainly not how teachers should teach. It moreover can be argued that more students are more likely to reach more learning goals, when teaching adapts to their learning needs.

Indeed, in ubiquitous computing programs across the country, teachers are making use of increased access to educational resources. Across implementations, researchers have found much greater use of Internet resources (Honey & Henriquez, 2000; Hill, Reeves, Grant, Wang, & Han, 2002; Zucker & McGhee, 2005) and significantly more presentations communicating findings (Honey & Henriquez, 2000; Hill et al., 2002). They have found a much greater variety of representations being used to explore, create, and communicate knowledge (Apple Computer, 1995; Honey & Henriquez, 2000; Bartels & Bartels, 2002; Danesh, Inkpen, Lau, Shu, & Booth, 2001; Hill et al., 2002; Roschelle, Penuel, & Abrahamson, 2004) including the use of a much wider variety of visual representations, spreadsheets and databases, simulations, and exploratory environments.

Teachers in RCET's SBCAC are also introducing their students to traditional, standards-based content in non-traditional ways. A kindergarten teacher, for example, encouraged her students to use digital photography, tessellation software, a music composition program, and the Logo robotic turtle to explore patterns. A fourth-grade teacher allowed his students to communicate what they had learned about plant biology through web pages, videos, and Powerpoint presentations, as well as in traditional written reports. A sixth-grade English language arts teacher had her students include scanned pictures, family trees created using Inspiration software, and family crests created with graphics software in the autobiographies, which had been a standard part of her curriculum for several years prior to her SBCAC experience. She told us,

> Some students used color coding systems to denote maternal and paternal lines and some used graphics to depict 'favorites' of their ancestors or to show marriages. ... Students used the Internet to access information about heraldry, concentrating on information about the meaning of specific symbols, colors, and shapes. Each student wrote several paragraphs about his or her coat-of-arms. The writing described why certain colors and symbols were selected. I have done this project with students several times; the work done in the SBCAC is by far the best I have ever seen.

As suggested by the previous quotation, students in these SBCAC classes learned the curricular concepts their teachers identified as important at least as well if not better than they would have learned them in a traditional classroom setting. We worked with teachers in the 2003/2004 and 2004/2005 cohorts to create pre- and post-tests on the big ideas in the units they taught during their time in the SBCAC. Averaged across classes, student pre- to post-test gains in the 2003/2004 school year were a full-effect size and student pre- to post-test gains in the 2004/2005 school year showed an effect size increase of 2.44. In-depth analysis of selected student work from each SBCAC class also provides evidence of deep conceptual understanding of curricular concepts across student ability levels.

We also documented changes in teaching practices when teachers moved from their traditional classroom settings to the ubiquitous computing environment of the SBCAC. Indeed, comparisons of teacher and student activities and the organization of interactions among students and teachers in their regular classrooms with activities and social organization in the SBCAC revealed meaningful differences between settings. The most noticeable difference involved student groupings (Table 1). In the SBCAC, teachers were nearly twice as likely to organize their students into small groups. In addition, teachers spent over two-thirds of their time at the front of their classes in their regular classrooms, whereas in the SBCAC they alternated their time between teaching from the front of the room, orchestrating presentations from the teacher station and moving among students. Teachers were also much more likely to spend time in lecture and discussion, and asking and answering questions in their regular classrooms than in the ubiquitous computing classroom, and spent a good deal more time on classroom management. In the SBCAC, teachers were much more likely to spend their time giving directions and demonstrations, supervising activities, and talking with their students than they did in their regular classrooms.

Other researchers are documenting similar changes in teaching. Across ubiquitous computing implementations, they are overwhelming finding that teachers are becoming more student-centered (Apple Computer, 1995; Ricci, 1999; Fung, Hennessy, & O'Shea, 1998; Honey & Henriquez, 2000; Norris & Soloway, 2004), more constructivist (Apple Computer, 1995; Rockman,

Table 1. Percentage of Class Time Students Spent in Identified Groupings Across Classes.

Student Groupings	Regular Classroom	SBCAC
Individual	12.96	8.52
Small groups	31.31	58.73
Large groups	7.78	0.00
Whole class	47.95	32.75

2003), and more flexible (Zucker & McGhee, 2005). They are developing lessons that are more project-oriented (Honey & Henriquez, 2000; Norris & Soloway, 2004) and more inquiry based (Ricci, 1999; Norris & Soloway, 2004), and, perhaps as a result, they are assigning more group work (Honey & Henriquez, 2000).

These documented changes in teaching approaches demonstrate a tendency for teaching to become more conducting and less instructing in ubiquitous computing environments. However, a good deal more rethinking must be done before the possibilities afforded by ubiquitous computing become generally manifest. In particular, rethinking needs to take place at the school and district levels and in schools of education before the culture of teaching can truly change.

Rethinking Boundaries

A second area in which teaching needs to be rethought for the potential of ubiquitous computing to be realized, that of anywhere/anytime learning, requires even more radical reimagining. Ubiquitous computing diminishes boundaries imposed by brick and mortar spaces and the school day. Mobile computing devices and online virtual spaces make it possible to extend teaching and learning beyond school walls and the school day. Many teachers have long sought ways to make learning more relevant, to bridge the gap between school and the "real" world. Ubiquitous computing can help bridge that gap, but a major rethinking of teaching practice will be necessary before such promise can be realized.

We have seen some indications of this potential in the SBCAC. For example, all students in our SBCAC classes receive mobile computing or handheld computing devices, which most teachers allow them to take with them 24/7. Many teachers encouraged their students to use these devices during the time they spent being bused to and from the SBCAC for journaling and other reflective activities. Most teachers also noted that such use of mobile devices resulted in improvements in both the quantity and quality of student writing. One teacher, for example, told us,

> The one benefit I've noticed is that they do write more with the [mobile computing devices]. And I believe that much as occurs with reading, the more you write, the better a writer you become.

Another teacher noted,

> Taking the [mobile computing devices] home resulted in everyone's homework always being done, and shortened the time frame for getting work done.

The students we interviewed concurred and told us that using mobile computers helped them organize their work better and made writing "more fun."

Mobile computing also helps teachers to take their classes into the world. For example, a fourth-grade class participated in an Ohio-wide stream quality project sponsored by state environmental agencies. They were assigned a local stream to monitor, which they did on fall and spring field trips during which they used digital probes to test water temperature, Ph, and stream flow as well as nets to collect and count organisms in their stream. They recorded their data as they collected it using handheld computers, which they also used to take pictures of the stream site. They then shared their findings with state officials and other classes across Ohio through videoconferencing and data sharing over the Internet.

Indeed, a third way we have seen ready access to ubiquitous computing break down barriers of space and time involves the Internet. Many teachers helped their students communicate with others via email, and most used video teleconferencing over the Internet to connect their students with experts on the topics they were studying, as well as with students in Mexico studying similar topics. All SBCAC teachers incorporated Internet research into the projects they assigned in very integrated ways that would not have been possible with limited access. In all these ways, teachers made the SBCAC less an isolated classroom and more a portal to the larger world.

Of course, these are very small examples when one considers the potential for teaching and learning outside the schoolroom and school day that are available now. Fully online classes are now being taken by over 10% of students enrolled in higher education (Allen & Seaman, 2004), and the number of virtual classes being taken by K-12 students is growing fast. The educational possibilities of cell phone technology (Prensky, 2005) and online gaming (Gee, 2003) are being seriously examined by researchers and educators, but rethinking teaching along anywhere/anytime lines is still tentative at best. It requires serious consideration.

Rethinking What is Taught

A third and final way teaching must be reconsidered involves rethinking what is taught. As McClintock (1999) suggests, we must rethink what knowledge is important and what it means to be literate in a digital world. Indeed, a unique consortium of leaders from government, industry, and education, the Partnership for 21st Century Skills (2003), argues that the emphasis of *No Child Left Behind* on core subjects is not enough, but rather that core subjects should include 21st Century content, that they should be taught and learned using 21st Century tools in a 21st Century context, and that learning should be measured using 21st Century assessments. Specifically, they contend that students need to learn how to "appropriately use digital technology and communication tools to access, manage, integrate and evaluate information, construct new knowledge, and communicate with others" (p. 6).

In the SBCAC, we are beginning to see teachers teach their students to use such tools. Participating teachers encouraged their students to use a variety of digital devices to help students explore their topics both in and outside the classroom. All teachers incorporated word processing, Internet research, and the use of mobile computing into their assignments. Most classes used concept-mapping, graphing, and spreadsheets to organize and explore ideas and data. All but the kindergarten teachers developed extended projects in which students demonstrated their learning through technology-based presentations. These included Powerpoint presentations and desktop publishing, but also the creation of websites and digital movies.

Most importantly, all the teachers utilized the available technologies to support their teaching and learning goals. Table 2 summarizes the digital representations used by classes in the 2003/2004 school year. Teachers in these classes used differing technologies to meet differing learning objectives, often in very creative ways. Their students learned to use a variety of digital technologies appropriately to access, manage, create, and communicate information. Participating teachers also developed ways of assessing technological products and explored new ways to use technology to enhance assessment of student learning, including electronic portfolios, electronic journaling, and/or observational software on their handhelds to assess student learning.

In their post SBCAC interviews and reflections, teachers noted the effects of ubiquitous access to computing on the kinds of representations of knowledge they used in their classes. For example, one teacher stated,

> The children all had electronic portfolios, and our "daily reflections" were done using the digital camera and my laptop. I also used a projector to type the daily reflections and have the children see what I was doing.

Another teacher commented on ways digital representations enhanced students' learning about the writing process itself,

> Students got a better idea of editing and publishing from being able to share their work publicly. Students also benefited from 1:1 access to computers in honing their information searching and evaluation skills. They became more reflective and better writers, perhaps through group revisions, and got good practice typing.

Table 2. Digital Representations Employed in SBCAC Classes in the 2003/2004 School Year.

Grade	Topic	Representations Used
7	Biography	Video conferencing (Mexico), Internet research, Powerpoint (including Vox Proxy audio), journaling on handheld computers, Inspiration (brainstorming), digital photography, digital video, timelines (Timeliner), graphs, Write Out Loud software (reads back text to improve writing), email
6	Family history	Digital photography, Inspiration (family crests, family trees), Internet research, Powerpoint, desktop publishing, journaling on handheld computers, video and audio recorders for family interviews, scanner (family photos), clipart, graphics software
5	What's wild?	Webquests, Powerpoint, Inspiration (concept map), Internet research, journaling on handheld computers, videoconferencing (Stream Quality project), science probes and sensors, spreadsheets, graphs (data analysis), digital photography, desktop publishing, digital video
4	Plant biology	Student-created videos (iMovie), student-created webpages (DreamWeaver), Powerpoint, science probes, time-lapse photography, digital photography, Inspiration (concept map), digital microscope, spreadsheets, graphs, BugScope, handhelds for data collection, videoconferencing (Mexico), email
3/4[a]	Flight	Digital photography, Photoshop, digital video, Powerpoint, Internet research, Inspiration, flight simulator, science probes, graphing software, timelines (Timeliner), scanner, spreadsheets, time capsule and journaling on handheld computers, video conferencing (NASA)
K	Patterns	KidPix (graphics package), digital photography, digital microscopes, scanned images (fabric), Logo turtle, audio recorders, music composition software, tessellation software, Paint program, email, group reflections using presentation system
K	Space	Digital photography, digital video, Internet (bookmarked websites), video conferencing (NASA), KidPix (graphics package), word processing on mobile devices, Powerpoint, digital KWL charts, presentation system, Elmo

[a]Third- and fourth-grade teachers from one district collaborated on a similar unit.

Indeed, most of the teachers we interviewed commented on the ways in which the use of digital representations enhanced and expanded students' communication and problem solving skills.

Of course, these examples also involve small steps. For the full potential of ubiquitous computing to be realized, what is taught must be systematically rethought across the curriculum at the school, district, and state levels.

RETHINKING LEARNING

If teaching needs to be reconceptualized to take full advantage of ubiquitous access to digital computing, it follows that learning must similarly be reimagined. Our work in the SBCAC has led us to believe that ubiquitous computing has the potential to make learning truly student-centered and that student-centered learning can also be higher-order learning. We believe that learning needs to be reimagined by both teachers and students to take advantage of the kinds of supports ubiquitous computing can provide for individual and social construction of knowledge. In particular, students need to be given, and to take, responsibility for their own learning. Four interrelated areas in which learning might be rethought in a more student-centered direction seem particularly relevant in a ubiquitous computing context. These center on engagement and motivation, individualization and choice, collaboration and peer learning, and learning for all students.

Rethinking Engagement and Motivation

Student-centered learning begins with engagement. An engaged student invests herself in learning activities, making learning, even learning that did not start out that way, student-centered. Digital technologies seem to engage students in learning. Indeed, students we interviewed told us time and time again that they thought they learned more in the SBCAC because of the "fun" they had using digital technologies. For example, one student explained, "I think you learn more if it's fun because if it's fun it helps you concentrate and listen." Another told us, "You want to have fun and learn at the same time. If you are bored you don't learn as much because you don't want to focus in to it."

The students we spoke with repeatedly used computer-based representations to describe a concept or demonstrate how they used a particular computing application to create knowledge. Overall, the majority of students we interviewed described in great detail the projects they were working on including key concepts represented in their work. Their engagement was palpable.

Teachers similarly commented on the sometimes profound effect ubiquitous computing had on student engagement and motivation, noting that these are necessary first steps in higher-order learning. For example, one teacher told us,

> Learning was more efficient, students were busier. There was some fooling around at the beginning, but in general students were more engaged, more motivated, more on task, freer.

The teachers we interviewed further noted that because students were more engaged in the SBCAC, they could pursue more complex and extended projects than they had in their regular classroom settings. Most thought ubiquitous computing seemed to be particularly supportive of project-based and inquiry learning precisely because of its power to engage students. One teacher, for example, told us,

> With my students, I've noticed they are really much more inquisitive. The higher achieving kids take learning to the next step, and I see the other kids trying to do the same. For instance, the other day while working on a unit addressing natural forces, the kids themselves wanted to create a rubric to analyze the material. I've assigned that to them before, but they never before told me that's what they wanted to do.

Another summed up her experience as follows,

> The most important thing that I learned is the power that technology has to both motivate students and keep them on task. I was able to work one-on-one with a lot of students because the others were so completely engaged in their own projects.

Indeed, all of the teachers we interviewed were surprised by how engaged and how motivated to learn their students were in the SBCAC. Many of them extended the activities they had planned to take advantage of it. Other ubiquitous computing researchers are documenting similar effects. They are finding improved motivation (Apple Computer, 1995; Ricci, 1999; Vahey & Crawford, 2002; Zucker & McGhee, 2005), engagement (Silvernail & Lane, 2004; Zucker & McGhee, 2005), behavior (Apple Computer, 1995), and even school attendance (Apple Computer, 1995; Stevenson, 1998) among students involved in ubiquitous computing initiatives. In addition, research shows such students are better organized (Ricci, 1999; Zucker & McGhee, 2005) and more independent learners (Apple Computer, 1995; Zucker & McGhee, 2005).

Thus, the first way educators need to rethink learning to realize the potential of ubiquitous computing is that they need to plan for and support student engagement. In particular, they need to think in terms of intrinsic, rather than extrinsic, motivation for learning and explore ways of using digital technologies to make learning "fun."

Rethinking Individualization and Choice

A second way in which educators need to rethink learning to realize the full potential of ubiquitous computing involves individualization of learning and student choice. Most teachers of the SBCAC teachers we interviewed said they were surprised at the way they could work with individual students or groups of students without worrying about what the rest of the class was doing. One teacher, for example, noted,

> It's much more student-centered there. The technology keeps them engaged so I can go around and do one-on-one.

Other teachers echoed this theme and pointed out that because management issues were reduced, they could give their students more independence:

> I also learned the value of open-ended software and letting the children have some independence when learning new software. It rejuvenated my teaching.

> I tried to give the students more choices about projects because of the different ideas I saw in the classroom.

It should also be pointed out that ubiquitous access to digital computing devices makes it much easier both to individualize learning and to give students choice simply because, as McClintock (1999) notes, it gives teachers and students access to a wealth of resources beyond the limited resources of the typical classroom. Not only does access to rich collections of materials in a variety of media formats make it possible for teachers to tailor activities for individual students, but giving students mobile computing devices allows them to individualize their own workspaces and so to make their learning their own in a very tangible way.

Teachers in the SBCAC began to take advantage of these rich possibilities and more importantly allowed their students to. They uniformly remarked on the high quality of student work that resulted. We analyzed the work of selected high, average, and low performing students from every SBCAC class, as well as the work of selected special-needs students in almost every class (some classes had no special-needs students). Many of the artifacts studied required students to utilize technology to organize, synthesize, or interpret information, describe patterns, create models or simulations using data or information they collected or selected, suggesting that teachers were making use of digital technologies not only to support individualization and student choice, but to support higher-order learning. Students responded with unique, creative, and high-quality work. In most of the student artifacts there was good evidence that students had developed a deep understanding of key concepts and ideas related to the content area they were studying, in that they were able to elaborate on specific concepts and make connections between concepts. In addition, the majority of the work samples supported big ideas with details and examples, facts, graphics, and symbolic representations in ways that demonstrated students' ability to communicate their learning.

Other research on ubiquitous computing initiatives also shows that the increased individualization of learning and opportunities for student choice afforded by ubiquitous computing can affect student learning (Siegle & Foster, 2000). Researchers have documented increased media literacy (Hill et al., 2002; Rockman, 2003), improved writing (Apple Computer, 1995; Ricci, 1999; Vahey & Crawford, 2002; Rockman, 2003), and, in some cases, increased scores on standardized tests (Stevenson, 1998; Honey & Henriquez, 2000).

This latter finding, as well as the pre- to post-test gains we documented in SBCAC classes, suggests that individualization and choice need not be sacrificed in the standards-based, high-stakes testing context griping American K-12 education today, at least not when they are supported by ubiquitous computing. Thus, a second way learning needs to be rethought involves taking advantage of ubiquitous computing to maximize individualized learning and student choice within a framework defined by specific learning goals. One way to approach this is suggested by the student work samples we reviewed. We saw that students better understood important concepts when they were guided to explore them in their own terms using a variety of digital resources. Indeed, researchers are finding that learning in ubiquitous environments is becoming more efficient (Apple Computer, 1995; Hill et al., 2002) and that students are becoming "experts" on particular topics (Apple, 1995; Norris & Soloway, 2004). A good deal more rethinking of learning along these lines, however, remains to be done.

Rethinking Collaborative Learning

A third way ubiquitous computing compels a rethinking of learning involves collaboration. Student-centered learning is not just individualized. Because learning is fundamentally a social activity (Vygotsky, 1978; Lave & Wenger, 1991), learning that is student-centered must also involve collaboration. Moreover, research suggests that collaborative learning can very positively affect learning outcomes (Johnson & Johnson, 1989, 1992). Ubiquitous computing affords unique supports for collaborative and peer learning activities. Indeed, researchers across the country have noted significant increases in collaboration, among students and between students and teachers, in ubiquitous computing classes (Apple Computer, 1995; Robertson et al., 1996; Hennessy, 2000; Sharples, 2000; Roschelle & Pea, 2002; Vahey & Crawford, 2002; Norris & Soloway, 2004).

For example, most mobile computing devices have beaming capabilities that allow students to easily share their work and/or work collaboratively. Several teachers in the SBCAC used such devices to support peer editing and believed it enhanced both the activity and the quality of the resulting student work. One teacher told us that the use of mobile computing *"also seemed to make individual sharing and peer tutoring work better."* Another commented,

> The biggest change has been in their weekly journals. We have been journaling all year and they have always written them but in using the [mobile computing devices], peer editing takes on so much more meaning when they can beam to someone rather than trading papers. With the [mobile computing devices] they are editing their own writing more and it keeps getting better.

Indeed, many teachers noted that being able to access each other's work digitally seemed to motivate students to create higher quality products. One teacher also commented that being able to share work on computer screens and over the presentation systems gave students increased pride in their work,

> The SBC experience also taught me the value of sharing student work. Giving a grade for a project is not enough, students need peer affirmation of performance.

Being able to share work on computer screens and across computing devices also seemed to facilitate collaborative group work. As previously mentioned, students in the SBCAC spent more than half their time working on collaborative group projects, much more time in such activities than they did in their regular classroom settings. Several teachers we interviewed remarked on how differently, and how much more successfully, group work progressed when all students had access to computing devices. One teacher, for example commented,

> Students interacted more and more freely. Bullying stopped and the class achieved a sense of itself much sooner than they would have in their regular classroom. At the beginning of the year, I gave students cards on which they told who they would like to sit near. I just redid them and found that they had changed dramatically. The SBCAC experience in some sense forced kids to interact with each other.

Students in some SBCAC classes also shared their work and collaborated with students in Mexico on particular projects, adding a multicultural dimension that clearly enriched their learning experience. Students in one fourth-grade class collaborated with students across Ohio and state environmental officials to measure water quality in Ohio streams. One class of kindergarten students collaborated with their parents over email. It is our belief that these kinds of collaborations just touch the surface of what is possible with ubiquitous computing. Online environments, for example, make all sorts of rich collaborations possible. Students online can engage in rich discussions asynchronously across space and time. They can participate in collaborative simulations and collaboratively create all sorts of products. They can share data, collaboratively analyze it and report their results.

Some people are experimenting with collaborative performances across distance. The possibilities are legion but we believe that they cannot be substantively realized until collaborative learning is radically reimagined to harness the potential of ubiquitous computing on a much larger scale, across schools, districts, and states, at the very least, but ideally at national and international levels.

Rethinking Learning for All Students

A final area in which learning needs to be reconceptualized to take advantage of ubiquitous computing involves learning for all students. Traditionally the special needs literature describes the use of assistive technology tools for supporting meaningful mainstreaming of struggling students or the use of intervention-based software to facilitate learning. In the SBCAC classroom, however, we found that students with special needs and lower abilities were achieving at high levels using the same technology tools as their peers.

Table 3 shows our ratings of student work samples for students in different ability groups averaged across classes. Work samples were rated on depth of analysis, understanding of concepts, and elaborated communications using a four-point rubric in each category for a possible total score ranging from three to twelve. As previously noted, all student work was of very high quality, but what stands out in the findings is that special needs students were completing work of the same quality as students identified as average learners and almost as high quality as the highest achieving students. This finding is supported by other research (Stevenson, 1998; Honey & Henriquez, 2000; Hill, Reeves, Grant, Wang, & Han, 2002) that is documenting similar achievements by special needs and low ability students in ubiquitous computing programs. It has important implications for educators regarding to student integration and accommodation issues. It also

Table 3. Average Conceptual Understanding Scores for Ability Groups Across Classes.[a]

	Average Score Across Classes
High ability	10.0
Medium ability	9.4
Low ability	8.5
Special needs	9.3

[a]Overall scores (possible range of 3(low) to 12 (high).

suggests that we need to rethink what and how special needs students can learn given ubiquitous access to digital computing devices.

Indeed, all the teachers we interviewed told us they were amazed at the work their lowest achieving students completed in the SBCAC, and remarked on the way ubiquitous computing seemed to "level the playing field" for students of varying abilities. For example, one teacher stated,

> I believe that I must always teach to my students' strengths and use those strengths to help students overcome their weaknesses. Technology levels the playing field for students, especially those students on Individualized Education Programs. Most of my students had strengths in technology and had the opportunity to become more accomplished. Technology helped my students to become empowered. Because of the variety of the hardware and software at the lab, all of my students were successful on some level.

Another said,

> In particular, the special education students bloomed. They could go at their own pace and technology seemed to emphasize their strengths as opposed to their weaknesses. It had a leveling effect.

These comments highlight an important way ubiquitous computing can facilitate all students' learning; digital computers support multiple representations of knowledge, and so a variety of meaning making. They allow students who are less facile in traditional classroom ways of knowing to learn in other ways, to find their own voices. *No Child Left Behind* legislation dictates that we support the learning of all students. Research on ubiquitous computing suggests that we can do so if we rethink learning to include multiple ways of knowing supported by ubiquitous access to computers.

RETHINKING TECHNOLOGY INTEGRATION

In the previous two sections, we have discussed how teaching and learning need to be rethought for the potential of ubiquitous computing (McClintock, 1999) to be realized. We have seen indications of how teaching and learning can indeed change in ubiquitous computing environments, and the positive effects that can have on student achievement. It is clear, however, that such positive effects will remain isolated indications until rethinking takes place on a much larger and more inclusive scale. We must radically rethink our notions of technology integration in education in ways that embrace not only ubiquitous computing, but the full potential for new approaches to teaching and learning that ubiquitous computing affords.

The first step in rethinking technology integration is simple but radical. We need to embrace ubiquitous computing. We need to view access for all students to a variety of digital computing devices wherever and whenever they need them as fundamental to the learning enterprise, as fundamental to learning, in fact, as ubiquitous access to books and writing materials. We need to see ubiquitous computing as essential. While this is a radical idea, it is not a ridiculous one. Consider, for example, the fact that education is the only knowledge industry today that does not view ubiquitous computing in this way. Consider as well that books were once the new technology. Ubiquitous computing is an essential part of meaning making in almost every aspect of our everyday lives, indeed in almost every aspect of our students' lives, except in school. Education must embrace ubiquitous computing or become irrelevant. Consider the fate of medieval scribes.

We must embrace ubiquitous computing and we must make it so. We must ensure that all students have access to a variety of digital technologies wherever and whenever they need them. This second step is possibly a little easier than first because once we realize ubiquitous computing is essential, we can seriously redirect our resources toward that goal. The state of Maine, for example, is moving toward ubiquitous computing by giving laptop computers to every middle school student in the entire state (Silvernail & Lane, 2004). Other initiatives are trying similar things on a slightly smaller but still significant scale. Across the country and around the world, schools, districts, and counties are implementing 1:1 computing initiatives (Rockman, 2003; Tatar, Roschelle, Vahey, & Penuel, 2003; Russell, Bebell, & Higgins, 2004; Johnstone, 2003; Zucker & McGhee, 2005). And momentum is growing (Wagner, 2005). It is important to remember, however, that as important as these first initiatives are, they are just steps along a path to ubiquitous computing. We need, for example, to rethink education to incorporate the digital devices most students have and use regularly; cell phones are an obvious example as are gaming devices. Most importantly, we need to rethink teaching and learning within a ubiquitous computing frame.

Indeed, we probably need to stop thinking about technology integration altogether. As critical as large-scale technology initiatives are today, they are device focused; they cannot be otherwise. Our thinking must go beyond implementation issues to reimagine the entire educational enterprise in light of the new possibilities, digital devices afford. Seymour Papert (2002) reminds us that we must guard against integrating technologies based on an educational culture that was shaped by conditions that no longer apply. In this chapter we have seen how ubiquitous computing makes possible new approaches to teaching that are more like conducting than instructing, that are not bound by school spaces and times, and that address 21st century knowledge, skills, and attitudes in meaningful ways. We have seen how ubiquitous access to computing can support student-centered learning that is more engaging, more individualized, more collaborative, and more inclusive than what we have come to expect. There are surely other ways teaching and learning can be reconceived in this brave new world.

   The Educator's Manifesto (McClintock, 1999) was written more than five years ago, a long time in terms of technology integration, the blink of an eye in terms of educational reform. It was written before *No Child Left Behind* changed the landscape of K-12 education in this country. Its central thesis is, however, if anything, more relevant now than when it was written. Serious consideration of the notion that digital computing has changed what is educationally possible in dramatic ways can help us begin to reimagine that landscape and transform education to meet the needs of today and tomorrow's knowledge society in ways that might surprise us all.

REFERENCES

Allen, I. E., & Seaman, J. (2004). *Entering the mainstream: The quality and extent of online education in the United States, 2003 and 2004*. Needham, MA: The Sloan Consortium.

Apple Computer (1995). *Changing the conversation about teaching, learning and technology: A report on 10 years of ACOT research*. Retrieved April 8, 2005 from http://images.apple.com/education/k12/leadership/acot/pdf/10yr.pdf

Bartels, F., & Bartels, L. (2002). *Reflections on the RCDS laptop program after three years*. Retrieved April 8, 2005 from http://www.learningwithlaptops.org/files/3rd%20Year%20Laptop%20Prog.pdf

Danesh, A., Inkpen, K., Lau, F., Shu, K., & Booth, K. (2001). Geney™: Designing a collaborative activity for the Palm™ handheld computer. *Proceedings of CHI, Conference on human factors in computing systems*. Seattle: WA.

Engelbart, D. C. A. (1963). conceptual framework for the augmentation of man's intellect. In: P. W. Howerrton & D. C. Weeks (Eds), *Vistas in Information Handling* (Vol. 1, pp. 1–29). Washington, DC: Spartan Books.

Fung, P., Hennessy, S., & O'Shea, T. (1998). Pocketbook computing: A paradigm shift? *Computers in the Schools, 14*, 109–118.

Gee, J. P. (2003). *What video games have to teach us about learning and literacy*. New York: Palgrave MacMillan.

Hennessy, S. (2000). Graphing investigations using portable (palmtop) technology. *Journal of Computer Assisted Learning, 16*, 243–258.

Hill, J. R., Reeves, T. C., Grant, M. M., Wang, S.-K. & Han, S. (2002). *The impact of portable technologies on teaching and learning: Year three report*. Retrieved April 8, 2005 from http://lpsl.coe.uga.edu/Projects/aalaptop/pdf/aa3rd/Year3ReportFinalVersion.pdf

Honey, M., & Henriquez, A. (2000). *More things that do make a difference for youth. Union City School District, NJ.* Retrieved April 8, 2005 from http://www.aypf.org/compendium/C2s18.pdf

Johnson, D. W., & Johnson, R. (1989). Computer-assisted cooperative learning. *Educational Technology, 26*(1), 12–18.

Johnson, D. W., & Johnson, R. (1992). Positive interdependence: Key to effective cooperation. In: R. Hertz-Lazarowitz & N. Miller (Eds), *Interaction in Cooperative Groups: The Theoretical Anatomy of Group Learning* (pp. 174–199). Cambridge: Cambridge University Press.

Johnstone, B. (2003). *Never Mind the Laptops.* New York: iUniverse, Inc.

Kay, A. (2005). The Dynabook revisited: A conversation with Alan Kay. *The Book and the computer: Exploring the future of the printed word in the digital age.* Retrieved May 26, 2005 from http://www.honco.net/os/kay.html

Kyle, B. (2000). Acute pencil shortage strikes state lawmakers. *Bangor Daily News.* Retrieved May 26, 2005 from http://www.papert.org/articles/laptops/acute_pencil_shortage.html

Lave, J., & Wenger, E. (1991). *Situated Learning: Legitimate Peripheral Participation.* Cambridge: Cambridge University Press.

McClintock, R. (1999). *The educator's manifesto: Renewing the progressive bond with posterity through the social construction of digital learning communities.* New York: Institute For Learning Technologies, Teachers College, Columbia University. Retrieved March 21, 2005, from http://www.ilt.columbia.edu/publications/manifesto/contents.html

Norris, C., & Soloway, E. (2004). Envisioning the handheld centric classroom. *Journal of Educational Computing Research, 30*(4), 281–294.

Papert, S. (1980). *Mindstorms: Children, Computers and Powerful Ideas.* New York: Basic Books.

Papert, S. (2002). Learners, laptops, and powerful ideas. *Scholastic Administr@tor, Fall 2002.* Retrieved May 26, 2005 from http://www.learningbarn.org

Partnership for 21st Century Skills (2003). *Learning for the 21st century.* Retrieved June 28, 2005 from http://www.21stcenturyskills.org/

Prensky, M. (2005). What can you learn from a cell phone? Almost anything. *Innovate* 1(5). Retrieved June 29, 2005 from http://www.innovateonline.info/index.php?view=article&id=83&action=article

Ricci, C. M. (1999). Program evaluation: New York City Board of Education Community School District Six laptop project. Paper presented at the annual meeting of the American Educational Research Association, Montreal.

Robertson, S. I., Calder, J., Fung, P., Jones, A., O'Shea, T., & Lambrechts, G. (1996). Pupils, teachers, and palmtop computers. *Journal of Computer Assisted Learning, 12*, 194–204.

Rockman, S. (2003). Learning from laptops. *Threshold, 1*(1), 24–28.

Roschelle, J., & Pea, R. (2002). A walk on the WILD side: How wireless handhelds may change computer-supported collaborative learning. *International Journal of Cognition and Technology, 1*(1), 145–272.

Roschelle, J., Penuel, W. R., & Abrahamson, L. (2004). The networked classroom. *Educational Leadership, 61*(5), 50–53.

Russell, M., Bebell, D., & Higgins, J. (2004). Laptop learning: A comparison of teaching and learning in upper elementary classrooms equipped with shared carts of laptops and permanent 1:1 laptops. *Journal of Educational Computing Research, 30*(4), 313–330.

Sharples, M. (2000). The design of personal mobile technologies for lifelong learning. *Computers and Education, 34*, 177–193.

Siegle, D., & Foster, T. (2000). Effects of laptop computers with multimedia and presentation software on student achievement. Paper presented at the annual meeting of the American Educational Research Association, New Orleans, LA.

Silvernail, D. L., & Lane, D. M. M. (2004). *The Impact of Maine's One-to-One Laptop Program on Middle School Teachers and Students (Report #1)*. Gorham, ME: Maine Education Policy Research Institute, University of Southern Maine Office.

Stevenson, K. R. (1998). Evaluation report: year 2: Schoolbook laptop project. Retrieved April 8, 2005 from http://www.beaufort.k12.sc.us/district/ltopeval.html

Tatar, D., Roschelle, J., Vahey, P., & Penuel, W. R. (2003). Handhelds go to school: Lessons learned. *IEEE Computer, 36*(9), 30–37.

Vahey, P., & Crawford, V. (2002). *Palm Education Pioneers Program: Final evaluation report*. Menlo Park, CA: SRI International. Retrieved April 8, 2005 from http://www.palm-grants.sri.com/PEP_Final_Report.pdf

Vygotsky, L. S. (1978). *Mind in Society*. Cambridge, MA: Harvard University Press.

Wagner, E. D. (2005). Enabling mobile learning. *Educause Review, May/June*, 41–52.

Zucker, A. A., & McGhee, R. (2005). *A Study of One-to-One Computer Use in Mathematics and Science Instruction at the Secondary Level in Henrico County Public Schools*. Washington, DC: SRI International.

DIGITAL PHOTO JOURNALS: A NOVEL APPROACH TO ADDRESSING EARLY CHILDHOOD TECHNOLOGY STANDARDS AND RECOMMENDATIONS

Cynthia Carter Ching, X. Christine Wang and Yore Kedem

ABSTRACT

The early childhood field is full of mixed messages about young children and technology. Research and policy standards stress the importance of computer use as a means to increase basic skills and develop information literacy, while also warning that over-use can lead to children's social isolation and reduced attention spans. It is within this ongoing debate that we situate our research on digital photo journals in a kindergarten/first-grade classroom. Students in our study used a digital camera to document their daily activities and created digital photo journals on the computer to represent their experiences and their surroundings. Our results suggest a novel approach to addressing current debates in educational technology for early childhood, wherein the digital camera and photo journals become explicit

Technology and Education: Issues in Administration, Policy, and Applications in K12 Schools
Advances in Educational Administration, Volume 8, 253–269
Copyright © 2006 by Elsevier Ltd.
All rights of reproduction in any form reserved
ISSN: 1479-3660/doi:10.1016/S1479-3660(05)08017-0

tools for exploring social networks, understanding and interpreting the
classroom environment, and achieving meaningful technology integration.

Early childhood educators are stuck between a rock and a hard place, when it comes to technology integration. On the one hand, educational technology standards and early learning research stress the importance of computer use for young children, as a means to increase basic skills and develop information literacy vital for success in the twenty-first century (ISTE, 1998; CoSUN, 2003). On the other hand, child advocacy groups and early socialization research warn that too much "screen time" can lead to children's social isolation and reduced attention spans (Cordes & Miller, 2000; 2004; Healy, 1998). Early childhood standards and policy organizations emphasize meaningful integration of technology into the classroom and curriculum (NAEYC, 1996); however, the vast majority of early childhood technology practice reveals children's incidental and peripheral classroom use of commercial, stand-alone software (Cuban, 2002). Many educators are clearly at a loss for what to do, and with good reason.

It is within this ongoing debate that we situate our research on digital photo journals in a kindergarten/first-grade classroom. In our work, we wanted to create and investigate an educational technology activity for young children that would be integrated into both the physical spaces and social fabric of the classroom, would be personally and socially meaningful, and would scaffold children's reflective and creative capacities. This chapter presents the results from a study of one kindergarten/first-grade classroom with 21 students and three teachers (one lead teacher and two assistants). Students used a digital camera to document their daily activities and created digital photo journals on the computer to represent their experiences and their surroundings. This chapter describes a novel approach to addressing current debates in educational technology for early childhood, wherein the digital camera and photo journals become explicit tools for developing and exploring social networks, understanding and interpreting the classroom environment, and achieving meaningful technology integration.

REVIEW OF RESEARCH

Computers are becoming quite commonplace in young children's environments: from preschools and elementary schools (Clements & Sarama, 2003b;

NCES, 2003) to libraries and other public spaces (CoSN, 2002), to children's own homes (Rideout, Vanderwater, & Wartella, 2003). An increasingly wide variety of applications and games are designed and marketed toward young children (Cuban, 2002; Postman, 1993). The National Center for Educational Statistics finds that in 2001–2002, the largest group of new internet users was 2–5 year olds (NCES, 2003). What exactly children are doing with their increased access and time on computers, and what are the benefits and potential risks of these activities remain largely open questions, however. These questions need to be examined in light of young children's cognitive and social development.

Research on early childhood development emphasizes the importance of rich social interactions with caregivers and others that scaffold children's linguistic, problem-solving, and reflective capabilities (National Research Council, 2000; Rogoff, 1990; Siegel, 1999). Particularly critical are peer and friendship networks, which are often topics of conversation and reflection for young children (Corsaro, 1985, 1997; Dyson, 1993). Studies also show that children actively construct their social environments through negotiating and establishing norms, and they create their understandings of these social networks through memory and narrative talk (Carere, 1987; Fernie, 1999; Fivush & Buckner, 2003). Consequently, social interaction and peer relationships are highly emphasized in the development of early childhood curriculum and activities (e.g., NAEYC, 1992).

The typical picture of a sole individual working determinedly on his or her "personal" computer seems on the surface somewhat at-odds with these developmental goals. Thus, many early childhood educators, researchers, and advocates repeatedly express concern that regular computer use by young children can lead to isolation, poor physical fitness, short attention spans, and a lack of opportunities to develop cognitively and socially with peers and adults (Rideout, et al., 2003; Healy, 1998). Some recommendations go so far as to suggest that, because of these risks, computer use in early childhood should be restricted or even postponed until later in development (Cordes & Miller, 2000, 2004). As a counterpoint to these recommendations, however, some research studies demonstrate that, despite an activity structure favoring independent use, young children are actually highly collaborative among themselves when working on computers (Freeman & Somerindyke, 2001; Clements & Sarama, 2003a; Wang & Ching, 2003). Additional research shows that young children's independent computer use, either in the classroom or at home, can result in increased basic skills and increased comfort levels with technology – both key components of future success in learning (NCREL, 2000).

It is obvious that early childhood educators, administrators, and policy-makers are receiving mixed messages about educational technology from the research and advocacy communities. Largely as a result of these mixed messages, there exists no firm consensus as to what the concrete practices for educational technology in early childhood should be. Standards for early childhood curriculum and teacher preparation, as well as recent federal policy and researcher recommendations, have managed to converge on the notion of "developmentally appropriate" computer use, and curricula in which technology is 'integrated" across a wide variety of areas, but these criteria remain vague without specific recommendations. Following are some examples of the language from policy, standards, and recommendations of this type (emphasis added in all):

• National Association for the Education of Young Children Early Child-hood Professional Preparation Standards: "Early childhood education candidates should evaluate and demonstrate *appropriate use* of technology with young children" (NAEYC, 1992).
• Recommendation appearing in *Young Children*, a professional develop-ment magazine for early childhood educators: "During the preschool years, children should have many opportunities to explore open-ended, *developmentally appropriate* software programs in a playful, supportive environment," (Murphy, DePasquale, & McNamara, 2003).
• National Association for the Education of Young Children Position Statement on Technology and Young Children Ages 3–8: "*Developmentally appropriate* software offers opportunities for collaborative play, learning, and creation," and "Computers should be *integrated* into the classroom physically, functionally, and philosophically," (NAEYC, 1996).
• United States Department of Education National Educational Technol-ogy Plan recommends that schools from pre-K through grade 12: "En-courage *ubiquitous access* to computers and connectivity for each student," and pursue "*high levels of integration* across all grade levels" (U.S. Department of Education, 2004).
• Recommendation appearing in *Childhood Education*, another practice-oriented journal: "The full potential of technology's tools is only realized when they are used effectively and in *ways that connect meaningfully to the ongoing curriculum* of the classroom and support creativity and critical thinking" (Bergen, 2000).

A common theme also echoed in the early childhood technology recom-mendations is that of supporting creativity and social engagement, as in the last quotation above; however, authors differ in the extent to which they assert that this goal can or cannot be achieved through technology use. In our view, the digital photo journal project addresses many of the mixed messafges and concerns of existing recommendations. The digital camera is highly portable, and its use by young children provides a somewhat unique approach to technology in the classroom, one that is not bounded by the physical location of "computers in the corner" (Cuban, 2002). In this project there exist multiple opportunities while taking pictures for children to interact with peers and teachers throughout the learning environment. Further, the activity of downloading pictures to the computer and creating photo journals also takes place in intimate conversation with an adult (a teacher or researcher), who not only provides technical help but also scaffolds children's reflection about their photos. Finally, and perhaps most importantly, social connections and scaffolded reflections are not only *afforded* in the digital journal project, they are *inherent* in the very nature of the task. Peers, teachers, and other parts of the classroom environment are visually represented on-screen and are the explicit topics of adult–child and peer–peer conversations.

For our goals of addressing existing standards and recommendations, we had two broad research questions. First, how does the digital camera project create meaningful technology integration within the physical space and learning environment? And second, how does the activity of making a digital journal provide children with opportunities for social engagement and reflection? These questions were addressed by collecting and examining video, fieldnote, and transcription data from children's picture-taking and journal creation activities.

METHODS

Site and Participants

This study was conducted in a K/1 classroom at a university-affiliated school in a Midwestern town. The participants consisted of one head teacher, two teaching assistants (one of whom is the fourth author), and 25 students. Of these students, 21 created finished photo journals. Gender and grade-level distribution of the participating 21 students was as follows: 8 boys (4 kindergarten, 4 first-grade) and 13 girls (6 kindergarten, 7 first-grade). The population of students was ethnically and culturally diverse.

Despite being located at a major university, the technology resources in this classroom were somewhat minimal. Only one digital camera was available for the project, and the classroom only had one powerful computer equipped with a connection for a digital camera and capable of running iPhoto (other computers in the environment were much older models). These more advanced technologies were also occasionally in use by the teaching staff and consequently not always available to students. In this sense, the classroom community we investigated was similar to other early childhood environments where technology is a limited resource.

Digital Photo Journal Project
The digital photo journal project took place during the 2002–2003 school year. Because there was only one digital camera available, students took turns on a daily basis taking pictures and creating their journals. When it was a student's turn to take pictures, he or she would be shown how to use the camera by a teaching assistant in the morning and then be given the camera for the rest of the day – during lunch, recess, lessons, choice time, etc. – to take pictures of whatever interested him or her. A researcher was present to either videotape or take fieldnotes while students took pictures.

Typically the next morning, but not more than two days later, the student then sat down with one of the researchers to create his or her journal. This process involved downloading all the pictures the student took, looking at each one, selecting which pictures to include in the photo journal, and then writing captions for each picture. Students dictated captions while the investigators typed, due to the fact that our students were all emerging readers and/or frustrated and slow typists. When researchers described for students the process of writing captions, they tended to frame it in very general terms, such as, "what do you want to say about your picture?" Only after a student had dictated a caption, would the researcher follow up with another question or two in the same vein as the student's initial comment. This open-endedness left the form and the content of captions entirely up to students. The entire journal creation process and accompanying student–researcher conversation was videotaped. At the end of the year, students displayed their finished photo journals (print-outs and soft copies) to their families and peers at an open-house night.

Data Collection and Analysis

Given that only one student per day could take pictures, and that each student's journal-creation process required the presence of a researcher to help and ask questions, the entire project and accompanying data collection spanned several months. With time required for gaining access, getting to know the children, becoming familiar with the environment, and obtaining parental content, all the investigators were present in the classroom during much of the school year (November through May). Final data sources included video and fieldnotes of the students taking pictures, students' finished journals, and video of the journal creation process and accompanying researcher–student discussions.

Video and fieldnotes of students' picture-taking were combined with general fieldnotes and reflective writing by researchers about their classroom observations; these data were examined using grounded theory methods (Strauss & Corbin, 1998) for emergent patterns in both student–photographer behaviors and general classroom activities. Analyzing students' journals and the journal-creation process required the creation of a unit of analysis that drew on multiple data sources. We matched up portions of student–researcher talk that corresponded to each of the pictures and captions in the finished journal (see Fig. 1 for example).

In Fig. 1, the top cell on the left is the student's picture, the bottom cell on the left is the caption the student dictated, and the cell on the right is the interaction between a researcher (the first author) and the student (Brenna[1]). At the end of our multi-source data merge, each child had an Excel[TM] file containing all the units corresponding to each of his or her pictures, captions from iPhoto[TM], and accompanying transcript segments, as above. Units were then coded according to multiple emergent criteria created using a grounded theory approach, and students were compared for gender and age differences in type of reflections. (As our emergent categories are themselves a major finding of the study, they will be described fully in Results.)

C: What do you want to say about this one?

B: I took this one because Julia doesn't know what she wants to get.

C: Um..Mmhm (typing)...why do you think she doesn't know what she wants to get?

B: Because she was standing there for a looonng time.

Caption:
I took this one because Julia doesn't know what she wants to get.

Fig. 1. Multi-Source Unit of Analysis for Journals.

Admittedly, the researcher–child exchange in Fig. 1 is somewhat short, only four conversational turns. This length is fairly typical for discussion of individual pictures. We found after the first few interviews, which were long and complex, that asking multiple questions about every picture in a child's camera file could result in the process taking several hours, particularly if the student had taken and chosen many pictures for his or her journal. Children became bored or restless and wanted to move on to other activities, so we learned to keep our interactions short, asking different kinds of probing questions about different pictures, rather than querying children about multiple aspects of each photo. As each child is unique, so too were their experiences taking pictures and creating photo journals. Our results, then, are not designed to be controlled or strictly comparable across individual children or demographic groups, but rather to give a sense of the broad spectrum of technology integration and reflection afforded by this type of curricular activity.

RESULTS

In this section, we focus on two main activities of the digital photo journal project: picture taking and photo journal creation. Our driving research question about how the digital camera would function as a classroom technology is informed by the video data, fieldnotes, and analysis of children's picture-taking activities as well as some observations of whole-class dynamics while children were creating their journals. Our research questions about the nature of children's reflections on their pictures are answered by our examinations of children's completed journals and accompanying student–researcher conversations. The results section is organized according to these two major activities – picture taking and photo journal creation – within which we address the research questions that are informed by each activity. In the discussion section, we draw across the whole project in describing implications for research and suggestions for classroom practice.

Achieving Meaningful Technology Integration

In the process of taking pictures, we found that children extended the physical space of technology use and integrated technology in their classroom activities in new ways. The nature of the social space surrounding the computer where children created their journals also changed. As we had hoped, the digital camera seemed to function in highly distinctive ways as a classroom technology.

The portability of the digital camera facilitated taking technology into physical and social spaces in the learning environment it had not been before. When the students took pictures, they traveled across a wide range of physical and social spaces in the classroom, including those that were relatively peripheral. Child photographers usually spent a great amount of time taking pictures of central activities identified by them at the beginning: for example, the rug areas during the whole group meeting, the playground during the outdoor activities, and the dinner tables during lunch time.

The space where the center activities took place somehow became a base. They took a variety of pictures there: initially they mostly focused on the people, their friends, the head teacher, or other teaching staff. After a round of pictures, they started to explore less obvious things, for example, friends' books and classroom objects. Then they gradually ventured to a more peripheral space: the calendar on the corner, a book shelf next to the desks. From time to time, they would venture to a different room, for example, the middle room or back room where individual projects were going on. This kind of venture out usually lasted for a few minutes. They would come back to their base rather quickly and explore different things more. They would also strategically switch between a photographer and a participant in the center spaces. The mobility of the digital camera allowed students to explore the entire learning space and pay attention to things that were relatively peripheral. In this way, the digital camera helped extend the physical and social space experienced by students.

Not only did the digital camera itself facilitate technology's presence in these alternative spaces, also the space around the most powerful computer became more meaningful for some students while children created their journals. Although the students had used computers for a project assignment earlier in the fall, in which groups made PowerPoint™ slides to share their investigations about measurement (see Wang, Hertzog, & Kedem, 2004), the most typical use of technology by children in this environment was as a choice activity. There existed a cohort of "usual suspects" who would routinely select computers as their daily choice activity, playing games such as Freddi Fish™ and Gizmos & Gadgets™. There were other children (mostly girls), however, who almost never paid any attention to the computer stations during regular choice time and stayed physically far away, preferring activities like puzzles and blocks, art, or dramatic play. Occasionally, a student's journal-creation process would take place during choice time, however, and this changed the attraction of the most powerful computer dramatically.

When a student was making his or her journal on the computer, the downloaded photos would be shown on-screen in large iPhoto[TM] "book" format – visually accessible to those in the immediate vicinity. For those children who typically avoided the computers during choice time, seeing a friend working on his or her photo journal – particularly a friend who had taken pictures *of them* on a previous day – was an irresistible draw. In order to better observe the process and catch a glimpse of themselves on-screen, these children would choose an activity closer to the computer, or bring over a puzzle, book, or some other choice object to an adjacent desk or rug space. Eventually, the pretense of other choices would be abandoned by some, and they would just stand behind the journal-making student and the researcher to watch.

Although child photographers were given the camera to take with them into all their activities and explorations for the day, the seamless integration of participation and documentation we had imagined was not exactly what took place. As it turned out, children found the camera too cumbersome to have with them all the time. So they typically found someplace to set it down while they played, worked with teachers, or engaged in other activities. Periodically, they would seem to decide of their own accord that it was time to take pictures, and they would then retrieve the camera from its location, take numerous pictures at a time while roaming around the room or outside, and then set the camera down again and return to their previous activity. Thus there seemed to be both temporal and conceptual shifts between students' normal roles and their photo documentation.

Opportunities for Social Engagement and Reflection

Overall, we found that children very much enjoyed creating their photo journals and talking with researchers about their pictures. Children displayed enthusiasm at the appearance of their pictures on the computer screen, and they often laughed out loud and drew researchers' particular attention to photos they found humorous. In our analyses we focused on children's finished journals, in terms of the pictures they selected and the captions they dictated, and on the researcher–student talk that accompanied each picture.

The content of children's journals tended to be very diverse. Not only did children take the camera into a wide variety of places, as discussed in the

This is a tessellation.   *Evan and Cameron are building a Lego structure.*   *Rachel is going to try another shot at the basket.*

Fig. 2. Topical Variety of Journal Content.

previous section, they also took many different kinds of pictures: object-focused pictures, pictures of individual people, pictures in the classroom, playground pictures, action-shots, still pictures, and pictures of teachers or other adults. Fig. 2 is an example of three different focal types of pictures, taken from three pages of the finished journal of one kindergarten student, Amy. The first is a shot of some finished student work from a mathematics lesson involving making tessellations with pattern blocks. The second is a picture of students working together on a choice time activity, in this case building with Legos. The third picture is an action shot taken of a peer about to shoot a basketball on the playground at lunch recess.

Making the journal proved to be an opportunity for children to think deeply about their early childhood classroom world, and to talk intimately with adults about many facets of their environment and the visual representations they created. As described in Methods, however, children's attention spans, as well as the number of pictures they selected for their journals, varied widely. Thus, the extent to which children were able to focus for an extended period on a single picture and reflect on its contents or contexts also varied. Sometimes students spontaneously generated a fairly deep reflection in dictating their caption, and sometimes the reflection would emerge in further conversation with a researcher. We decided to give these spontaneous and emergent reflections equal weight in developing a descriptive framework.

Consistent with a grounded theory approach (Strauss & Corbin, 1998), when we went to analyze children's captions and talk about their pictures, we first created an exhaustive list of all the different kinds of thinking we saw children doing regarding their pictures, and then we collapsed that list into several broader categories. Revisiting the data after collapsing the list ensured that our broader categories were still exhaustive enough to capture the variety of reflections we saw. In the framework, we came up with the description of our data, children seemed to have four basic approaches to talking about their pictures. Within these broad approaches, a few meaningful and distinguishing subcategories were also maintained.

The first category is a *descriptive* approach, wherein children would simply say what was on the screen. Within this category there are different types of descriptive utterances, as represented in Fig. 2: one being an announcement of the subject of the picture (e.g., "This is a tessellation"), and another being a sentence describing the activity represented (e.g., "Evan and Cameron are building a Lego structure"). An additional example is shown in Fig. 3, cell D, in which a student describes his picture of the weather calendar.

The second category is an *explanatory* approach, wherein children described the reasoning behind why they took or chose particular pictures.

(A) *This is Adrienne, she is my best friend.*

(B) *This is Brenna putting her hand on her cheek because she's tired.*

(C) *This is Yore sitting at a table during lunch time.*

(D) *This is the weather calendar.*

Fig. 3. Student Reflections.

Reflections in this category revealed the child photographer's intent while taking pictures, or the child's decision to include particular pictures from his or her camera dump in the photo journal. An example of an explanatory approach is found in Fig. 1, where Brenna says, "I took this picture because Julia doesn't know what she wants to get."

The third category is a *situative* approach, which relays the physical, temporal, or social context of the picture. This approach situates the immediate photographic subject within a broader understanding of some aspect of the learning environment. A social situative approach always described pictures of people, and the student photographer would discuss the subject of the picture in relation to existing friendship networks: either their own, as in Fig. 3, cell A, or others' friendship groups (e.g., "Sam and Bryan always sit together"). Figure 3, cell C contains an example of a different kind of situative reflection from first-grader Amy's journal, wherein she situates a picture in the temporal progression of the school day: lunch time.

The fourth major category we identified is an *interpretive* approach to reflection. One kind of interpretation we saw children engaging in was attribution, in which children would fill in details about the talk, thoughts, or feelings of the people in their photos. Sometimes these attributions would take the form of giving voices to the people in their pictures, as in Paige's journal when she comes to a picture of Julia with a book covering her face and dictates that the caption should be: "Julia's saying, 'Don't take my picture!'" Another type of attribution is to make statements or inferences about the internal states of photographic subjects. As an example, in Fig. 3, cell B, kindergartener Lily says that Brenna is "tired" in her caption, an attribution as to Brenna's internal state.

Taken together, the results from our journal-creation analysis suggest that the activity of making a digital photo journal provides an opportunity for multiple kinds of complex reflection and connection to children's social networks as well as a distinct and promising approach to technology integration in early childhood education.

DISCUSSION

The results of our research indicate that the digital photo journal project was effective at facilitating the integration of technology into the physical spaces and social fabric of the classroom, and it served as an opportunity for students to reflect on their environment and social networks in conversation with an adult.

Given our interest in understanding children's world from their perspective, however, there remains an open question in the issue of technology integration. We wonder if children actually think of the digital camera and the computer as being related to one another in some categorical way. We as researchers are excited about the ability to escape the confines of the desktop station and take technology into kitchens, playgrounds, and bathrooms, but does it matter to our students? They have been raised with these artifacts, so do they even conceive of a separate class of objects known as "technology" and thus notice its unusual entry into alternative spaces? Perhaps this notion of "technology" is a distinction that belongs to a previous generation, those of us still struggling with the "before" and "after" of the computer revolution. This is definitely a direction for future research, the results of which could have a profound impact on how we think about technology and young children.

Despite the relative smallness of the digital camera in relation to a desktop computer, there was still definitely an issue of portability in our data, in that students found they could not carry the camera with them at all times. This alerts to us a potential need in the educational technology market, another area, which is often focused on software rather than smaller peripherals or creative technologies. We see a need to design handheld technology that is appropriately sized for younger children, because as we discovered, what is marketed as being pocket-sized or wearable around the neck for adults is not so for young children. Many features of the digital camera owned by the school were also not friendly to children; consequently we did not make use of them. Children did not use the real-time delete or review/edit features of the digital camera, but rather they treated it like a film camera with a picture window, snapping pictures one right after the other. They waited until the journal-creation process to select the best or most interesting pictures for their journal. While this was good for us as researchers, in that we heard children's reflections aloud during the journal-creation process, we wonder how the entire activity might be different, and might afford different kinds of thinking, if children could not only achieve a more fluid synthesis of participation and documentation through increased portability, but also have a simpler interface to select and edit their pictures in real time as they were being taken. Currently, we do not have the available technology to answer these questions.

In addition, we believe this study has some important implications for early childhood classroom teachers. Many teachers are already using a digital camera in their classrooms for their own purposes. In one study, a kindergarten teacher, Feldman (2003) used a digital camera to create portfolios to assess students' progress. This represents progress toward technology integration in early childhood education; nevertheless, the technology mostly remains as the teachers' tool. The photo journal project reported in our study promotes student-centered and meaningful technology integration, and it also proved to be effective in promoting students' reflections; thus, this approach would be highly useful in many school programs. We believe the photo journal activity would not be difficult to replicate or approximate in other classrooms; following are some insights for organizing the project. First of all, the project should give students flexible time to explore the digital camera; however, some demonstration and tutoring of how to use the camera at the beginning would be useful. Second, it is critical to provide scaffolding in the journal creation stage, and not just because students may need some help with writing captions. This stage provides opportunities for students to reflect on their work, their social and cognitive activities in the classroom, and their social networks, but students require assistance and probing questions to reflect most productively. Finally, the digital photo journal project would work best in a classroom culture that encourages exploration and offers freedom for children to explore. The project-based curriculum (Katz & Chard, 2000) in the classroom we investigated is conducive to these types of activities and also provides for student choice and flexible usage of space. But early childhood teachers who are not engaged in a fully project-based curriculum may reap benefits from a digital camera project as well. Because students' use of digital cameras allows teachers to see the classroom world through children's eyes, this activity may enable teachers to examine their own beliefs about children as learners and fellow participants in the learning environment – a necessary and often difficult step in the process of realizing student-centered technology integration.

In conclusion, the digital photo journal project provides a unique lens through which we might refigure our perspectives on young children and technology. Rather than articulating how technology use can be a *context* for social negotiation, as we have argued in the past (Wang & Ching, 2003), here we have created a curricular activity wherein technology becomes an explicit *tool* for developing and exploring understandings of self, others, and the classroom environment. We have articulated a new focus not just on children's social interactions and developing understandings *around* technology in the classroom, but on children's developing understandings being realized *through* technology as an instrument for meaningful integration and social and personal reflection.

NOTES

1. All participant names have been changed, in both the text of this paper and in the data examples shown.

REFERENCES

Bergen, D. (2000). Linking technology and teaching practice. *Childhood Education, 76*, 252–253.

Carere, S. (1987). Lifeworld of restricted behavior. In: P. A. Adler & P. Adler (Eds), *Sociological studies of child development*, (Vol. 2, pp. 105–138). Greenwich, CT: JAI.

Clements, D., & Sarama, J. (2003a). Strip mining for gold: Research and policy in educational technology – A response to "fool's gold." *Educational Technology Review, 11*(1). Online: http://www.aace.org/pubs/etr/issue4/clements.cfm08/11/05http://www.aace.org/pubs/etr/issue4/clements.cfm. Retreived 08/11/05.

Clements, D., & Sarama, J. (2003b). Young children and technology: What does the research say? *Young Children, 58*(6), 34–40.

Consortium for School Networking (CoSN). (2002). Digital leadership divide. Online: http://www.cosn.org/resources/grunwald/digital_leadership_divide.pdf. Retrieved 08/11/05.

Cordes, C., & Miller, E. (2000). *Fool's gold: A critical look at computers in childhood*. College Park, MD: Alliance for Childhood. Online: www.allianceforchildhood.net/projects/computers/computers_reports.htm. Retrieved 08/11/05.

Cordes, C., & Miller, E. (2004). *Tech tonic: Towards a new literacy of technology*. College Park, MD: Alliance for Childhood. Online: www.allianceforchildhood.com/projects/computers/pdf_files/tech_tonic.pdf. Retrieved 08/11/05.

Corsaro, W. A. (1985). *Friendship and peer culture in the early years*. Norwood, NJ: Ablex.

Corsaro, W. A. (1997). *The sociology of childhood*. Thousand Oaks, CA: Pine Forge Press.

CoSUN. (2003). *Bridging the gaps: School, home, and student achievement*. Washington, DC: Consortium for School Networking.

Cuban, L. (2002). *Oversold and underused: Computers in the classroom*. Cambridge, MA: Harvard University Press.

Dyson, A. H. (1993). *The social worlds of children learning to write in an urban primary school*. New York: Teachers College Press.

Feldman, D. (2003). iPhoto & iMovie for assessment & portfolios. Presented at the Annual Conference of National Association for the Education of Young Children, Anaheim, CA.

Fernie, D. (1999). *The honeymooners: Teachers and children co-construct the school culture of a preschool*. (ERIC Document Reproduction Service No. ED325210).

Fivush, R., & Buckner, J. (2003). Creating gender and identity through autobiographical narratives. In: R. Fivush & C. Haden (Eds), *Autobiographical memory and the construction of a narrative self* (pp. 149–167). Mahwah, NJ: Erlbaum.

Freeman, N. K., & Somerindyke, J. (2001). Social play at the computer: Preschoolers scaffold and support peers' computer competence. *Information Technology in Childhood Education Annual*, 203–213.

Healy, J. (1998). *Failure to connect: How computers affect children's minds – for better or worse*. New York: Simon & Schuster.

International Society for Technology in Education (ISTE). (1998). *National Educational Technology Standards for Students.* Online: http://cnets.iste.org/students/NETS_S_standards.pdf. Retrieved 08/11/05.

Katz, L., & Chard, S. C. (2000). *Engaging children's minds: The project approach* (2nd ed.). Stamford, CN: Ablex.

Murphy, K., DePasquale, R., & McNamara, E. (2003). Meaningful connections: Using technology in early childhood classrooms. *Young Children, 58*(6), 12–18.

NAEYC. (1996). *Young children and technology – ages 3–8: A position statement of the National Association for the Education of Young Children.* Washington, DC: National Association for the Education of Young Children (NAEYC).

NAEYC & NAECS/SDE (National Association of Early Childhood Specialists in State Departments of Education). (1992). Guidelines for appropriatee curriculum content and assessment in programs serving children ages 3 through 8. In: S. Bredekamp & T. Rosegrant (Eds), *Reaching potentials: Appropriate curriculum and assessment for young children*, (Vol. 1, pp. 9–27). Washington, DC: NAEYC.

National Center for Education Statistics (NCES). (2003). *Young children's access to computers in the home and at school in 1999 and 2000.* Washington, DC: US Department of Education, National Center for Education Statistics.

National Research Council. (2000). *How people learn: Mind, brain, experience, and school.* Washington, DC: National Academy Press.

North Central Regional Laboratory (NCREL). (2000). Computer-based technology and learning: Evolving uses and expectations. Naperville, IL: NCREL. Online: http://www.ncrel.org/tplan/cbtl/toc.htm. Retrieved 8/11/05.

Postman, N. (1993). *Technopoly: The surrender of culture to technology.* New York, NY: Vintage Press.

Rideout, V., Vandewater, E., & Wartella, E. (2003). *Zero to six: Electronic media in the lives of infants, toddlers, and preschoolers.* Menlo Park, CA: Henry F. Kaiser Family Foundation.

Rogoff, B. (1990). *Apprenticeship in thinking: Cognitive development in social context.* New York: Oxford University Press.

Siegel, D. J. (1999). *The developing mind: How relationships and the brain interact to shape who we are.* New York, NY: Guilford Press.

Strauss, A., & Corbin, J. (1998). *Basics of qualitative research: Techniques and procedures for developing grounded theory* (2nd ed.). Thousand Oaks, CA: Sage.

U.S. Department of Education, Office of Educational Technology. (2004). *Toward a new golden age in American education: How the internet, the law and today's students are revolutionizing expectations.* Washington, DC: U.S. Department of Education.

Wang, X. C., & Ching, C. C. (2003). Social construction of computer experience in a first-grade classroom: Social processes and mediating artifacts. *Early Education & Development, 14*, 335–361.

Wang, X. C., Kedem, Y., & Hertzog, N. (2004). You really need to measure: Scaffolding young children's reflections with PowerPoint presentations. *Journal of Research in Childhood Education, 19*(2), 159–174.

PERSONAL, PROFESSIONAL, TECHNICAL, AND INSTITUTIONAL FACTORS INVOLVED IN DEVELOPING A COMPUTER-INTENSIVE ENGLISH CURRICULUM

Judith A. Federmeier and Renee T. Clift

ABSTRACT

This chapter discusses the factors that impact successful incorporation of technology in public schools, specifically in the area of English instruction. Based on the experiences gleaned from a five-year high school/ university partnership, the authors identify areas of concern (professional identity, public perception, administrative support) as well as areas that lead to success (cooperative relationships, willingness to redefine roles, focus on student needs).

High school students' and teachers' use of computers has definitely increased in the past few years. Data from the National Center of Education

Technology and Education: Issues in Administration, Policy, and Applications in K12 Schools
Advances in Educational Administration, Volume 8, 271–286
Copyright © 2006 by Elsevier Ltd.
All rights of reproduction in any form reserved
ISSN: 1479-3660/doi:10.1016/S1479-3660(05)08018-2

Statistics (Condition of Education, 1999) indicated that 95.7% of 11th graders reported using computers at home or at school to write papers or stories. The same data show that their use of computers in schools increased from 5.7% in 1984 to 15.3% in 1996. A 2003 NCES survey of a represent-ative sample of U.S. public schools documented that nearly 100% had In-ternet access and that 82% of schools with Internet access offered teachers professional development opportunities to learn how to integrate Internet use into the curriculum (NCES, 2005, February). Interestingly, however, in 2001–2002 only 49% of teachers reported that at least one computer for every four students in a classroom was essential to their teaching (NCES, 2005, March).

Given these recent statistics, along with Cuban's (2001) contention that classroom computers are seldom used to transform teaching, we feel that it is important to go into a more detailed analysis of what it might mean to transform one's classroom and one's teaching from simply having one desk-top computer with Internet access available to fully integrating computers into the curriculum. Furthermore, we feel it is important to look at this transformation across several years and across the related dimensions of per-sonal and professional growth and technical and cross-institutional support through the eyes of the teacher – the major actor in any teacher change effort.

In this chapter, we provide a detailed account of one high school English teacher's (Judy's) decision to create a computer-intensive environment for all of her high school English classes, the people and the factors that made this possible (including Renee's role within the process), and what we have, jointly, learned from this experience. We first worked together because of our participation project funded by the U.S. Department of Education that we called METER (Mathematics, English, Technology Educational Re-sources). After the METER funding ended, we continued to meet to talk about what we had learned and were continuing to learn about improving school-based and university-based instruction with and without using tech-nology. Many of our data points for this chapter come from ourselves, our evaluation reports for a project in which we both participated, and the technical reports of people who have collected and analyzed data on us. Judy was a co-author of several evaluation reports and was also one of the subjects for a technical report and an early research report. Renee was a project director and helped supervise the creation of the technical reports and the early research report, and she was also responsible for annual eval-uations of the entire project. To prepare this chapter we reviewed our notes, the annual evaluations, and the technical reports. All technical reports can be found at http://www.ed.uiuc.edu/meter/. We then constructed a joint narrative of our experiences in which Judy's voice predominated, followed by a summary of what we have learned, incorporating our work with that of other recent technology integration projects.

This chapter addresses district and building level administrators, university staff who work with schools, and technology directors in districts where all resources – staff, money, equipment, and time – are scarce. We offer an insight into how districts might leverage their participation with university projects and how buildings can encourage and support teachers as they begin to incorporate computer and Internet technologies into their curriculum. Because Judy's voice is predominant, our work privileges the teacher's voice, not that of researcher or of external partner. Thus, we provide an insider's view of what makes technology integration in a content area both possible and desirable. We argue that learning to do so takes time and support from many people at many levels across the district and the external partners. We further argue that studying the impact of computer use should be a multi-year project and should take both individual and contextual factors into account.

A JOINT NARRATIVE OF OUR EXPERIENCES

Judy: In Spring 1989, the principal of Danville High School in Danville, IL, asked four high school teachers (two English and two math) if they would be interested in participating in a program with the University of Illinois at Urbana-Champaign. Our goal would be to use technology to improve education for both high school students and university teacher education students. As a veteran teacher, I was thrilled to have this opportunity to learn about technology and refine my teaching skills to fit into the twentieth/ twenty-first centuries. I also always wanted to work with prospective teachers, and this program would give me the opportunity to do that. University personnel and high school teachers spent the first year getting to know one another, brainstorming ideas for activities, and designing the project. At first we considered videotaping high school classroom sessions for viewing and analysis by the college students. However, this turned out to be much too burdensome for us because of the mechanical demands of videotaping while teaching, the time demands of previewing tapes, editing, shipping, etc. Then we thought about using Internet-based video for sharing educational activities and discussions. Potential teachers could observe our classrooms in real-time without having to drive back and forth from the university, and they would be able to interact directly with teachers as well as students.

Renee: I had never worked with Danville High School before, and I was excited about getting to know new teachers who might be willing to work with our prospective teachers. I was even more excited about developing a way to design field experiences for our teacher education students, which would enable us to "visit" classrooms around the state. The high school served a very diverse student population, with about two-thirds of the students qualifying for free or reduced lunch. Many of the students had little to no access to computers at home – or at school. School computer access was limited to over-booked labs and students were not able to accomplish even simple tasks like logging on to a network, searching the web, or using e-mail. We thought that this setting would be a perfect pilot test site for trying out new ways to use technology in teacher education.

My technologically sophisticated colleagues agreed that education had yet to tap the potential of real-time video over the Internet, and we bought equipment for video conferencing that connected over telephone lines because they were simple to use and, we thought, suitable for a school that was not yet technology-intensive. I did not envision that what we would be doing was documenting failure. The 2002 year-end report from the project technology team (Buell & Levin, 2002) concluded, "Nearly two years after our initial attempt to implement videoconferencing for METER, we remain cautiously optimistic about the potential for video-over-IP communication between the College of Education and Danville High School. We know more about where the problems are, we have solved several, and we understand more about what we still do not know. We have not reached our destination yet, but we appear to be headed down the right path." I was less convinced; I was ready to try something new – and potentially less frustrating.

Judy: During the second year of the grant, university personnel set up the units at the university and the high school, and we tried several times to connect. In one session, high school students attempted to discuss a novel with university students; another time practicing teachers tried to hold a question/answer session with teachers-in-training. Although several of our trial connections after school hours often worked very well, when we tried to connect during the school day (a time when the Internet was being used more heavily), either the picture or the audio or both would fail, making the sessions frustrating, if not totally unproductive. After a year of planning and another year of trying, we determined that we would need a different focus for our work.

To find that focus, we went back to our early discussions. At that time, English teachers could only use a school computer lab two weeks a year for word processing when their classes wrote research papers. The university loaned computers to both project English teachers, giving us the capability to get students to work on computers regularly and to offer lessons that used technology throughout the curriculum. With the available computers, I re-designed several of my regular classroom activities to have students work with computers. I signed up for an online quiz site (http://www.quiz-lab.com). I would input the documents, students would complete them, and the site would e-mail scores to me. Using another online site (http://www.teacherweb.com), I created a WebQuest for our study of poetry using the computers as stations for groups to rotate through. I began practicing using Office applications so that I could create PowerPoint presentations and teach students how to do so. Students were incredibly receptive to using the computers in all these ways, so we felt encouraged to make computers more available on a regular basis.

We approached the university about the idea of creating a wireless laptop computer lab that would make it possible for each student to work on a computer and would also encourage collaborative learning because of the mobility of the hardware. We began the next year by focusing on getting a computer lab setup and finding software that would enable students to make greater use of the computers in the English classroom. With the help of the technology experts at the university and the high school, we designed a laboratory located between the classrooms of the two English teachers, us-ing movable tables and chairs to make the lab as flexible as possible. We got a laser printer and color inkjet printer to enable students to complete project-oriented learning assignments. We ordered licenses for Inspiration software and Office products as well as Big Myth software to use in mythology study.

Renee: The flexible funding and the ability to make changes within and across the five years of our project was the only thing that saved our re-lationship with Danville High School and the English teachers. We could not accomplish our original goals, but we could let the school and the teachers determine new goals. I felt that the university's credibility remained intact and I began diverting financial and staff resources toward this new project. Jim Buell, a graduate student on the technology team was very interested in learning more about how the English teachers would work with the mobile lab (Computers on Wheels, or COWS) and so he both supported the teachers' use of technology and documented the process (Buell, 2003). Judy's story goes beyond his documentation, however, in that she chronicles the personal efforts she and her partner invested into making the lab a reality.

Judy: My partner (another English teacher) and I spent evenings and weekends with student volunteers cleaning, painting, and setting up the lab. It took until December for all the equipment and furniture to be delivered and set up. Once the lab was ready, we began using it on a daily basis, and students enjoyed the simple projects we attempted: gravestones for Julius Caesar and the conspirators, instructional posters for poetry study, PowerPoint presentations of individual stories from the King Arthur legend, and biographical vignettes of authors chosen by students. As I worked through these projects, I found that I had to be a self-learner. Anyone who has talked to young people who seem to be "experts" with technology usually say they have gotten to that point by "just messing around" with the equipment. My partner and I had to be willing to "mess around" with the Internet in order to learn the breadth of what is "out there" and with a variety of software programs so that we could become experts with Microsoft Office productivity tools. A university-sponsored summer workshop known as the "Moveable Feast" helped us learn more about this software; my partner began a master's program in technology, which helped us learn even more. I found that working with my usual lessons and adapting them to use Office programs was the simplest way to begin to incorporate technology into the English curriculum, because they lend themselves to immediate use in a language arts curriculum where, by definition, the focus is on effective communication and using visual/oral stimuli to reach out to others. However, even a simple task like inserting a graphic and resizing it requires a knowledge base that most students do not have. To be able to teach them, I had to spend hours teaching myself and practicing first.

Quickly realizing that we would accomplish more if we worked together, my partner and I shared skills and knowledge and made suggestions for success from our own experiences. Because we had some reassigned time from the grant, we collaboratively planned a unit for doing research, designed materials, found websites, and created a rubric that we both could use. This decreased the workload for both of us and helped to ensure that we offered only high-quality learning materials to students. In addition, we consulted with other teachers for input on all these activities and shared our products with them since all English teachers must teach a research unit. We felt that by sharing responsibilities, successes, and failures, we were modeling collaborative work to reduce competition and jealousy among other staff members who otherwise might perceive us to be singled out as "favored" teachers who were "allowed" to use the technology, go to training workshops, co-plan, etc.

Then we focused on rewriting both unit and daily lesson plans to include technology. We wanted to make students more responsible for their own learning, and we wanted to focus on active learning. So we tried to figure out what the students could "do" to accomplish the skills we knew they needed. Our students created PowerPoints about grammar and sentence structure and taught the class mini-lessons. Students used Publisher to create pages of a mock textbook, business cards for Shakespeare, and travel brochures for the Globe Theater. They wrote essays that they hot-worded to informative Internet sites they found. Students shared their work with other members of the class, and we added performance evaluations and rubrics to our repertoire of grading techniques.

We purposely tried to keep adding familiarity with new programs and techniques using technology to our curriculum. One area where we felt less than competent was web page creation, so when university personnel invited the four METER teachers to have an expert train them to create a personal web page for student/parent access to resources, homework assignments, and e-mail communication with the teacher, we got involved immediately. Once I felt comfortable with FrontPage, I used my new skills to create WebQuests for Shakespeare and Dickens units that required students to complete inter-related projects and share what they learned. Students enjoyed the WebQuests so much that the four METER teachers decided to plan training for any interested district teachers who would like to learn how to create their own web pages. Once they had done that, they would have the technology skills to apply to designing WebQuests for their classes as well.

Renee: Judy's and her partner's enthusiasm and commitment were paramount in making things happen, but the above account leaves out part of the story. Because of the grant, the teachers were able to have an extra, collaborative planning period for four years. They were also able to directly access university professors, staff, and graduate students who knew a good deal about technology and troubleshooting and who knew whom to contact in order to resolve problems. In addition, the Danville School District, like many other Illinois school districts at the time, did not have a technician assigned to the high school exclusively, and the district technology coordinator was understaffed and overworked. My role, along with that of our technology team, was to help the district develop capacity and to be the outside agent of pressure. The grant enabled the high school to hire a full-time technician (the district paid one-half of his salary; the grant the other half). My job became one of making sure that my staff and the technician were able to help get the lab up and running and to run interference for the teachers. The high school principal was then able to leverage the pressure I exerted into something he could use within the district. But neither he nor the teachers were doing anything for me, for the university, or for the U.S. Department of Education: they were doing it for the students.

Judy: I watched students blossom in their abilities on the computers, and they responded very positively to the project-based learning that I encouraged. I found several extremely useful online sites including http://www.flashcardmachine.com (students or the teacher can input major concepts for students to review in a flashcard format), http://www.nicenet.org (teacher can upload worksheets so that they are immediately available to students both at school and at home – wherever the Internet is available), and http://www.learningtowrite.net (an online English writing and grammar site with exercises and tests). By adding these learning venues to the students' daily activities, I took further steps to make the students' learning computer-intensive.

During the fourth and fifth years of the project, I maximized my use of technology in class. Students became adept at going online to access the materials they needed, either materials I had created or available Internet sites that they could use for learning. Booting up the computer, manipulating online tests and quizzes, editing papers and sharing them with others, and e-mailing attachments to one another as they created projects became as natural as picking up a pen and taking out paper to work. I found that I seldom had to xerox and distribute worksheets. Textbooks became support materials for students' learning, and they turned to one another much more often than they turned to me to get help with assignments. My goal of using technology as an integral part of education seemed to be working; I still controlled the direction of the learning, but neither a textbook nor I was perceived as a "font" of answers.

Renee: Judy's and her partner's early use of technology and her students' responses were highlighted in the local paper and Judy became the subject of a doctoral student's early research project (Buell, 2003). We were successful in documenting Judy's thoughts about technology integration and about the technology-intensive activities she put in place. What we were not able to do was to conduct an evaluation of the impact of her changes on her students. Why? Because any type of quasi-experimental design would have meant that some of Judy's students might not be able to have access to the computers and Judy thought that this was not within her ethical and professional boundaries. I was never able to convince her or her partner to work through some kind of comparative study of students' use of technology and, once I understood the basis of their resistance I quit trying. We do know that Judy continued to further develop her teaching after her partner moved to California and Buell moved to another project. And, because this account covers six years, we can see that once a teacher makes a commitment to using technology more intensively and if the environment offers more opportunities to continue learning, the synergy that results can be impressive. By this time, I was out of the picture – I no longer needed to run interference.

Judy: As a collaborator with Renee, I felt pulled in two directions. I certainly wanted to cooperate with her research plans and recognized that knowing how technology impacted individual students would be valuable information. On the other hand, as a teacher, I could never forget that my first responsibility was to my students. I had to make sure all of the young people I influenced every day received the benefits of the available resources, even if that meant we did not have the comparative data for students who did an assignment using technology and for students who had to do the same work without the benefit of the technology. What I did instead was try to expose the students to as many varied types of technology and applications as possible and observe which ones benefited them the most. Thus, I could provide qualitative data even if I could not provide quantitative results.

In my effort to expose students to technology, I got involved with a district-sponsored PALM Handheld Computers Project (a Palm™ is a portable computer is small enough to be held in one's hand). Students learned to use PALM handheld computers in conjunction with their wireless laptops to write, answer questions, do review exercises, and take quizzes. Students quickly became comfortable with beaming ideas to one another and syncing their PALM handheld computers assignments to the computers so that they could send them to me for evaluation. The university offered several classes that I took to learn how to create interactive quizzes using PowerPoint and how to use Adobe Photoshop.

As my teaching evolved, so did my need to keep learning. Incorporating technology enlivened my interest in my profession because I perceived that I was doing a better job of serving my students much more effectively. Granted, the first few years were really difficult. I never had enough time to teach as well as spend the time I needed to learn skills myself, adapt lessons, find sites, etc. However, despite the stress and tension, I truly believe that I developed into a much more creative, effective teacher. Once I had become a technology-dependent teacher, my teaching could never stay the same, and I felt that it would never become stale. It would be very hard now for me to go back to the "old" classroom setup without the availability of computers because I observed firsthand how the computers motivated students, developed their thinking and problem-solving skills, and encouraged independence in learning as well as effective collaboration.

Renee: Things often change rapidly in school districts and in school–university partnerships. The first principal at Danville High School is now the Superintendent and the second principal became the Associate Superintendent in 2004. Judy retired from teaching in 2005. One of her student teachers, who is also one of my former students, has been hired to take her place. We do not know what will happen to the rapidly becoming outdated wireless lab, but we suspect that it will become institutionalized and modernized if enthusiastic teachers find supportive administrators who will work with grant savvy professionals – whether they are university-based or not. We discuss this in more detail in our joint reflections on what we have learned from our work together.

REFLECTING ON EXPERIENCES: JUDY

In my experience as an English teacher working with a computer-intensive curriculum, I found new meaning in Polonius's advice in Hamlet: "This above all: To thine own self be true." To be true to themselves, I learned that teachers changing the curriculum may find themselves in very awkward positions. They often must defend themselves when colleagues critically comment, "Well, no wonder the kids like your class. You just let them play on computers all the time." They have to answer to department heads when they cannot quite cover all of the "curriculum" outlined in the Board of Education policies. They must fight for time from the tech support people working on the attendance software to keep their equipment up and running for the students. To become computer-intensive instructors, we found that as educators we had to redefine the role of the English teacher in the classroom. Most teachers plan and work within the framework of their past successes and failures, but for many experienced (and even novice) teachers, the world of the computer-based language arts classroom is entirely new, so teachers have no previous experiences to fall back on.

Our ultimate goal was to promote student achievement for all English students at the high school. To do that we not only had to change our roles, but we also had to allow the students' roles to change. In a computer-intensive English classroom, the students assume responsibility for their own learning to a much greater degree. I had to be willing to give up "control" and "leadership" in the classroom to allow students to assume responsibility for their own learning by working together to gain skills and knowledge. Often students with partners or in small groups collaborated, providing one-on-one instruction to each other in computer skills and content-based learning. Because people learn best what they teach to others, the inter-student instruction fostered high levels of understanding in students. Such computer-based instruction individualized in another way as well: Special needs students could proceed at their own pace and could use modifications provided by the technology to help them learn. I am sure that once class-rooms have such innovations as voice-recognition software, tablet PCs, and handwriting recognition, teachers will be able to encourage students of varied abilities, learning styles, and skill levels to be successful in the class-room. The benefits of using technology were not immediately apparent; it took several years before I started to feel comfortable with a computer-based curriculum and the changes it brought about, and I often questioned whether I still had control of the learning in our rooms.

Of course, the teacher truly does maintain control, even though students take more responsibility for their own learning. I still decided when in-struction best lent itself to whole group work, small group projects, part-nerships, or individual activities. I learned to control through planning, not lecturing – I formulated questions, posed problems to investigate, chose websites, asked for alternative responses, etc. Much of my work was "be-hind the scenes"; then I observed while students took on the responsibility for their own learning. Such control allows the teacher to guide students to "learn how to learn" what is important. To provide this guidance, I had to internalize using technology as an integral part in my lesson planning just as I naturally incorporated textbooks, reading guides, pens and paper, etc. in a "regular" classroom. In addition, computer-intensive classrooms require very effective classroom management and discipline skills to ensure that the equipment is treated properly and used appropriately. I composed and dis-tributed guidelines for usage, sent them home, and required parent signa-tures. Then I consistently enforced those rules, with no exceptions. Finally, I had to build in new routines for myself to lock and secure everything before I left every single day.

I found that I also had to rethink my ideas about what and how I taught. One typical concern we faced in terms of using computers in the English curriculum was to question the time required to teach computer skills before the students could work on their English. Knowing that students come into the room with a wide variety of computer skills – I had some who did not know their way around a keyboard, some who had never used a mouse or touch pad, some who did not know what a drop-down menu was – many people raise valid concerns about how much time becomes devoted to computer-based lessons in an already-crowded curriculum. In fact, many teachers have experienced the feeling of having an over-packed curriculum, most of which they feel they only gloss over. There is never enough time to "really" teach the writing process, to reinforce reading skills, to give students practice speaking clearly. When the curriculum involves computers, teachers must also teach students how to log on to the network, how to save work properly, how to navigate the icons, programs, commands, error messages, etc. All that instructional time is time lost to English. Ideally, students would learn many of these skills through vertical articulation of curriculum with elementary and middle school teachers. However, in districts like ours that are taking first steps toward a computer-intensive curriculum, that may not be possible, and teachers may just have to accept the sacrifice of some English-teaching time to computer-teaching time.

What does the teacher have to gain from such sacrifice? I found that students who work with computers tend to be more motivated and show more interest in their work. I had students coming into class daily asking, "Do we get to use the computers today?" Students can see more connections of their learning to real-life situations, and they become engaged learners. Rather than listening to books being packed into book bags and watching students start to get out of their seats the last five minutes of the period, I heard students complain that they needed more time and watched them do a few more keystrokes as I called attention to their need to print or save. When I was teaching writing with computers, I found that students were more willing to revise and to rewrite, simply because it was so much easier than redoing the work by hand. In addition, final products were much neater and easier to read, saving me a lot of evaluation time.

I also found that computers gave my teaching versatility. Technology changes very quickly. Just working on the Internet forced me to learn new things regularly and keep my teaching up-to-date. I knew that sites that were readily available for use might disappear in a short time. I had to learn how to search the Internet efficiently and judge the validity and usability of sites. These are valuable skills that will help to keep anyone's lessons up-to-date as well as provide a way to model for students how to remain current in their learning.

I found that my students and I gained a sense of pride when using technology to create products in English. They could see concrete examples of learning that looked much more professional and polished. In advertising, graphics, sounds, movement, and music entice people to pay more attention to the product offered. In the same way, professional-looking documents, posters, business cards, brochures, etc. entice students to pay attention to what they are studying. Teachers are, in essence, salespeople who must analyze their audience and appeal to their interests and needs. Although a minor consideration, I found that attractive worksheets and quizzes did motivate young people to pay more attention to what they were doing. By creating such documents themselves and then teaching students to do the same, teachers empower their students to take an active part in their own learning and earn a sense of pride in what they do.

JOINT REFLECTIONS

Together we have thought about what our work means along four dimensions: personal, professional, technical, and institutional. We feel that any school or district that hopes to incorporate more technology into the curriculum should consider all four factors. The institutional commitment to change is crucial (Ringstaff & Kelley, 2002) not only in terms of allowing teachers to think about change, but being willing to change themselves. For example, in many districts, Boards of Education must approve curricula for the schools, and they must be willing to allow teachers to rewrite standard, long-accepted guidelines to accommodate the demands of using computers in the classroom. Evaluators and administrators must also accept change in the teacher/student roles. When observing a computer-intensive lesson, they may not see the teacher "doing" much lecturing or writing on the board or using overhead transparencies. Often, the teacher's work occurs before the lesson, and the students become the "doers" while the teacher becomes a planner and facilitator.

We concur with Garthwait and Weller's (2005) conclusion that establishing a computer-based curriculum also involves a financial commitment and commitment to training. After providing the equipment first, the METER resources were necessary for things such as replenishing supplies of ink and paper, new batteries, and parts for the computers when they malfunctioned.

But financial commitment is not sufficient. In their study of a partnership for implementing technology across the curriculum, O'Bannon and Judge (2004) concluded that access, ongoing support, and professional development were important in facilitating change. Training in hardware and software is important; providing time and resources for messing around while one learns is important; and tolerating the inevitable mistakes and failures while learning progresses is important. Teachers in the high school and in the university who deal with the technical side of incorporating technology into instruction need a lot of support. Choosing what to buy is the first challenge. It is important to have someone familiar with hardware and software features, the jargon surrounding these features, and the ability to understand the relationship between teaching and learning and hardware and software. Setting up and installing hardware and software is often the second challenge. Technical experts need input on room arrangements, numbers of special needs students, outlet requirements, safety issues with wires and peripheral placement, etc.

Once ready to "teach" with technology, the educator side of the technology support staff becomes important. In addition to workshops and one-on-one lessons in software applications and network issues (passwords, logging on procedures, how to save effectively etc.), technicians who are willing to share their expertise with staff members help overcome insecurities by empowering teachers to troubleshoot problems on their own. As Judy notes, "My most valuable asset in learning to teach with computers was a technician who said 'call me any time' and meant it, who didn't laugh when I asked what I now know were ridiculous questions, who patiently walked me through procedures step-by-step and then waited while I wrote down the steps because I knew I wouldn't remember! Because I knew that help was just a phone call or page away, I felt less insecure and was more willing to take the steps needed to incorporate computers into my daily lessons."

The professional relationships among staff are essential. What our work demonstrates is that what Judy has accomplished is not about Judy alone. At the very least it is the synergy among:

• Judy working with a partner
• Judy working in a school that wished to participate in a school–university project
• Judy working within a project that allowed the teachers to make most of the decisions
• Judy having access to resources beyond the project
• Renee and Judy working within a project that permitted flexible parameters, changes in goals, and changes in structure
• Renee having both direct and indirect access to many, many people with technical expertise and a commitment to the project
• Renee and Judy being able to talk honestly and openly about challenges, opportunities, frustrations, and clashes.

There is a tremendous potential in enabling teachers to rethink what it means to "teach" and to provide them with collaborators who are willing to take risks and experiment. By sharing equipment, lessons, resources, successes, and failures, teachers are better able to meet the new challenges posed by the Internet and by rapidly changing software. Challenges, frustrations, failures, joys, and successes are an enduring part of teaching – and technology brings its own set of issues. Teachers who want to incorporate technology must realize that they cannot do it all at once and, also, must have many opportunities to ask for help from other teachers, from university partners, from administrators, from technology experts, from their spouse, from their children, from their students. No one person has all of the knowledge necessary for the many parts that make up a technology-intensive environment. Acknowledging that up front and then designing the professional and inter-personal infrastructure around collaboration will prevent a good deal of unnecessary frustration or, at worst, the decision that the change is simply not worth the effort.

In summary, what might initially appear to be a series of personal decisions such as participation in the project; deciding to abandon and unproductive line and take up a new one; creating a new setting for teaching and learning; facing and working through technical and not so technical obstacles; learning and continuing to learn; and sharing that knowledge with others, is far more complex. The personal decisions we both made would not have resulted in anything without the knowledge, support, advice, and commitment of a lot of other people. Creating a computer-intensive environment is, just that, an environment. Creating a livable and dynamic technology-rich curriculum is very possible, but not without attention to the conditions that support the people who occupy that space.

REFERENCES

Buell, J. (2003). *COWs in the classroom: Technology introduction and teacher change through the lens of activity theory.* Unpublished manuscript. University of Illinois at Urbana-Champaign.

Buell, J., & Levin, J. (2002). Videoconferencing and the METER project: A METER technical paper. Retrieved July 26, 2005, from http://www.ed.uiuc.edu/meter/Documents/POLYCOM_2002.pdf

Condition of Education. (1999). Student computer use. *Education Statistics Quarterly, 1*(3). Retrieved July 11, 1005, from http://nces.ed.gov/programs/quarterly/vol_1/1_3/3-esq13-b.asp

Cuban, L. (2001). *Oversold and under used: Computers in the classroom.* Cambridge, MA: Harvard University Press.

Garthwait, A., & Weller, H. G. (2005). A Year in the life: Two seventh grade teachers implement one-to-one computing. *Journal of Research in Technology Education, 37*, 361–377.

National Center for Education Statistics (NCES). (2005, February). *Internet access in U.S. public schools and classrooms: 1994–2003.* Retrieved July 6, 2005, from http:// nces.ed.gov/surveys/frss/publications/2005015/

National Center for Education Statistics (NCES). (2005, March). *Computer technology in the public school classroom: Teacher perspectives.* Retrieved July 11, 2005, from http:// nces.ed.gov/pubs2005/2005083.pdf

O'Bannon, B., & Judges, S. (2004). Implementing partnerships across the curriculum with technology. *Journal of Research in Technology Education, 37*, 197–213.

Ringstaff, C., & Kelley, L. (2002). *The learning return on our educational technology investment.* San Francisco, CA: WestEd. Retrieved June 24, 2005, from http://www.wested.org/ online_pubs/learning_return.pdf

SUPERINTENDENT LEADERSHIP FOR TECHNOLOGY INTEGRATION IN PUBLIC EDUCATION

Richard C. Hunter

ABSTRACT

Today, public schools are under considerable pressure to integrate computer technology into their instructional programs. Results from studies of computer technology usage in public education and its impact on student achievement have not been very promising. Yet, schools are expected to purchase more computers and to incorporate them into classroom instruction. This paper examines several theories of leadership and decision making related to technology integration in primary and secondary schools and their impacts on public education. Finally, a number of leadership strategies for public school superintendents to better integrate computer technology in the instructional programs of public schools are presented.

THEORIES OF LEADERSHIP

There are many issues of leadership impacting on the usage of computer technology in public schools. Before discussing them, several leading theories of leadership that influence outcomes in public education are discussed. Owens (2001, p. 233) reported more than 350 definitions of leadership and

Technology and Education: Issues in Administration, Policy, and Applications in K12 Schools
Advances in Educational Administration, Volume 8, 287–300
Copyright © 2006 by Elsevier Ltd.
All rights of reproduction in any form reserved
ISSN: 1479-3660/doi:10.1016/S1479-3660(05)08019-4

identified two crucial elements that must be present in any schema of leadership (p. 234). These elements existed in Sergiovanni's (2006, p. 172) description of leadership, which was viewed as a process for leaders, acting alone, seek to influence the behavior of others. Machiavelli (1519, pp. 13–14) indicated that leaders, who inherit positions of power, are merely required to follow the methods of their ancestors and to be adaptable to unforeseen situations in order to maintain control. Today, Kowalski (2003, p. 182) described leadership as filled with complexities and as being highly unstructured. He maintained leadership is not just about making decisions about how to do things, but is more importantly about making decisions about what should be done. This is the major problem with leadership. For, making decisions about what should be done is not as easy as it seems. Unfortunately, individuals are fallible and not only make wrong decisions, but often make decisions about the wrong things.

In order to minimize these problems a number of theoretical constructs of leadership have been created. McGregor (1978, p. 18) developed two theories of leadership, Theory X and Y. Theory X recognized workers dislike their jobs, are lazy, and must be prodded or coerced by their supervisors to get work done. Theory Y, on the other hand, is based on assumptions that people are good and will exercise self-control to get work done. Burns (1978) developed two theories of leadership that are quite different. Transactional leadership focuses on the extrinsic motivational needs of followers; while transformational leadership is based on the view that leaders are not merely power brokers, but work with followers to increase each other's functioning, over time (p. 20). Today, Burn's contributions to leadership have shaped the way we think about leadership in public education. Sergiovanni (2006, p. 162) indicated that moral leadership is derived from the obligations of teachers and their feelings for each other, their students, and the school. Moral leadership is powerful and leads to a sense of interdependence and allows people to share the commitment of the school. Another theory of leadership is servant leadership where the leader's role is to run interference for his workers, making sure workers have complete control of their destiny at every level in the organization (Naisbett & Aburdene, 1985). Sergiovanni (2006) suggested a progressive leader should not be dictatorial; instead they should encourage others to share the responsibility of leadership. This theory is called shared leadership and is a method designed to aggregate what is done by leaders and followers (pp. 172–173). Zalesznik (1989, p. 15) said that,

Leadership is based on a compact that binds those who lead and those who follow into the same moral, intellectual, and emotional commitment.

This gives meaning to the following statement by Owens' (2001, p. 239):

> Leadership is not something that one does to people, nor is it a manner of behaving toward people: it is working with and through other people to achieve organizational goals.

The leadership administrator's exhibit in the discharge of responsibilities is influenced by one of these perspectives of leadership. In addition, there are several approaches to decision making that impact on educational leadership.

DECISION MAKING

Matthews and Crow (2003, p. 164) presented a continuum of seven approaches to decision making practiced by school administrators. These approaches range from types of decision making that are totally unilateral to those that are fully collaborative. Descriptors for the seven approaches to decision making are unilateral, consulting, advisory, sharing the problem, collaboration as an equal participant, group consensus, and shared governance.

Today, school administrators who desire to lead schools to achieve greater student success must learn to operate on the end of the continuum that point toward collaboration. They must also involve their faculties and others in the formulation of a vision for the schools.

VISION

Daft (1999) indicated a vision links the future with the past, motivates workers, provides meaning for work, and identifies standards for the organization. He further stated that a vision is not just a dream, but is an ambitious view of what a school can become. Daft also identified five themes of effective visions: The themes include broad appeal, dealing with change, encouraging hope, reflecting high ideas, and defining the journey. Senge (1990, p. 10) maintained that leaders of learning organizations cannot learn apart from the organization and must empower the organization to learn. Starratt (1993, p. 145) indicated the leader's vision is what motivates them to become a player in the drama of schooling. In addition to leader's personal vision, there is also a collective vision that is used to provide direction for a school; thus, defining the future of the school. These visions must be developed with all stakeholders, including administrators, teachers, staff, parents, and even students (Matthews & Crow, 2003, p. 151). It has been said, that you cannot arrive at a place, if you do not know where you are going. So, the formulation of a shared vision is important to the success- ful operation of a public school or any organization for that matter. Nev- ertheless, it is the pre-eminent responsibility of school administrators to design and implement educational programs that effectively serve children (Norton, Webb, Dlugosh, & Sybouts, 1996, p. 51.

BACKGROUND ON TECHNOLOGY

Before discussing the use of technology in public education, we will define what is meant by technology in public education. Avci (2001, p. 16) re- minded us the primary use of technology in public education is to describe the use of computers in instruction and administration. However, he rec- ommended that schools should use more descriptive definitions of technol- ogy, so students will understand technology, as a product of human ingenuity. Further, he maintained students should understand that every- thing used today is a result of human ingenuity and science, thus they are forms of technology. Tooms, Acomb, and McGlothlin (2004, pp. 14–15) identified four phases of computer technology in public education. The first phase in the 1960s involved the use of mainframes, primarily for admin- istrative tasks. Phase two in the 1970s involved the use of personal com- puters for administration, teaching, and students. Phase three in the 1990s involved the Internet and provided a different level of communication. Phase four is still evolving and is represented by wireless technology, which has produced handheld computers able to communicate with the world over the Internet. Technology advances from Phase four are creating problems for public education. Tooms et al. indicated schools use of wireless tech- nology is producing considerable change in public education. Students are bringing handheld computers to school. Moreover, schools are no longer required to wire each computer or to install large computer labs to enable students to access the Internet (p. 18).

USE OF TECHNOLOGY

The use of technology in public education is continuing to experience tre- mendous growth. Glennan and Melmed (1996, p. 424) indicated between

1983 and 1995 the student to computer ratio nationwide was reduced from 125 to 9. Grunwald (2004, p. i) reported over 8 in 10 homes, with children, have computers connected to the Internet. In addition, Roberts (2004, p. 225) said, we have experienced phenomenal growth in the use of technology in schools.

> In 1994, slightly more than one-third of schools and just 3% of classrooms had access to the Internet. Today, all elementary and secondary schools and over 92% of classrooms are connected.

He further reminded us today's students were born in the Information Age and have been surrounded by video, computers, and DVD and MP3 players. Johnson (2004, p. 8) indicated today's students are text messaging and sending digital photographs to each other on cell phones. They also use handheld computers or PDAs that provide word processors, spreadsheets, presentation programs, and digital photography. Moreover, high-end PDAs and laptops are presenting virus problems for school wireless networks. Because of this, some school districts are considering whether to ban students from using their own laptops or PDAs in schools. School leaders are also considering whether to expand the usage of such devices in their schools by issuing them to students.

One of the important questions regarding the use of computers and the Internet is whether there is a gap in the usage for various income, age, and racial groups. Kuttan and Peters (2003, pp. 24–25) revealed home Internet access for households earning $35,000 to $49,000 increased from 29.9% in 1998 to 46.1% in 2000. However, families earning less than $25,000 in 1999 experienced only a modest increase in home access of the Internet, 7.9–9.7% in 2000. The income gap is largely responsible for this difference and can be observed in the following statistics on home computer ownership. During the period identified above, 25% of families who earned $30,000 owned a computer, compared to 80% of families who earned $100,000. Servon's (2002, p. 201) study of computer availability in Seattle, Washington, contained information on various groups. She found only 56% of persons over 65 years of age had access to computers, while a much higher percentage of younger residents did. She also indicated 52% of African-Americans, 70% of Whites, and 80% of Asian-Americans had access to computers. Zehr (2000, p. 1) indicated the overall percentage of schools with at least one computer connected to the Internet increased from 89% to 95% from 1998 to 1999. However, the nation's poorest schools made no progress during this period. These data indicate even after government intervention, there is still a digital divide regarding the usage of the Internet and access to computers for students from poor families in the United States.

EVALUATION OF TECHNOLOGY

Research on the use of technology in public schools is mixed and overall is not very promising. Norris, Sullivan, Poirot, and Soloway (2003, p. 15) reported a potential positive impact on computing technology on K-12 education; however, the reality of the impact over the past 25 years had been essentially zero. Bielefldt (2005, p. 340) reported no significant effect on math and reading achievement, relating to computer access in schools for K-12 students. Kuttan and Peters (2003, p. 80) and Cuban (2000, p. 1) indicated computing in K-12 education had not produced positive results, as relates to students achievement. On the other hand, NCREL's (1999, pp. 2–3) synthesis of research on technology and student outcomes revealed a small, positive, significant ($p < 0.05$) effect when compared to traditional instruction. Also, the Massachusetts Department of Education's (1998, p. 1) review of the *Milken Report*, indicated under the right conditions students may experience increased test scores by using computer technology. Why has there been such limited success with computer technology in public education?

PROBLEMS WITH TECHNOLOGY

There are problems impacting on the success of computers and K-12 student achievement. The Massachusetts Department of Education said, "There is a big difference in having technology and using it effectively" (p. 1). Cuban (1999, pp. 1–4) indicated the public should not bash teachers for not being able or interested in providing experiences to increase student use of computer technology. Rather, he cited the contradictory advice of computer experts on what teachers should do with students as a primary cause behind the limited use of computers by teachers in classroom instruction. The advice of computer experts has changed with each decade and has produced different expectations for what teachers should do regarding the use of computers in classrooms. Cuban indicated 70% of teachers have very effectively used computers at home surfing the Internet. Moreover, students have the skills needed to successfully use technology in schools. Nevertheless, teachers are not using computers for instruction; nor are they permitting students to do so. Cuban reported the structure for teaching has not changed overtime, which is different from the radical paradigm shifts experienced in business and industry. Unfortunately, high school teachers are still teaching 150 students each day and in classes that are only 40–50 min long. This traditional organizational arrangement has limited the type of computer integration teachers can use in their classrooms. There are a number of additional problems limiting the success of computer technology in classrooms. They are as follows:

- Beem (2002, p. 6) pointed out it is difficult for school districts to keep up with the technology brought about by the Internet. They are also experiencing difficulty attracting and maintaining competent personnel to keep computer systems operational. New computer systems require a higher level of technical skills, than were required before the Internet. In the past, part-time teachers were able to keep old computer technology running. Now, school districts are required to employ highly trained individuals, who are in short supply. These individuals also command higher salaries than schools can afford to pay.
- Zhao and Frank (2003, p. 808) presented several factors that have slowed the integration of computer technology into classroom instruction. These factors include:
  - The process for teachers to integrate computer technology in their classrooms takes time, and time is something teachers do not have.
  - Schools are slow to implement change. They continue to resist new instructional methodologies and to rely on traditional methods of instruction.
  - Schools are social organizations, and some believe they are at odds with new computer technology.
  - Most teachers believe direct teaching or lectures are the best means of transferring knowledge to students, not computers.
  - Many teachers do not hold positive attitudes about the use of technology in K-12 education.
  - The constant changing nature of technology works against its being effectively integrated into classroom instruction. School districts are publicly funded institutions that cannot easily replace old computers and software with new ones. Also, as soon as teachers understand how to use the old computers and software, there are new and more powerful ones to replace the one they just learned to use.
  - The unreliable nature of computer technology and the 40–50 min instructional period organizational arrangement of high schools do not facilitate teachers investing large amounts of time preparing lessons to

integrate computers into instruction. Further, computers do not always
work and usually there is no one at the school who can repair them
before the class period has ended.

COST OF TECHNOLOGY

Since, we are not experiencing great success with computer technology in
public education, why are we continuing to spend large sums of money on
this innovation? How much are we spending on computer technology in
public education? According to Hurst (2005, p. 34) we have spent millions of
dollars on computer technology, and people are beginning to understand it is
an ongoing cost that will never terminate. According to Technology Counts
(2005, p. 8) schools spend an average of $103 per pupil each year on ed-
ucational technology, two-thirds of which is spent on hardware. The state
with the highest expenditure for technology in 2005 was New York, $196.3
million; while Mississippi was the lowest, $318 thousand. Although en-
rollments in these states vary significantly, these data suggest there is still a
digital divide in public education. Borja (2005a, p. 18) indicated many states
have faced huge budget deficits. Because of this, many educational programs
have been reduced. Actually, most states have relied on the federal government to provide funds for computer technology. Trotter (2005a, p. 30a)
reported the largest expenditures for technology was awarded by Congress
on the recommendation of former President Clinton. The E-Rate program
had provided $2.25 billion annually and had given a total of $14.3 billion to
various organizations by 2004–2005. These funds are used to discount the
costs of telecommunications services, Internet access, and internal connections with priority for schools and libraries serving low-income students or
rural areas. However, Trotter (2005b, p. 26) reported President Bush had
asked Congress to eliminate funding for the major federal grant program
that annually provided nearly a half-billion dollars for technology in schools.
This proposed cutback may occur at a time when many school computers are
due for costly upgrades or replacement. President Bush also recently an-
nounced his, "National Education Technology Plan." The Plan contained
seven recommendations. They are: (1) strengthen leadership, (2) use budg-
eting innovations, (3) improve teacher training, (4) expand broadband internet access, (5) use more digital content, (6) integrate data systems, (7)
harmonized goals with the E2T2 grants. Finally, New Jersey has changed the
states' administrative code to use $6.8 million from the Schools Construction
Corporation to wire and build computer technology infrastructures in K-12

schools. Other states are using funds for other sources to address computer technology needs in this period of budget deficits.

Why are we continuing to spend great sums on computer technology in public education? First, the information age is here to stay. Second, computer technology has been very successful in business and industry. Computers have lead to increased rates of productivity for American workers. Because of this, there is great anticipation that similar increases in productivity will be realized in the public educational system. This is a faulty assumption. The present structure and purposes of public education do not lend themselves to increased productivity; unless, the paradigm for delivering knowledge to students is dramatically changed. One effort to create a new system of delivering knowledge to public school students is Cyber Schools. Borja (2005b, p. 22) reviewed the status of Cyber Schools, which educate children over the Internet, instead of relying on traditional classroom instructional methodologies. Today, 22 states have created Cyber Schools. Florida has the largest and best-funded Cyber School. There is an obvious problem with this approach. Who will look after the students, while their parents are at work? Babysitting has become a primary, although unspoken, responsibility of public schools and is a significant stumbling block to greater use of Cyber Schools. Third, the financial structure of public education was mentioned earlier as not permitting schools to keep up with advances in computer technology. The public educational system is not able to buy the newest computer technology, thus is incapable of performing up to standards in the new millennium. Fourth, public education lacks needed research and development on how to integrate not only the newest computer technology into classroom instruction, but how to adapt future computer technology into teaching. Public schools also do not have the economic resources to devote large numbers of highly trained and talented computer and instructional specialists to the task of developing better ways to integrate computer technology into classroom instruction. Instead, the public educational system relies on the private sector whose profit motive has resulted in the K-12 system being pushed into buying new equipment before it has mastered the old hardware. Fifth, it must be repeated that teachers do not have the time to spend hours in curriculum development modifying methods to better integrate computer technology into teaching. Integrating computers into instruction represents a major paradigm shift for public education, which will require a significant commitment of time and economic resources. Public education does not rank high enough in the scheme of governmental priorities to achieve this goal. Moreover, educational computer technology policy appears to be

shifting away from the goal of integrating computer technology into classroom instruction.

CHANGE IN POLICY

Technology Counts (2005, p. 8) indicated a major shift in education technology policy has occurred as a result of the *No Child Left Behind Act of
2001*. Under the Clinton administration, federal education technology policy
was devoted to opening new educational horizons. The Bush administration,
on the other hand, is committed to using computer technology as a tool to
analyze student achievement data. States and school districts are now spending millions of dollars to provide online student-data systems to help teachers
plan better for instruction. This will leave fewer funds to train and support
teachers to integrate computer technology into their instructional programs.

LEADERSHIP FOR TECHNOLOGY

As mentioned earlier school leadership is complex. Fullan (2001, p. 147)
provided four ways to view the complexity of school leadership. They are:
(1) changes are more complex than most realized, (2) difficult dilemmas exist
regarding deciding what to do, (3) administrators need to act differently in
various phases of the change process, and (4) advise received should be
viewed as guidelines, not steps that must be followed. Given this understanding of leadership and the problems of integrating technology into instructional programs in schools, what can leaders do to enhance the usage
and success of computer technology in public education?

   School superintendents should do the following to ensure that computer
technology is supported and expanded in their communities. Teachers need to
be better supported to integrate computer technology in classrooms. Several
leadership strategies for public school superintendents, based on the research
on leadership and computer technology presented in this paper, were designed to improve the integration of computer technology into the instructional program of schools. The strategies support each other and are marked
with appropriate symbols to indicate the time it might take for a school
district to implement them. The symbols for the strategies are: short range,
1–3 years (S); mid range,4–6 years (M); and long range, 7–10 years (L):

- A long-range vision for a school district regarding integrating computer
  technology in student instruction would be developed with participation

from all important stakeholders in the community. Once, the vision is created it would be communicated widely throughout the school system and community. The vision statement would be updated periodically, as new computer technology is developed. (L)

- Professional development for teachers, curriculum specialists, and principals to assist them with modeling and computer technology integration in classrooms would be an ongoing effort. (S)
- If the district is large enough, it would create and operate a Cyber School. This school would be funded like other schools in the district. It would provide instruction for students who are unable to operate in the traditional school environment and for students who attend regular schools and desire to earn extra credit. Small school districts would be encouraged to collaborate with neighboring school districts. (M)
- A department in the school district would be created whose mission is to integrate computer technology in the curriculum of the school district. Curriculum and technology specialists would staff this department. This structure would facilitate the development of lessons on how computer technology would be used to deliver knowledge to students in every academic subject. This group would also provide technical assistance and professional development for school administrators and teachers. (S)
- A partnership program for technology development with business, industry, employee unions, parent groups, and other community leaders would be developed. The primary purpose of this partnership would be to obtain resources to support implementation of the vision for integrating computer technology into the instructional program of the school district. (S)
- A consortium of large school districts to fund a think tank on technology integration in public education would be established. Local colleges and universities would be asked to participate in this consortium. This group would comprise curriculum and computer technology specialists and academics. They would be given responsibility for keeping up with technological advances and for development of applications for integrating new computer technologies into classrooms instruction. Information from this group would be shared with the district's staff of curriculum and technology specialists. (M)
- A demonstration school to show teachers how to integrate computer technology in classrooms would be created. Local colleges and universities would be asked to participate in this school. All teachers from the district would be required to spend a number of days in this school. Larger districts would need to create more than one demonstration school. The district's curriculum and technology specialists would help to monitor the

teacher's work at this school. Reports on what teachers learned and are able to do after being involved in the school would be shared with district curriculum and technology specialists and school administrators. (M)

- Funds to provide release time for teachers for professional development, planning, and curriculum development on integrating computer technology in their curriculum would be funded. Teachers would be released for curriculum development after they spent time in the demonstration school. This work would also be supported by the district's curriculum and technology specialists. (M)
- Develop a plan to upgrade the district's computer technology infrastructure. The goal is to make the district's computer capability state of the art with regard to wireless Internet-based equipment. This effort would require collaboration with local business and industry to define the school district's needs and to implement corrective actions to keep it up-to-date. (L)
- The district would provide greater technical assistance to keep equipment operating effectively in schools. School-based curriculum/technology specialists would be employed. There would be one full-time person for every school of 600 students or so.
- The district would seek to secure an understanding with the teacher union and others regarding supporting ways to alter the traditional instructional paradigm in schools that might mitigate against teachers effectively integrating computer technology in classrooms. Schools can create longer class periods by using models, such as Block scheduling, which provides more instructional time for teachers.

CONCLUSION

Educators have a tremendous leadership challenge in integrating computer technology into the public school instruction. They face many obstacles in accomplishing this task, including a shortage of funds to repair and upgrade an aging computer technology infrastructure. But hardware is the least of the problems and the one most easily addressed with additional economic resources. The most difficult problems will require time, ingenuity, collaboration, and the embracing of a comprehensive and ambitious vision calling for computer technology to be fully integrated into every aspect of the district's instructional curriculum. This is not an impossible dream, but with strong, determined, steady, and transformational or better, yet, servant leadership, it is possible to create a new paradigm for schooling in the 21st century, one that recognizes the power of computers to transmit knowledge to students in public schools.

REFERENCES

Avci, H. I. (2001). Misuse of the word technology in schools. *The Illinois School Board Journal*, *69*(5), 16–21.

Beem, K. (2002). Tech Support. *The School Administrator*, *6*(59), 6–10.

Bielefldt, T. (2005). Computers and student learning: Interpreting the multi-variant analysis of PISA 2000. *Journal of Research on Technology in Education*, *37*(4), 19–32.

Borja, R. R. (2005a). State support varies widely. *Education Week's Technology Counts 2005*, *24*(35), 18–24.

Borja, R. R. (2005b). Cyber schools status. *Education Week's Technology Counts 2005*, *24*(35), 22–23.

Burns, J. M. (1978). *Leadership*. New York: Harper & Row.

Cuban, L. (1999). The technology puzzle. *Education Week*, *18*(43), 1–4.

Cuban, L. (2000). Is spending money on technology worth it? *Education Week*, *19*(24), 1–3.

Daft, R. L. (1999). *Leadership theory and practice*. Fort Worth, TX: Dryden Press.

Fullan, M. (2001). *The new meaning of educational change* (3rd ed.). New York: Teachers College Press.

Glennan, T. K., & Melmed, A. (1996). *Fostering the use of educational technology: Elements of a national strategy*. Santa Monica, CA: RAND.

Grunwald, P. (2004). *Children, families, and the Internet: National survey and report*. Prepared by Grunwald Associates, San Mateo, CA. The report is available at www.grunwald.com, p. i.

Hurst, M. (2005). Schools eye future costs. *Education Week's Technology Counts 2005*, *24*(35), 34–39.

Johnson, D. (2004). Ban or boost student-owned technology? *The School Administrator*, *10*(61), 8.

Kowalski, T. J. (2003). *Contemporary school administration: An introduction* (2nd ed.). Boston, MA: Allyn & Bacon.

Kuttan, A., & Peters, L. (2003). *From digital divide to digital opportunity*. Lanham, MD: Scarecrow Education.

Machiavelli, N. (1519). *The Prince*. New York, NY: Bantam Books.

Massachusetts Department of Education. (1998). *1998 EdTech update report: Milken report study* (pp. 1–5). http://www.doe.mass.edu/edtech/etreport/1998/milken.html

Matthews, L. J., & Crow, G. M. (2003). *Being and becoming a principal: Role conceptions for contemporary principals and assistant principals*. Boston, MA: Allyn & Bacon.

McGregor, D. (1978). *Leadership and motivation*. Boston, MA: MIT Press (1966).

Naisbett, J., & Aburdene, P. (1985). *Re-inventing the corporation*. New York: Warner.

Norris, C., Sullivan, T., Poirot, J., & Soloway, E. (2003). No access, no use, no impact: Snapshot surveys of educational technology in K-12. *Journal of Research on Technology in Education*, *36*(1), 15–21.

North Central Regional Education Lab (NCREL). (1999). Quantitative synthesis of recent research on the effects of teaching and learning with technology on student outcomes (pp. 1–5). Chicago, IL: NCREL. http://www.ncrel.org/tech/effects/results.htm

Norton, M. S., Webb, L. D., Dlugosh, L. L., & Sybouts, W. (1996). *The school superintendency: New responsibilities, new leadership*. Boston, MA: Allyn & Bacon.

Owens, R. G. (2001). *Organizational behavior in education: Instructional leadership and school reform* (7th ed.). Boston, MA: Allyn & Bacon.

Roberts, L. G. (2004). Harnessing information technology for international education. *Phi Delta Kappan, 86*(3), 225–228.

Senge, P. (1990). *The fifth discipline: The art and practice of the learning organization*. New York, NY: Doubleday.

Sergiovanni, T. J. (2006). *The principalship: A reflective practice perspective* (5th ed.). Boston, MA: Allyn & Bacon.

Servon, L. J. (2002). *Bridging the digital divide: Technology, community, and public policy*. Malden, MA: Blackwell Publishing.

Starratt, R. J. (1993). *The drama of leadership*. London, England: Falmer Press.

Technology Counts. (2005). Electronic transfer: Economic and policy forces are moving technology dollars in new directions. *Education Week, 24*(35), 8–9.

Tooms, A., Acomb, M., & McGlothlin, J. (2004). The paradox of integrating handheld technology in schools: Theory vs. practice. *Technological Horizons in Education Journal, 32*(4), 14–24.

Trotter, A. (2005a). E-Rate: The road ahead. *Education Week's Technology Counts 2005, 24*(35), 30–31.

Trotter, A. (2005b). Federal role seen shifting. *Education Week's Technology Counts 2005, 24*(35), 15–17.

Zalesznik, A. (1989). *The managerial mystique: Restoring leadership in business*. New York: Harper & Row.

Zehr, M. A. (2000). Poorer schools still lagging behind on Internet access, study finds. *Education Week, 19*(24), 1–2.

Zhao, Y., & Frank, K. A. (2003). Factors affecting technology uses in schools: An ecological perspective. *American Educational Research Journal, 40*(4), 807–840.

ABOUT THE AUTHORS

Diana Betout is a graduate student at the University of Illinois, Department of Curriculum and Instruction. She is studying teacher education. She plans to pursue her career as an elementary teacher.

Nicholas C. Burbules is Grayce Wicall Gauthier Professor in the Department of Educational Policy Studies at the University of Illinois, Urbana-Champaign. He has published widely in the areas of philosophy of education, technology and education, and critical social and political theory. He is also the current editor of *Educational Theory*.

Thomas A. Callister, Jr. is professor of Education and Chair of the Education Department at Whitman College in Walla Walla, Washington where he teaches courses in the foundations of education. His research focuses on the impact of new technologies on educational practice and policy.

Tawana L. Carr is a doctoral candidate in the Department of Educational Administration and Policy at Howard University. Ms. Carr currently serves as a Non-Categorical Special Education teacher for Fairfax County Public Schools in Virginia. As a Non-Categorical Specialist she works with children that have disabilities ranging from autism to Down syndrome. She earned her Masters in Education from the Ohio University. Her research interests are in the areas of computer-assistive technology, academic achievement, and educational policy.

Bryan Carter is an assistant professor of English at Central Missouri State University. He specializes in African-American literature of the 20th century with a primary focus on the Harlem Renaissance and has a secondary emphasis on visual culture. He has published numerous articles on his doctoral project, Virtual Harlem and has presented it at locations around the world. In the spring of 2004, he served as Professeur Invité at the University of Paris IV-Sorbonne where he taught Digital Communications and Cultural Studies. Dr. Carter has also been one of the forerunners in the Department of English and Philosophy in the use of technology in the classroom where recently he has incorporated desktop videoconferencing, podcasting, internet radio broadcasts and blogging into each of his courses. Being a strong supporter of online collaboration, Dr. Carter actively connects his classes with those of colleagues in Sweden, France, and at universities in the states. "Using digital communications helps to expand the world-view of my students in ways that, prior to the evolution of these tools, was more difficult. Students love it."

Cynthia Carter Ching is assistant professor of Educational Psychology at the University of Illinois Urbana-Champaign, where she resides in the divisions of Cognition, Learning, Language, Instruction, & Culture (CLLIC) and Child & Adolescent Development. She received her Ph.D. in Psychological Studies in Education from UCLA in 2000. Ching's research focuses on three areas: collaboration and negotiation around computers in the classroom, gender and technology, and technology and identity. Her work has appeared in *Journal of the Learning Sciences*; *Early Education & Development*; *Computers in Education*; *Journal of Science Education & Technology*; *Education, Communication, and Information*; and *Urban Education*.

Renee T. Clift is professor of Curriculum and Teacher Education in the Department of Curriculum and Instruction, where she serves as the Associate Head for Graduate Programs. Before coming to the University of Illinois at Urbana-Champaign in 1990, she was on faculty at the University of Houston, and, prior to that, a high school teacher in Florida public schools. She holds a Ph.D. in Curriculum & Teacher Education from Stanford University. In collaboration with others, she has developed and implemented the Novice Teacher Support Project, a project to facilitate the development of novice teachers out of college for less than 4 years. She is also the Acting Director of the Illinois New Teacher Collaborative, a partnership of universities, businesses, professional organizations, and others interested in attracting and retaining talented and committed teachers. Her research addresses: (1) cognitive, social, and emotional processes that influence the transition from student to teacher; (2) roles of technology in teaching and teacher education; and (3) factors that promote retention in and satisfaction with the teaching profession. Her current research projects include longitudinal study of English teachers who graduated from UIUC in 2002 and an exploration of the potential of electronic conferencing to link novice teachers with mentors in five sites across Illinois.

Nicole S. Clifton is a doctoral candidate in the Department of Educational Administration and Policy at Howard University. Currently, she serves as an Assistant Principal in Alexandria, Virginia. She earned her Bachelor of Science degree in the arts and sciences, in addition to her masters degree in education administration and supervision, both from Tennessee State University. Her research interests lie in the area of the achievement gap, the impact of technology on education as it relates to technology access for underserved students, in addition to the effect of ubiquitous or 1:1 computing on underserved students.

Dale Cook is the director of the Research Center for Educational Technology at Kent State University and Summit Professor for Learning Technology. He devotes his time to the advancement of learning technology efforts, especially at RCET and its SBC Ameritech Classroom. Dr. Cook also serves as a faculty member in the Educational Administration program in Kent State's College and Graduate School of Education and is involved in a partnership with the College of the Bahamas, where he teaches courses on a regular basis. His current interests include ubiquitous computing, the integration of mobile devices in formal and informal learning environments, and capacity building in learning environments such as the Bahamas.

Saran Donahoo is an assistant professor in the Department of Educational Administration and Higher Education at Southern Illinois University – Carbondale. She earned both her doctorate in higher education administration and her M.A. in history at the University of Illinois at Urbana-Champaign. She completed her B.A. in secondary education at the University of Arizona. Her research interests include history of education, legal issues affecting education, educational policy, and educational diversity and equity.

Mustafa Yunus Eryaman is the managing editor of the *International Journal of Progressive Education*, and the associate editor of the *Turkish Journal of Educational Policy Analysis and Strategic Research*. He received his B.S. from Gazi University, Ankara in Turkey, and M.Ed. from University of Missouri-Columbia, USA. He is now a Ph.D. candidate at the University of Illinois at Urbana-Champaign. He is also the president of International Association of Educators at the University of Illinois, and a member of the international advisory board of the International Association of Qualitative Inquiry.

Judith A. Federmeier is a retired public school English teacher with 22 years experience at the high school level. From 1990 to2005 she taught honors English and rhetoric as well as freshman English classes at Danville High School in Danville, Illinois. She also taught rhetoric and freshman English at Schlarman High School in Danville; German and English at Mitchell High School in Mitchell, Nebraska; and freshman and sophomore English at York High School in Elmhurst, Illinois. She received her bachelor's degree in English Education from Northern Illinois University and her masters degree in Educational Administration from Eastern Illinois University. Judy served as committee chairperson of the DHS North Central accreditation team, served on the School Improvement Team for several years, participated in the METER program to encourage the use of technology in high schools and for teacher training, and mentored seven student teachers during the last 10 years of her career. She took advanced training in gifted education, webpage and webquest development, Office©programs, use of Inspiration©, and teaching writing. Her focus the last seven years of her career included (1) using internet-based sources to individualize education, (2) shifting English curriculum to project-based learning, (3) using TriBeam© and PALM© applications and software to enhance student learning, and (4) adapting standard curriculum to computer-based study.

Ellen S. Hoffman, EdD, is an associate professor in the Department of Educational Technology at the University of Hawaii at Manoa and the Director of the Center for Research on the Internet and Schools at Eastern Michigan University. She was the founding director of an educational digital library, Michigan Teacher Network, and the Principal Investigator on three National Science Foundation digital library grants focusing on schools. Her background includes 20 years experience in instructional technology management in education at all levels from K-12 to college.

Barbara Hug is an assistant professor of Science Education in the Department of Curriculum and Instruction, College of Education at the University of Illinois at Urbana-Champaign. She is interested in how students learn in technology-rich learning environments. Her research has focused on elementary and middle age students.

Richard C. Hunter is a professor of educational administration and former head of the Educational Organization and Leadership Department at the

University of Illinois at Urbana-Champaign (UIUC). He was a professor and chair of Educational Leadership Program at the University of North Carolina at Chapel Hill and has worked in the public schools as a superintendent in the cities of Richmond, Virginia; Dayton, Ohio; and Baltimore, Maryland.

Yore Kedem is a doctoral candidate in the Curriculum and Instruction Department at the University of Illinois at Urbana-Champaign. His research interests lie mainly in the field of aesthetics education with emphases on music performance teaching and learning, and mentoring relationships in music studios. In these projects he concentrates on qualitative methods and applying philosophical and hermeneutic ideas to both methodology and findings. In addition to teaching in diverse fields and contexts, he collaborates in research projects on technology integration in early childhood and literacy in special education.

John K. Keller is the director of Instruction for the Indiana Humanities Council where he leads the smartDESKTOP Initiative. He is also an adjunct professor for Indiana Wesleyan University where he teaches in the Transition to Teaching and Masters in Education programs. John's research interests include the professional development of teachers, school transformation, and instructional design. After graduating from a homeschool program, John received his baccalaureate from Grace College, his masters from Indiana University, Ft. Wayne, and, for six years, taught 5th and 6th grade in the public schools of Warsaw, Indiana. He holds a Ph.D. in Instructional Systems Technology from Indiana University.

Annette Kratcoski is a senior researcher in the Research Center for Educational Technology at Kent State University. Since joining RCET in Fall 2000, Annette Kratcoski has been involved in research focused on the impact of ubiquitous technologies on teaching and learning. Prior to joining RCET, Annette worked as a speech-language pathologist in clinical and school settings and also in special education and curriculum coordination in the public schools. She holds bachelors and masters degrees in special education and has earned her Ph.D. from Kent State University in Speech-Language Pathology.

Yi Mei Lin serves the Research Center for Educational Technology as a Senior Researcher Educational Consultant. She received her B.A. in Mass Communication and Masters in Educational Technology. Her research interests have been focused on computer supported collaborative learning

(CSCL), computer-mediated communication (CMC), online learning community, technology appropriation, and the development of educational multimedia/hypermedia. She has presented work related to evaluation and assessment of technology appropriation, learning, and collaboration in different learning environments at several national and international conferences. Prior to her work at RCET, Yimei was a graduate instructor in Interface Design, Networked Learning Systems Foundations, and Introduction to Web Development at the University of Missouri-Columbia and a design consultant in the Graphic Education Corporation. She holds a doctoral degree with a major in Information Science and Learning Technologies from the University of Missouri-Columbia.

Tim Linder is a doctoral candidate for Information Science and Learning Technology from the University of Missouri. He specializes in designing websites, interactives, 3D animation, virtual reality, and video production. Several of his developments can be found at the Smithsonian Institution, the St. Louis Science Center, The Children's Museum of Manhattan, and many more. He is an instructor for digital media and game development for the University of Missouri – Columbia and the University Vaxjo-Sweden.

David M. Marcovitz is associate professor in the Education Department and Director of Graduate Programs in Educational Technology at Loyola College in Maryland. He received his Ph.D. in Education from the University of Illinois at Urbana-Champaign where he studied support for technology in elementary schools. He has taught computer applications and computer programming at the high school level, and he has worked as a technology specialist in a high school. Prior to coming to Loyola College, Dr. Marcovitz taught in the educational technology program at Florida Atlantic University. He was hired by Loyola College in 1997 to develop a Masters program in Educational Technology, the program which he directs and for which he teaches many of the classes. His scholarly interests include support for technology in the schools and multimedia design by teachers and students. He is the author of the 2004 book, *Powerful PowerPoint for Educators*.

Marcia A. Mardis is an assistant professor in the Library and Information Science Program at Wayne State University in Detroit, MI and a Research Investigator at the School of Information at the University of Michigan Ann Arbor. Prior to these roles, Marcia was the project director of an educational digital library, Michigan Teacher Network, and member of the leadership of four National Science Foundation digital library grants. She served as a school library media specialist for 10 years in Michigan and Texas.

Barbara Monroe, associate professor of English, is the Coordinator for the English Education program at Washington State University. She has published several journal articles on teaching with technology, including *Computers and Composition, English Journal*, and *Kairos*. Her book *Crossing the Digital Divide: Race, Writing, and Technology* examines the forms and norms that define the communication – both on and offline – of students in four low-income schools when those schools first entered the Information Age. Coyotelike, Barbara likes to cross boundaries – institutional, disciplinary, and cultural – as evidenced in her scholarship and her fieldwork.

George Reese is the director of the Office of Mathematics, Science, Technology Education in the College of Education at the University of Illinois at Urbana-Champaign. He is interested in designing professional development opportunities for mathematics and science teachers. His research has focused in examining the professional development of mathematics and science teachers.

Jason Schenker is a senior researcher in the Research Center for Educational Technology at Kent State University. He worked as an evaluator on a variety of programs at several Ohio school districts over the past three years before joining RCET in July of 2004. He received a B.A. in psychology and music from Heidelberg College, and obtained his M.A. in industrial/organizational psychology at the University of Akron. He is currently completing his doctoral degree in Evaluation and Measurement at Kent State University. His interests include statistics and data analysis, quantitative and qualitative research methods, and measurement theory. He has also acted as an instructor, teaching assistant, and tutor for research methods and statistics classes.

David Williamson Shaffer is an assistant professor of Learning Science in the University of Wisconsin-Madison Department of Educational Psychology, and a research scientist at the Academic Advanced Distributed Learning Co-Laboratory. He studies how new technologies change the way people think and learn.

Sharon Smaldino is the LD & Ruth G. Morgridge Endowed Chair and Director of the College of Education Partnership Office at Northern Illinois

University. She has taught courses in distance education, technology integration, and professional standards. She has co-authored several books, including *Teaching at a Distance: Foundations for Distance Education, Instructional Technologies and Media for Learning*, and with Dr. Herring, *Planning for Interactive Distance Education: A Handbook*. She has conducted numerous workshops related to distance education. Dr. Smaldino is the current AECT President.

Kurt D. Squire is an assistant professor in Educational Communications and Technology at the University of Wisconsin-Madison, and a research scientist at the Academic Advanced Distributed Learning Co-Laboratory. He studies video games and the educational applications of game technology.

Matthew J. Stuve is an associate professor and the director of Educational Technology Programs in Teachers College, Ball State University. Dr. Stuve was co-principal investigator of a PT3 project from 1999–2003 during which he developed web portals for K-12 collaboration and assessment. His research interests include educational informatics, digital and representational literacies, and technology in teacher education. His Ph.D. is in Educational Psychology from the University of Illinois at Urbana-Champaign following baccalaureate and masters degrees in Industrial Design and Educational Computing, respectively, from Purdue University.

Karen Swan is the RCET research professor in the Research Center for Educational Technology at Kent State University. Dr. Swan's research has been focused mainly in the general area of media and learning. She has published and presented both nationally and internationally in the specific areas of programming and problem solving, computer-assisted instruction, hypermedia design, technology and literacy, and asynchronous online learning. Her current research focuses on the latter, on ubiquitous computing, and on student learning in technology-rich environments. Dr. Swan has also co-edited a book on social learning from broadcast television, and has authored several hypermedia programs including *Set On Freedom: The American Civil Rights Experience for Glencoe* and *The Multimedia Sampler for IBM*, as well as three online courses. She served as project director for the technology strands of three rounds of federally funded research on literacy learning as part of the National Research Center for English Learning and Achievement, and directed large scale, multi-year investigations of Integrated Learning Systems for the city of New York as principal investigator for the Computer Pilot Program and the Integrated Learning Systems Project. Dr. Swan serves on the national Ubiquitous Computing Research Advisory Board, and on the program committees for several international education and educational technology conferences. She is the Editor of RCET's new online *Journal of the Research Center for Educational Technology*, an Effective Practices Editor for the Sloan Consortium, and is the Special Issues Editor for the *Journal of Educational Computing Research*. In this vein, she co-edited a special issue on handheld and ubiquitous computing.

Claudine Taaffe is a doctoral student in the Department of Educational Policy Studies at the University of Illinois. She is currently researching the role of technology in under-served, urban schools using Critical Race Theory as her methodological lens.

Kona Renee Taylor is a doctoral student in the Curriculum and Instruction Department at the University of Illinois (Urbana-Champaign). She holds a M.S. degree from Illinois State University at Normal in Quantitative and Cognitive Psychology, as well as undergraduate degrees in Psychology and History. Her current research interests include the use of simulations and virtual reality technology to explore cognitive and emotional dispositions related to teaching and learning.

Tracey M. Taylor is a student at Jackson State University majoring in Elementary Education. In 2003 she served as an ambassador for Jackson State University while studying at the University of Fort Hare in Alice, South Africa. After graduation she plans to pursue her Ph.D. in Educational Policy Studies at the University of Illinois at Urbana-Champaign.

Sharon Y. Tettegah is a faculty member at the University of Illinois, at Urbana Champaign. She holds appointments in the Department of Curriculum and Instruction, Math, Science, & Technology Division Beckman Institute, National Center for Supercomputing Applications and The Department of Educational Psychology. Her research focuses on the use of simulation and virtual reality technologies to investigate pre-service and in-service teachers, and children's moral emotions, identity, and cognitions related to teaching and learning. Dr. Tettegah holds an M.A. in Curriculum and Supervision, a Ph.D. in Educational Psychology and post graduate work in online teaching and learning. Prior research and publications include multicultural education and technology articles. She was the guest editor of a Special issue on *Urban Education and Technology*, and published articles in *Tech Trends*, and *Multicultural Education Journals.*

Mark van 't Hooft is a technology specialist and senior researcher for the Research Center for Educational Technology. His current research focus is on the use of handhelds in K-12 education, especially in the area of social studies education. He has published his research findings in journals such as the *Journal of Educational Computing Research*, the *Journal of Research on Technology in Education*, and *Social Education*, and has presented at national and international conferences such as SITE, NECC, and AERA. In addition, he has been the conference chair for two RCET conferences on handheld technology in the K-12 classroom. Dr. van 't Hooft holds a B.A. in American Studies from the Catholic University of Nijmegen, the Netherlands, and an M.A. in History from Southwest Texas State University. He received his doctoral degree with a dual major in Curriculum and Instruction (Social Studies Education), and Evaluation and Measurement in August 2005.

Eun Won Whang is a doctoral student in Curriculum and Instruction at the University of Illinois at Urbana-Champaign. She finished her undergraduate in Early Childhood Education at Chung-ang University, and her Masters in Computer Science at Western Illinois University. She specializes in instructional technology, interested in using Web as a tool for learning and research.

X. Christine Wang is assistant professor of Early Childhood Education at the State University of New York at Buffalo. She obtained her Ph.D. from the University of Illinois at Urbana-Champaign in 2003. Her research interests include young children's learning and collaboration in technology-rich environments, sociocultural research, and early childhood education in international contexts. She is also interested in qualitative research methods and video ethnography in particular. Dr. Wang has published articles and book chapters in these areas. She is recently guest-editing a special issue on "Technology in Early Childhood Education" for the journal *Early Education and Development*.

Michael Whitney heads adaptive technology and accessible web creation for Disability Support Services at Southern Illinois University – Carbondale and is also the coordinator of the Adaptive Computer Technology & Website Design HECA grant project. In addition to his MA in Rehabilitation, he is working on his doctorate in higher education administration at Southern Illinois University.

Dawn G. Williams is an assistant professor of Educational Administration and Policy at Howard University. She holds an M.A. and Ph.D. in Educational Policy from the University of Illinois. Her research and writing has focused on educational inequities as they exist across ethnicity. Her scholarship and teaching interests include mixed methods research and educational policy as it affects urban settings. Dr. Williams is author and co-author of numerous articles and book chapters that highlight the impact of several educational policies on students of color.

Lisa C. Yamagata-Lynch is an assistant professor in the Department of Educational Technology, Research, and Assessment at Northern Illinois University. She has taught courses in technology education, teacher professional development, and educational research methods. She has peer-reviewed articles published on school–university partnerships, technology education, and sociocultural theory.

SUBJECT INDEX

SET UP A CONTINUATION ORDER TODAY!

Did you know that you can set up a continuation order on all Elsevier-JAI series and have each new volume sent directly to you upon publication? For details on how to set up a **continuation order**, contact your nearest regional sales office listed below.

To view related Educational Research series, please visit:

www.elsevier.com/education

30% Discount for Authors on All Books!

A 30% discount is available to Elsevier book and journal contributors on all books (except multi-volume reference works).

To claim your discount, full payment is required with your order, which must be sent directly to the publisher at the nearest regional sales office above.